Frederic Harrison

Annals of an Old Manor-House, Sutton Place, Guildford

Frederic Harrison

Annals of an Old Manor-House, Sutton Place, Guildford

ISBN/EAN: 9783337151591

Printed in Europe, USA, Canada, Australia, Japan

Cover: Foto ©ninafisch / pixelio.de

More available books at **www.hansebooks.com**

ANNALS OF AN OLD MANOR-HOUSE

SUTTON PLACE, GUILDFORD

Frontispiece

ANNALS

OF AN

OLD MANOR-HOUSE

SUTTON PLACE, GUILDFORD

BY

FREDERIC HARRISON

New and Abridged Edition

London
MACMILLAN AND CO., Limited
NEW YORK: THE MACMILLAN COMPANY
1899

Rights of translation reserved

TO

Sidney Harrison

LESSEE OF SUTTON PLACE

WHICH HE HAS OCCUPIED FOR A GENERATION

AND HAS DONE SO MUCH TO PRESERVE

THIS EDITION OF ITS ANNALS

IS INSCRIBED BY

HIS BROTHER, THE AUTHOR

PREFACE

ONE by one the old buildings of our country are perishing by accident, neglect, or wanton destruction; their memory passes away, and their place knows them no more. When the passion for covering this island with railways and factories shall have done its worst, our great-grandchildren will hardly possess a fragment of the older work to recall to their eyes the beauty and the life of England in the past. And so it becomes a sort of social duty for those to whom chance has thrown it in their path to preserve such wreckage of old things as the tempest of change has left —any relic that they find still mouldering in the flotsam and jetsam of time.

Thus I came to put together in spare days of leisure some memorials of a very beautiful and most interesting house, which is a landmark in the history of art, and has not a few associations with the history of our country. During the last twenty-four years I have often found there a time of peace and quiet thought; and pacing up and down the court, and watching the hues of russet and orange in the mouldings, or the evening light as it glowed through the jewelled quarries in the oriels, I became curious to know a little more about the builders and the building of it. From what movement of art did it spring? Whence came those amorini over Tudor gates, and the Italian arabesques in those Gothic traceries? What manner of life did these walls witness and serve? Of what kin were the men whose devices are recorded in the painted glass? As, one by one, I learned to recognise the story they could reveal, and had found how curiously the house was connected with the tempestuous days of the eighth Henry and his three children and successors, as I traced all the circumstances of the strange and bloody tragedy which set its mark upon these walls almost before the mortar in them was dry, I began for myself a connected record of the place.

A well-known historian used to say to me, "Sink a shaft, as it were, in some chosen spot in the annals of England, and you will come upon much that is never found in the books of general history." So I sunk my shaft in this spot, and tried to understand a bit of local history, as seen from a single manor and a particular family and house. I tried to identify SUDTONE, as it is described in Domesday, and to make out the meadow, and the land or arable, the woodland "of 25 swine," and the mill. The fortunes of the manor sway back and forwards during feudal times, as the fortunes of England itself. Ten times it fell back into the hands of the Crown; ten times it was granted to royal favourites or ministers; eight times it was lost by attainder, forfeiture, or surrender between the days of the Conqueror and the days of the Tudors; till at length Henry VIII. grants the ancestral domain of the last of the Beauforts, his father's mother, to the soldier and minister of his own who built the house.

I have often pictured to myself the veteran gazing at his newly finished home when his only boy lay headless in the fresh grave on Tower Hill. I would wonder if he still continued to entertain here his fierce master, and still put his faith in princes. It would seem so, for he kept his honours and his wealth; and in the inventory of his goods for the proving of his will is a "grete carpete to lay under the Kyng's fete." And we find his widow soon after sending presents of game and "swete bagges" from this house to the Princess at Guildford. And then I would try to conceive with what feelings the son of that slaughtered youth came to receive the daughter of Anne Boleyn in the house which his father had not lived to inherit, which he himself owed to the slayer of that father. With what thoughts, I have often asked myself, did Elizabeth keep state in the hall associated so closely with the death of her mother and the wayward passions of her father, where are still to be seen the emblems of Catherine of Aragon and Jane Seymour, of Mary and Gardiner, of a succession of chiefs from both camps in that furious revolution?

And the old Duke of Norfolk, the hero of Flodden, and Lord Berners, the friend of Caxton, both the colleagues of the founder, and Stanley of Derby, the famous Chamberlain, and Paulet of Winchester, the famous Treasurer, do their emblems commemorate their presence here? And the calm proud face on the canvas of Zucchero, which smiles as she might have smiled in welcome to the Queen, that Dorothy Arundell who had lived to see some twenty of her relations die as traitors in the Tower, did the past become to her a dream; and as she did the honours of her home, did she find it a natural incident of life that attainder should fall on the head of her father, and her mother, and her aunt, and her husband's father, and on her relations of both sexes and of every degree on her father's and her mother's side?

And then that later Sir Richard Weston, who made the canal upon the Wey, and who laboured so much in agriculture, how came he to keep his house safe and his estate intact in the great Civil War which shook and battered down so many of his neighbours around him? How come we to find in his windows designs from the fancy of the Parliament Poet, and also the portrait of King Charles?

These men and women were nothing to me or to mine, no more than any other names in the history of those days; their house and their pictures and their escutcheons do not belong to mine or to me, who am but a passing visitor amongst them. But I came to love the old place, the very brickwork and the weeds and lichens which have clung round the mouldings, the swallows twittering round the tiles, and the deep glow of the painted glass. So, bit by bit, my notes grew into a connected account of the house and its vicissitudes. And as the owner pressed me to work into it the memoranda which he had collected in manuscript, and the hints of many artistic and antiquarian friends, I found it convenient for the curious in art, and the neighbours who might visit it, to put the rough sketch I had gathered together into print.

So this book is but the expansion of a catalogue or manual that I began long ago for the use of our friends. To any special acquaintance with art or with antiquities of any kind I can make no sort of pretension. I have sought, since no one else was disposed to do so, to make a record or inventory of that which is passing away before our eyes. I am neither professed historian nor antiquary, and I certainly am no genealogist or herald. I am trying merely to rub the dust and weeds from the tombstones of the past, as "Old Mortality" would do in pious reminiscence of departed saints. My part is but to scrape and copy the inscription on the neglected stone, to learn who lie beneath, that I may keep their memory green. In giving some portion of my leisure to the study of the place, I feel as if I were repaying a personal debt that I owe to a spot endeared to me by the recollection of hours of perfect peace; above all, as if I were fulfilling a duty to my father, who lived and died in these walls, and who laboured so lovingly to preserve them. And I now must add to these memories those of my mother and of my brother Lawrence, who were in succession occupiers of this house until the close of their lives.

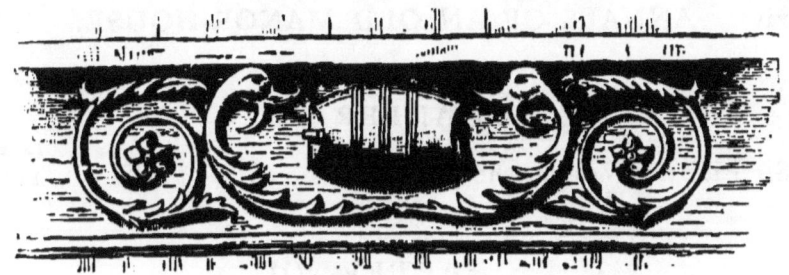

CONTENTS

CHAPTER I

Introductory 1

CHAPTER II

Vicissitudes of the Manor of Sutton . . . 18

CHAPTER III

Part I.—Before the Reformation—Sir Richard Weston the Elder, Builder of the House . . 39

Part II.—After the Reformation 65

Part III.—Westons, Knights of St. John . . . 82

CHAPTER IV

Sir Francis Weston, the Son and Heir . . . 89

CHAPTER V

Sir Henry Weston 107

CHAPTER VI

Sir Richard Weston, the Agriculturist, 1613-52 . . . 120

CHAPTER VII

From the Civil Wars to the Present Time . . . 134

CHAPTER VIII

The House 151

CHAPTER IX

The Quadrangle 171

CHAPTER X

The Great and the Panelled Hall 182

CHAPTER XI

The Long Gallery, Tapestries, Portraits, and Escutcheons 188

CHAPTER XII

The Painted Glass 199
Coats of Arms, etc., in Windows 204

INDEX 243

NOTE

This edition is a small and abridged form of the quarto work published in 1893 by Messrs. Macmillan and Co. The elaborate illustrations and coloured plates have been omitted, with the exception of some head- and tail-pieces, as well as the Appendices with the Pedigrees of Weston, Howard, Copley, Shelley, and other families, the Wills of the Westons, Grant of the Manor, and Inventory. For these and other details reference must be had to the larger and original work.

The estate is still the property of F. H. Salvin, who holds it by devise from his cousin, the last male of the Weston family. It has been occupied under a lease since 1874 by the family of the author.

CHAPTER I

INTRODUCTORY

SUTTON PLACE is an ancient manor-house on the banks of the Wey in Surrey, about 4 miles from Guildford and as many from Woking; and it was built between 1520-30 by Sir Richard Weston. It was the work of a great building age; Henry VIII., in the words of the old chronicle, was "the onlie phœnix of his time for fine and curious masonrie"; for this was the age of Hampton Court, Christ Church, Oxford, and Trinity College, Cambridge; of Thornbury, Hengrave, Grimsthorp, Kenninghall, and Layer Marney. It was built in the first outburst of the new art, which in Europe is called Renascence, when Henry was the successful rival of Francis and the Emperor Charles, and nearly in the centre of one of the most creative moments in art which our country has ever seen. The house is almost contemporary with some of those exquisite châteaux of the age of Francis which are still preserved on the Loire. Like them it possesses Italian features of a fancy and grace as remote from the Gothic as from the classical world. Like them, as was every fine work of that age, it is the embodiment of a single idea, of the personal sense of beauty of some creative genius; and thus it stands apart in the history of house-building in Europe, a cinquecento conception in an English Gothic frame.

Here the airy and fantastic grace of the Renascence, as we find it at Pavia and Blois, has lighted up a mass of Tudor Gothic. Yet withal there is no single classical feature, nor one that recalls the florid style of the Stuarts. It is as if some prophetic genius in art, saturated with Southern ideas of beauty, had been seeking to develop here a new English style, which should be as little military or Gothic as it should be classical. Had our builders continued on these lines of thought, it is possible that our architecture might never have fallen beneath the domination of Palladio, and yet might have worked clear of the imitation feudal castle and the mesquin inanity of debased Gothic. But the idea, to whomsoever it belongs, perished with him. Sutton Place remains the single extant production of a peculiar and suggestive type of Renascence Gothic.

The material in which it is built, like much in the conception itself, is Italian rather than English. It is one of the very few ancient buildings still remaining in our country which are made of terra-cotta and brick without any dressing of stone. The use of terra-cotta, not merely as a superimposed ornament, but as a constructive element, is exceedingly rare and instructive. And in this house the terra-cotta is used, not only with profusion for purposes of ornament, but precisely as stone is used where a building of brick is dressed with stone. Mullions, dripstones, string courses, turrets, arches, parapets, groins, and finials are all moulded in fine terra-cotta with delicate designs. After 380 years of exposure the mouldings remain almost as perfect as when they were cast; nor in the main does the terra-cotta show any sign of yielding to natural decay. The mass and the completeness of the terra-cotta work is hardly equalled by any old work in England. Now that our builders are seeking to acclimatise anew this potent resource of construction, it is of special interest to observe the methods in use in the bold attempt made to introduce terra-cotta as material for building more than three centuries and a half ago.

The house, too, has the singular fortune to retain, at least on the outside, its original form, and to be quite free from later additions. Save that one side of the court has been removed, the principal quadrangle, as seen from within, is in every essential feature exactly as the builder left it. Nor, except by the removal or the renewal of some mullions, has the exterior on any side suffered any material change. It is not, like so many of our ancient mansions, a record of the caprice, the ambition, the decay, or the bad taste of successive generations. No Elizabethan architect has added a classical porch; no Jacobean magnate has thrown out a ponderous wing with fantastic gables and profusion of scrolls; no Georgian squire has turned it into a miniature Blenheim, or consulted his comfort by adding a square barrack. Sir Richard Weston, were he to return from his long sleep with his descendants in Trinity Church at Guildford, would find his way to the doorway in the court, and would recognise his home, worn and dimmed a little in these 380 years, but, it may be, mellowed by time into a peculiar charm, softened by the mosses and the lichens on the cornices, and the wallflowers and the ferns which nestle beneath the traceries of the bays.

This unity and peace, which seem to rest on the old house almost as on a ruin or a cloister whence modern improvements are shut out, are doubtless due to this: that from its building till to-day the place has remained in the same family, and that a family debarred by adherence to the ancient faith from taking active part in the world of affairs. The hall itself was built before the Reformation, as the emblems and arms of Catherine of Aragon remain to witness. Under Elizabeth the house was searched as a secret receptacle of priests. In the next century the heir married the heiress of an eminent Catholic leader. According to the tradition of the family, the mass has been continuously celebrated within its walls, more or less openly, from the time they were raised until the other day when the new chapel was built in the park. During the civil wars and the last century the penal laws pressed heavily on Catholics, and after the civil wars the family took no part in public. Being neither wealthy, nor ambitious, nor busy, they clung to the old place, and they left it to hold its own with time, unaltered and unimproved. Thus it comes about that whilst the famous mansions of England bear the marks of succeeding generations, this one has remained with the unity and the pathos of a ruin, and still with but little of structural decay.

It has another feature which is of much account in the history of manners, and marks one of the great epochs in the history of architecture. It is, if not the earliest, at least one of the very first extant specimens in

England of a mansion-house built wholly as a peaceful dwelling, and entirely without any thought of defence. Down to the end of the fifteenth century all houses in the country of any importance or size were built either as actual castles and castellated mansions, or at least in the form and in the spirit of a castle. Narrow windows, turret staircases, cramped doorways, an irregular plan, battlements, embrasures, and dominant towers were the first necessities of a home to a wealthy and powerful chief who was living on his own estates. Penshurst, Haddon, Sudeley, Warwick, even Thornbury and Kenninghall, are all castles originally built with ideas of war, and gradually transformed under habits of peace. They are in spirit Gothic and feudal. When fifty years later, in the piping times of Bess, Longleat and Woollaton were built, when the Cecils, the Sackvilles, and Willoughbys were designing their new and stately palaces, all notions of a castle were abandoned. But early in the reign of King Henry VIII. it required an effort of the mind to perceive that the wars of the barons were over; that a gentleman might live at his ease under protection of law and the king's peace.

In Italy and in France men had long been building palaces instead of castles. As we shall see, Sir Richard Weston had gone on an embassy to Francis I. in 1518, and was taken across France at the very time when the new châteaux were building. It was natural that the minister and courtier who had attended in full bravery at the Field of the Cloth of Gold, and who was the trusted colleague of Wolsey, should be one of the first to raise in England a country house in our modern sense, instead of an imitation castle. Here, at any rate, Sir Richard built him a dwelling which would hardly resist the assault of a burglar; symmetrical, airy, light, and commodious, with large and regular windows, with an even and balanced façade, with wide hall doors opening on to the green; with no towers, winding stairs, moat, battlements, or outer rampart, but merely and simply a quiet country home. Here is nothing feudal; all is peace and art, and the art is rather Southern than Northern in idea. To conceive such a home was to inaugurate a peaceful revolution in manners.

It is well known how deeply, all through the sixteenth century, the ruling classes in England and in France had absorbed that New Life and New Art which in Italy had been fully developed in the century before. The Machiavellian turn for craft, secrecy, and suddenness of stroke, the passion for the beautiful, the revolt against the feudal habits of war and the old traditions of religious art, —all these colour the politics, the poetry, and the manners of the age. Henry loved the artists of Italy as much as did Francis; Wolsey lived surrounded by Romans; and Thomas Cromwell had his training in Italy itself. Weston's brother, the Prior of St. John's, spent much of his life in command at Rhodes, and they both belonged to a family which had served as Knights of St. John, and had seen foreign service for generations. Here, then, was exactly the combination best fitted to introduce into English homes that Southern grace, that colour and delight in life, that New Birth of beauty which warm the whole sixteenth century in England, and with which Surrey and Raleigh, Spenser and Shakespeare, so deeply filled their souls.

Sir Richard Weston was one of those skilful, wary, and trusty servants of the Tudors by whose energy and craft they established a strong personal government in England.

He was made Knight of the Bath in 1518, and in 1519 he was named with three other "sad and ancient knights" as gentlemen of the Privy Chamber. He was subsequently Master of the Court of Wards, Treasurer of Calais, and Under-Treasurer of England. In 1518 he was sent on an embassy to Francis I. with his brother, the Prior of St. John's, and Sir T. Boleyn. In 1520 he accompanied the King in state to the Field of the Cloth of Gold. In 1523 he took part in the campaign in France, and he served under the Duke of Suffolk in the siege of Boulogne. In 1521 he received a grant from the King of the royal manor of Sutton, and in 1530 he received a further grant of lands at Clandon and Merrow. His only son and heir, a personal playmate and minion of the King, had been married to a rich heiress by the King's favour in 1530, and in 1532 he was made Knight of the Bath at the coronation of Anne Boleyn. Four years afterwards that son was executed on Tower Hill as one of the reputed lovers of the Queen. Yet the father, mother, and widow remain at Sutton and enjoy and accept the favour of the King. They send presents to the royal family when they pass near them at Guildford. In 1539, but three years after the catastrophe, we find the old knight still at Court. He is chosen with other knights to attend the reception of Anne of Cleves in 1539. Then follow quickly the divorce of Anne, with the marriage and execution of Catherine Howard.

All these Sir Richard lived to witness. He died in 1542. For thirty-three years he was the trusted minister and servant of Henry; he had held his offices under Wolsey and under Cromwell, through the Reformation, the Six Acts, and the Pilgrimage of Grace, and all through Henry's first five marriages. He lost his son, but not his head; his patrons, but not his estates. The wild surging of those times from Catholic to Protestant professions, the deadly conflicts of that reign between mighty nobles and low-born ministers, did not shake Weston from his place, his offices, or his King's favour. In 1521, in the heyday of Henry's renown and the full ascendency of Spain, he received the grant of the royal manor of Sutton. In 1525 Wolsey writes to ask for him from the King the Chancellorship of the Duchy of Lancaster. In 1539 Cromwell, who devised the marriage with Anne of Cleves, was all-powerful. Weston is one of those chosen to receive her in honour, as his son had been appointed to wait on Anne Boleyn. The very next year Cromwell is overthrown and brought to the scaffold as a traitor in the Tower. Two years afterwards Sir Richard himself dies peacefully at home; his goods are inventoried at Sutton, and his executors are Sir Christopher More of Loseley, Fitzwilliam the Earl of Southampton, Sir John Russell, then Lord Admiral, and founder of the house of Bedford, and Lady Weston, the widow. Truly such a man who had weathered so many storms of Henry's passion in rule, in religion, in friendship, and in love, and is tranquilly laid to his rest full of years and of honours, must have been of the order of men to which belonged Paulet, he who said, "I am the willow, not the oak."

The vicissitudes and ironies of such a career give one a vivid sense of the tremendous whirlpool in which the Reformation and its consequences kept men revolving in the days of Henry. Here is an officer of state who serves the King for thirty-three years, and retains the confidence successively of Warham, More, Wolsey, Cromwell, Southampton, and Russell; who was a courtier through all the negotiations with Louis XII., with the Emperor, with

Francis I., with the German princes. He goes on an embassy to Francis I.; he names his only son after that king. He who had obtained his grant under Wolsey, and had adorned his house in honour of Queen Catherine, accepts the new order of things under Cromwell, and procures for his boy a place about the person of Anne Boleyn. His brother is the prior of a great monastic house, who dies of grief at the dissolution; Sir Richard himself undoubtedly dies a Catholic, and yet he is chosen to welcome the Protestant Anne of Cleves, and makes Russell of Woburn the executor of his own will.

When the son is beheaded as a traitor, the Constable of the Tower who executes the warrant is the knight who had been chosen with the father, eighteen years before, to be one of the four personal companions and advisers to the King. Yet the grandson lives to marry the cousin of Anne Boleyn, a cousin also of Catherine Howard, of Lady Jane Grey, and of Lord Surrey. The old knight himself serves first with the Bourchiers, the Fitzalans, the Howards, the Stanleys, Berkeleys, and Brays, whose arms and coronets and garters he so proudly displays in his hall, and then with the new men, the Paulets, Fitzwilliams, Wriothesleys, Gardiners, and Russells. In the end he leaves his will to be executed by the personal confidants of Henry; and to this very day we find in his house a portrait of the Emperor, the devices of Aragon and Castile, the pomegranate of Catherine, the phœnix arising from the flames of Jane Seymour, the arms of Bishop Gardiner, and the arms and portrait of Queen Mary side by side with the devices of Elizabeth and the portrait and escutcheons of her cousin and hostess.

And what a wreck and ruin after all was the old man's

life! With what bitterness and hopelessness of heart in his last years must he have looked across the links of the Wey and beheld the fresh beauty of his newly-risen house. There is a certain accord between the fortunes of the knight and the fortunes of his master; and the home which the minister built him on the ancestral manor of the King has shared in the blight which crushed the lives of both. It is still overshadowed by the catastrophe which snatched from the one his wife and from the other his son. Bright and promising was the fortune of Henry and the fortune of Sir Richard when these walls first rose in the freshness of their fanciful grace. But the only son who had played within them as a boy never lived to inhabit the house he had watched in the building. He who gave the estate in his bounty cut off the first heir to it in blood and shame. He who obtained the estate by the King's favour lost the son who should have inherited it by the King's fury. And the two men so strangely linked seemed still to have lived on in relations of intercourse, nay almost of friendship, as if their calamities had come to them by some inscrutable destiny, as if the father could as little blame the King as the King could blame the father. And now as we look on the building where 360 years ago the bereaved father lived on with the dead son's widow, it seems to bear traces of the tragedy and the ruin with which it began. One wing and the gateway are gone; one remaining wing is desolate and bare. Huge stacks of chimneys tower up, but are never warmed by a fire; the chapel and the chapel bell are gone; the amorini still dance and sport, but under mosses and weeds; decaying casements creak in the wind, and ivy encumbers the arabesques upon many an empty mullion.

Sir Francis who died on Tower Hill left an only child

in his father's house. The child grew up to be Sir Henry Weston, a soldier and a politician. He served with distinction in the last siege, when Calais was lost for ever in 1558. He was made Knight of the Bath with ten other gentlemen at the coronation of Elizabeth. In the next year he was High Sheriff of Surrey, and in the year following he was elected to Parliament as Knight of the Shire. Cousin by marriage of Elizabeth herself, and son of the man who had died in the same condemnation with her mother, he was in favour with the Queen. Two years after her accession she visited him in this house, and stayed in it three days. Many years later we find her again dating despatches to her ambassador from hence. It is probable that she was often here, as it stood on the way to Loseley, Cowdray, and other houses which she constantly visited. One of these visits of the Queen was the occasion of a serious fire, a fire of which traces remain, and which apparently destroyed one wing in some irreparable way. Kings and queens alike were destined to be dangerous friends of the house.

Sir Henry had married a lady (her portrait still hangs in the hall) whose family history was yet more tragic than his own, as her birth was far more illustrious. As he was the son of the man who had been executed as a traitor in 1536, so she was the daughter of Sir Thomas Arundell of Wardour and of Margaret Howard, both attainted in 1552 in the *coup d'état* that struck down the Protector Somerset. Sir Thomas Arundell was a nephew of Grey, Marquis of Dorset, and thus great-grandson of Mary Tudor, the sister of Henry VIII., once Queen Dowager of France. He was a nephew of that Henry Grey, Duke of Suffolk, who was beheaded in 1554, of Leonard Grey, who was beheaded in 1541, and of

Thomas Grey, who was beheaded in 1554; he was cousin therefore of Lady Jane Grey, who was beheaded with her husband, Guildford Dudley, in the same year, at the accession of Mary. He was a cousin also of Catherine Seymour, the unhappy victim of Elizabeth, who died prisoner in the Tower in 1567. Indeed ten of Lady Weston's near relations on the father's side had perished on the scaffold. But on her mother's side the havoc had been even greater. Her mother was attainted but not actually beheaded in 1552; her mother's sister was Catherine Howard, the queen who was executed in 1542; her mother's cousin was Lady Rochford, sister-in-law of Anne Boleyn, who was beheaded in the same year; her mother's cousin also was Anne Boleyn, who had been beheaded along with Sir Henry's father in 1536. Margaret Howard was great-granddaughter of the famous "Jockey of Norfolk," who was killed at Bosworth, granddaughter of the second Duke of Norfolk, who after being attainted by the Tudors and spending three years in the Tower, lived to be the victor over James IV. at Flodden; she was niece of the third Duke of Norfolk, who was attainted in 1546, and of Thomas Howard, who died prisoner in the Tower in 1536; she was cousin of Lord Surrey, the poet, who was beheaded in 1547; of the fourth Duke, who was beheaded in 1572; of Philip, Earl of Arundel, who died prisoner in the Tower in 1594; and she was sister-in-law of Ann Howard, who was attainted and died in prison in 1542. For two generations from the building of it the masters and mistresses of Sutton had worn mourning in their hearts, if not in their hall, for almost every head that had rolled on Tower Hill.

The career of Sir Henry and his house in the reign of Elizabeth seems to have closed as darkly as the career of

Sir Richard in the reign of Henry. From the time when the tremendous conflict with Spain shook the throne of the Queen, as the internecine war of assassination on the one side and executions on the other began to grow fiercer, it seems that the position of Sir Henry became less brilliant or less secure. After 1570 we find him in no public office. In 1569 he receives from Sir Thomas Copley, a desperate Catholic recusant, who ultimately ended his career fighting on the Spanish side, a letter imploring his intercession from his "loving neighbour and assured pore friend." Sir Henry's great-grandson married the descendant of this very man; it is possible that the knight interceded for the exile to his own cost. From this time the fortunes of the house, which still remained Catholic, seemed to fade. They sought no alliances with the great houses whose family burial-place was by Tower Hill; they avoided the perils of the Court, and they took no public employment. It would seem almost as if they lived more constantly on the Clandon estate, and ceased to reside in a house darkened by so many memories and seriously injured by the fire.

One other effort alone was made in the next century. Sir Richard Weston, the grandson of Sir Henry, and fourth in descent from the founder of the house, was in possession of the manor from 1613 to 1652. He seems to have occupied himself enthusiastically with agriculture, travelled much in Holland, and wrote a valuable treatise which introduced some new devices of scientific husbandry. He made known in England not only several foreign products, but the Dutch system of canals with locks, and for years he was occupied in obtaining an Act for his canal upon the Wey. By what skill he succeeded in carrying his project through the reign of King Charles, and then got his Bill passed by the Parliament of the Commonwealth, we have not succeeded in learning. He was a neighbour and a collateral connection of Richard Weston, Earl of Portland, the favourite of Charles, High Treasurer, and Royalist minister.[1] And yet Sir Richard, who had been made a Royal Commissioner by Charles I., and was a known Catholic and Royalist, lived peacefully for years under the rule of the Parliament, and is buried in Guildford, full of honour, in the high tide of the Commonwealth.

He married his son to the heiress of Gatton, and thereby the Westons obtained the splendid estates and quarterings of Copley. They sold the Clandon estates to Sir R. Onslow; they seem to have refitted the house at Sutton, placing the family residence in the undamaged side, and probably they built the new quadrangle on the western side, now the offices. From this time the family is heard of in history no more. Their children and fathers, their uncles and cousins no longer lay their head on the block. No kings or queens are again ever welcomed at Sutton. The fortunes of the family not only disappear from the annals of England, but they hardly are traceable in the annals of the county. They mind their lands beside the Wey, nor think of adding a brick to the old place that was now too large for their estate. The stirring traditions of Sutton Place end with the Commonwealth, where for the most of our famous mansions the stirring traditions begin.

From that day till our own the silent process of decay has slowly gone on with but little violent change. No structural additions were made to the house; one ruinous wing was pulled down in the last century; the pictures,

[1] See further particulars below as to Sir R. Weston, 1645-50.

the furniture, the parchments have gradually been lost to sight. Some few portraits remain—Queen Mary and the hostess of Elizabeth; the Weston who married the heiress of Gatton; William Copley, her grandfather; the last of the direct line of the founder; the ladies of the last century and the collateral Westons, to whom it passed in 1782. But of the glass in the hall the choicest and rarest part is happily preserved. The red and white roses united, the Tudor portcullis and the crown of Henry, the hawthorn and the monograms of Henry of Richmond and Elizabeth of York, the arms of the archbishop who married them, of Richard, whom Henry Tudor defeated and slew at Bosworth,—these remain of the same workmanship as the fragments in the chapel of Henry VII. in the Abbey at Westminster, and are evidently the work of the same school. There are the coats, too, of the finest period of painted glass in England, magnificent specimens of that wonderful art, in the arms with crown and garter of Henry, of Catherine of Aragon, of the Duke of Norfolk of Flodden, of the two Earls of Derby, the successors of the husband of Margaret Beaufort. There, too, remain in the richness of their colours the arms or devices of the men with whom the founder had served as a colleague and friend—Stephen Gardiner, and Fitzalan, Earl of Arundel, and Lord Berners, and Sir Reginald Bray, and Sir Walter Dennys. And above, of a later age, and in less conspicuous quarries, may be found the coats of Cecil, Paulet, Vane, Shirley, Coke, and Onslow.

The glowing blazons of these mighty and stormy personages which gleam across the hall like ghosts in a dilapidated house are all that remains in Sutton to recall its connection with the great. For two centuries and a half it has neither sought nor found such relations. Within the last eighty years its possession has passed in the same family five times, and only twice has the son succeeded the father. The pressure of the penal laws of religion has hardly yet been redressed. Happy (in an antiquarian sense) is the house whose annals are a blank. The restorer, the improver, the architect, and the landscape gardener have no scope for their art. Time and our forefathers have the long-drawn fight to themselves.

Thus it has come to pass that the genius of the place has retained in no scanty degree the peace and retirement of a ruin. The gently-gliding circles of the Wey, where it issues through the gate in the chalk at Guildford, wind round the house in long enfolding reaches, which on three sides alike shut it off from the neighbouring country. The water meadows stretch for miles from the foot of the wooded bank on which the house is placed. Far beyond them, on the ridge between Guildford and Farnham, lies the ancient track of the pilgrims from the west to the shrine of St. Thomas at Canterbury. Above Guildford the Chapel of St. Catherine and the Chapel of St. Martha crown the western and the eastern hills. Through the gap where the Saxons bridged the Wey at Guildford the glades of Surrey reach in broken vistas to the weald. To the east, head away in the distance, in sweeps of woodland and copse, the downs of Effingham and Clandon and Horsley. Broad open upland is all around, nor has our nineteenth century as yet broken the spell. One may watch the brickwork and the mouldings that the old knight raised in the heyday of the merry king without disturbance from the world or an echo of busy life. One listens to the cooing of the wood-pigeon in the shady masses of the limes; one may watch the kingfisher skim the unruffled bosom of the Wey and the heron at work in the shallows. And in the evening there comes across the warren the murmur of the tumbling bays—the invention that the younger Sir Richard brought out of Brabant,—and the beat of the water-wheel of the mill, which is the mill recorded by the Conqueror in his Domesday.

CHAPTER II

VICISSITUDES OF THE MANOR OF SUTTON

THE manor of Sutton, lying quietly out of the way in a home county, with nothing of any distinguishing character about it, supplies a good example of the vicissitudes which befell thousands of estates in England between the Conquest and the battle of Bosworth. Encircled in the reaches of the Wey a little below Guildford, it was far from the great tide of civil war which rolled so fiercely in Plantagenet times through the Midland and Northern counties. It was not near any great stronghold or battle-ground, nor did it form part of any rich and coveted tract of land. And yet during four centuries it is continually changing hands, passing from the Crown to the Crown favourites; back again to the Crown, and thence into a new line. It is held in turn by a succession of men and women famous in English history, and the domestic annals of this unobtrusive manor form a rude outline of the history of England.

Though not very valuable in itself, and not forming part of the great vantage-grounds of war, it was sufficiently desirable, inasmuch as it lay not far from the valley of the Thames, and was conveniently placed between the important town of Guildford and the capital to be worth possessing by statesmen and favourites of the Crown. It is thus during four centuries tossed about like a racquet-ball from chief to chief, as were scores of estates in the south, if they were worth the having. It passes successively to eight or ten families. More than ten times it is forfeited to the Crown. At least ten times the owner of it or the immediate heir to it is beheaded, attainted, or killed in civil war. It passes from king to baron, and back from baron to king, from Red Rose to White Rose, from York to Lancaster, and during the Wars of the Roses it is not easy to say at any given time to whom it belongs in law. It is held in turn, amongst other owners, by the Conqueror, by his favourite Robert Malet, by King Stephen, by his son William, Earl of Warren, by Henry II., by King John, by the Lords Basset, by Roger Bigod, Earl of Norfolk, by Hugh Despenser, by Edward III., by Edmund of Woodstock, half-uncle of Edward III., by Roger Mortimer, Earl of March, by John, Earl of Kent, by Joan, the Fair Maid of Kent, afterwards wife of the Black Prince, and by Thomas, Earl of Kent, her son. Thence it passed by marriage to John, Earl of Somerset, the son of John of Gaunt. At last, by the death of various Beauforts who fell in battle or on the scaffold in the Wars of the Roses, the inheritance ultimately passed, in 1468, to Margaret, Countess of Richmond, the mother of Henry VII. Of course during the reign of the house of York the manor was actually possessed by the Crown in the time of Edward IV. and Richard III. But after the battle of Bosworth, in 1485, Henry VII. put his mother in possession of the estate. She included it in her marriage settlement with Thomas, Earl of Derby, and at her death, in 1509, she left the manor to Henry VIII., her grandson.

During the stormy times of Angevins and Plantagenets the unfortunate manor seemed to grow less and less valuable. At each inquisition the value dwindles below its rating in the age of the Confessor. In three centuries the arable land diminishes from 500 to 300 acres, then to 130 acres, and in 1353, the date of the Statute of Labourers, between the battles of Crecy and of Poictiers, we find the inquisition run thus:

"1. A ruinous messuage valued, after reprisals, at £0 0 0
2. A dovecote, intirely ruined, as appears on
    view of the same . . . . . 0 0 0"

Such was the result of three centuries of feudalism.

But feudalism practically ended with the battle of Bosworth. Henry VIII. and his grandmother quietly retain the property for thirty-six years. Then in 1521 Henry grants the estate to a favoured comrade and friend to build himself a stately mansion; and from that day to this the property has remained in the same family, and descends peacefully from father to son or from kinsman to kinsman, save only that the ancient spell of treason, attainder, and beheading seems so far to cling round the manor, that hardly had its last grantee covered in the roof of his new home when his only son and heir was convicted of high treason and beheaded in one of the passionate outbursts of his fierce benefactor and king.

The hapless lad's son grew up to enjoy in peace his grandfather's home, though his own wife in turn had seen nearly a score of her near relations die on Tower Hill in the wild hurly-burly of the Reformation settlement. Thenceforth the manor peacefully descends from father to son for three centuries; and (what is not a little singular) the place which during the Wars of the Roses had changed its owner almost with every great battle remained perfectly undisturbed during the great civil war of the seventeenth century. The home of a devoted Catholic and Royalist family, of the same name and stock as that of one of Charles's most unpopular ministers, a house within an hour's walk of a stout Puritan town, and within a day's ride of Winchester and of Basing House, has not an escutcheon defaced or a window broken. The portraits of Dorothy Arundell, the hostess of Elizabeth, of Mary Tudor, the crowns, the garters, the red and white roses, the emblems of royal and noble persons, leopards and fleur-de-lys of England, and the arms and crest of Weston, kinsman of the hated Earl of Portland —all stood uninjured in the great hall whilst Oliver's fierce Ironsides were sweeping by to the storm of Basing House. And Protectorate, Revolution of 1689, and Hanoverian dynasty leave the stubborn, Jacobite, and non-juring race unbroken, though cruelly disabled by sequestration and fine.

And now at length, after more than eight centuries, on the very spot where the Confessor had his hunting lodge, they build a chapel of the old faith and dedicate it to St. Edward, and continue to worship after the ancient rite in despite of Tudor reformations and Elizabethan persecutions, and in despite of Roundheads, Whigs, and Georgian penal statutes. The manor of Sutton is thus one of the very few estates still remaining in England of which we can positively assert that it has never for a day passed away from Catholic hands, and wherein the mass has been continuously celebrated since the times of our Saxon kings.

The manor of Sutton, which is a member of Woking parish, and evidently so named as the southern hamlet of the Woking village community, was originally, we are told, held by the Saxon kings. King Edward the Confessor had there a hunting lodge, on the hill about three miles north of Guildford, close by the modern church of St. Edward and the priests' house, *Vine Cottage*. A clump of birch trees marks the remains of a very ancient well, always called St. Edward's Well, within which fragments of old pottery and of very early encaustic tiles have been found. The spot is still known as the "Manor Field."[1]

Edward the Confessor, it appears from the Survey, had granted the manor of about 500 acres to one Wenesi. The account given in the Domesday Survey (1082-1086) is as follows:—

SUDRIE.—XXVIII—
TERRA ROBERTI MALET—IN WOKINGES HUNDREDO—

ROBERTUS Malet tenet SUDTUNE. Wenesi tenuit de rege Edwardo. Tunc se defendebat pro v hidis, modo pro iii hidis. Terra est iii carrucarum. In dominio est una, et v villani et v bordarii cum ii carrucis. Ibi vi servi, et unus molinus de v solidis, et xx acrae prati. Silva de xxv porcis. Tempore Regis Edwardi, et post, valuit viii libras, modo c solidos. Hanc terram saisivit Durandus, et dicunt homines quod iniuste habet, nam nemo corum brevem regis vel liberatorem vidit.

---

[1] Information supplied by F. H. Salvin, from MSS. and relics in his possession. The account of the manor of Sutton down to the grant to Sir R. Weston is taken from Manning and Bray, i. 120 *et seq*. They have been followed by Brayley, *Surrey* (1850), vol. ii. 16.

In English it would run thus :—

The land of Robert Malet, in Woking Hundred.
Robert Malet holds Sudtune. Wenesi held it of King Edward. It was then rated for 5 hides; now for 3 hides. The arable land is 3 plough-teams. There is 1 in demesne, and 5 villains and 5 bordars, with 2 plough-teams. There are 6 serfs, and 1 mill of 5s. a year, and 20 acres of meadow. Woodland to feed 25 swine. In the time of King Edward, and afterwards, it was valued at £8: now at 100s. Durand has seized this land: but the homage present that he hath it without right, for that none of them hath seen the King's writ, or any one who gave him livery of it.

When Wenesi held this manor of the Confessor, and at the date of the Conquest, it was assessed at five hides, and valued at £8 per annum (or say about £500 of our currency). At the time of the Survey, twenty years after the Conquest, the assessment was reduced to three hides, valued at £5. It actually contained, however, about 300 acres of arable and 20 acres of meadow, with woodland for 25 swine.[1] The right of pannage would probably extend over 50 acres at least. The mill is valued as equal to 15 acres (roughly about £15 of our value). Of the manor, 100 acres were in demesne, occupied by the lord himself, 200 acres were occupied by 5 villains regardant, or attached to the soil, and tenants of the class which ultimately developed into copyholders, and 5 cotter tenants, bound to supply the lord's establishment, and there were 6 serfs, the lord's personal property, and acting as his domestics.

Thus an estate of about 400 acres in actual use

---

[1] The *hide* was a measure of *rateable value*, not of actual *area*. The *carruca* was the plough-team, and gave a rough measure of *area*. See Pollock (Sir F.) and Maitland (Professor F. W.), *History of English Law before Edward I.*, 2 vols., second edition, 1898.

supported and was worked by 16 resident tenants, and was valued at something like the equivalent of £400 per annum of our currency. The value of it was much about what it would be now; but the tenants, about one to each 25 acres, would be more in number than would now be found on it.

Besides the King and the Churchmen, who together hold the greater part of the county, there are only mentioned in the Survey about twenty holders of land in all Surrey. Every one of them appears to be a foreigner, and not one a native Englishman.[1]

The manor of Woking, which at the Survey was held by the King in demesne, was retained by the Crown as a royal manor until the reign of Henry II. But the manor of Sutton, in the same parish, had been granted to a subject by the Confessor, and was again continually separated from that of Woking by the Conqueror and his successors.

The Conqueror gave Sutton, along with immense possessions in five other counties, to Robert Malet, son of that William Malet to whom, with Toustain, the White, and many paladins, the mighty William entrusted the consecrated banner at the battle of Hastings, and whom he charged with the interment of Harold. William Malet, one of the most favoured of his chieftains,[2] and ancestor of the house of Malet, which lately served the Crown in Berlin, died about 1071 in the campaign against Hereward, but the Conqueror heaped estates on

---

[1] "Kent, Sussex, *Surrey*, became above all other shires the prey of the spoiler."—Freeman, *Norman Conquest*, v. 41.

[2] Freeman, *Norman Conquest*, iii. 466, 514; iv. 472. "William Malet, well-nigh the only Norman on whom Englishmen can look with personal sympathy and honour."

his son Robert. As he had no other manor in Surrey, that of Sutton was apparently worth having by a royal favourite. Henry I. made Robert Malet Great Chamberlain of England; but on his taking part with Robert, Duke of Normandy, in the conspiracy of the Duke against his brother, as did most of the Norman barons, Robert Malet was banished and his property confiscated (1102).

On the forfeiture of the estates of Robert Malet, Henry I. gave his possessions to Stephen of Blois, the son of Adela, the daughter of the Conqueror; and he, on coming to the throne as King Stephen, granted the manor of Sutton to his own son William, afterwards Earl of Warren. As there is no trace of any castle of importance on the manor, and as the adjacent manor of Woking remained in the hand of the Crown, there is no reason to suppose that during the terrible twenty years of Stephen's reign this particular district suffered especially from feudal anarchy. When Henry II. came to the throne in 1154 he, in accordance with a previous treaty, restored to William of Warren the lands which his father had held as a subject, and Sutton was amongst the vast estates of the popular prince.

On the death of William, Earl of Warren, Morteigne, and Surrey, in 1160, the manor of Sutton again reverted to the King. Henry II. gave it to one Urric, and it was confirmed to his sons by Richard I. It was then valued at £8 (say, vaguely, about £300).[1] Urric, called the Engineer, left it to a son; but on his death without

---

[1] Money values in ancient times cannot be reduced to any modern equivalent. The older writers gave arbitrary equivalents by multiplying by 12, 20, or 40, and they are sometimes followed here. But they have no real authority, and are not adopted by good modern authorities.

heirs it again reverted to the Crown. King John then granted it to Gilbert Basset, son of Lord Basset of Wycombe; and in the family of Basset the manor remained for upwards of seventy years. The manor of Sutton was now again united with that of Woking, and it remained so joined for the 300 years which separate the Great Charter from the time of Henry VIII. Though the great house of Basset were owners from the reign of John till the end of the reign of the third Henry, the estate descended rapidly through the family. Gilbert Basset died young from an accident in the hunting field, and his infant son followed him immediately to the grave. His next brother having been killed in battle, the estate descended to the third brother, Fulc, Bishop of London; and on the speedy death of Fulc, to Philip, a fourth brother. Philip was one of the barons who fought for the King at the battle of Lewes, 1264, and there was made prisoner along with his royal master. On his death, some years later, his inheritance passed to Aliva, his only surviving child, formerly wife of Hugh Despenser, the famous Justiciary, but now the wife of Roger Bigod, Earl of Norfolk.

The mighty baron, the Earl Marshal, who in a famous scene bearded the greatest of the Plantagenets,[1] possessed the estate in right of his wife; but on her death, in 1283, he was forced by law to surrender it to her son by her first husband. Hugh Despenser had been killed at the battle of Evesham in 1265; but he left by Aliva Basset a son, Hugh Despenser, Earl of Winchester, father of Edward II.'s wretched favourite, who was executed like him in 1327. And thus, for the fifth time since the Conquest, the manor reverted to the Crown.

[1] See Stubbs's *Constit. Hist.* i. 132.

On the death of Philip, the last of the Bassets, and on the claim of Roger Bigod to the inheritance in right of his wife, an inquisition was taken in the year 1272. It consisted of a tenement of the value of 1s. In the 200 years which had passed since the Great Survey the 300 acres of arable land had sunk to 145. There were 17 cocks and hens of the yearly value of 1s. 5d. (nearly half as much again as the "tenement"), the customs and services of the villains amount to £3 : 18 : 2, and the total value is £17 : 3 : 6. The whole was held of the King in chief by the office of Mareschal and the render of a pair of buckskin gloves furred with minever.

Roger Bigod, the great Earl Marshal, on the death of his wife, Aliva, attempted to hold her estates on the plea of having issue by her born alive—as the lawyers still call it, as *tenant by the courtesy of England.* But a jury being impanelled to inquire into this plea, Roger, Earl of Norfolk, thought fit to withdraw from trial and surrender the estate. It seems a strange and somewhat pettifogging proceeding of so mighty a baron; for he could hardly have been ignorant whether or not his lamented spouse had borne him a son who would be her heir. And it seems to show that in 1283, in the days of the "*Statute of Merchants*" and "*Quia Emptores*" and the rest, the law-courts of our English Justinian were strong enough to deal even with an earl marshal. At any rate Earl Bigod withdrew and left young Despenser in possession of the estate. He was not then of age; but he retained it for forty-four years, till his own death in 1327.

Hugh Despenser lived to be Earl of Winchester, and father of Edward II.'s arrogant favourite. He shared in the overthrow and death of his king and his son, and was attainted and hanged in the furious revulsion of feeling which swept into space the wretched Edward of Caernarvon. The manor, of course, was forfeited to the Crown. The very first year of his reign Edward III., or those who acted in his name, gave the manor to his half-uncle, Edmund of Woodstock, second son of Edward I., by Margaret of France. Three years later Edmund engaged in a conspiracy against the hated tyranny of the infamous Isabella, the queen mother, and her favourite, Roger Mortimer, Earl of March. He had short shrift, and was beheaded in 1330; and again the manor reverted to the Crown. The manor was found on inquisition to have fallen again in value. It is now worth altogether only £12 : 7 : 5½. The "tenement" of Bigod's time, worth 1s., is now a "ruinous messuage," £0 : 0 : 0. The arable and the meadow lands have both fallen in value; there is a "warren" of 2s. but the "cocks and hens" have disappeared. However, such as it is, with Woking and other estates, Roger Mortimer obtained a grant to himself and his sons.

But the triumph of Mortimer was short. A few months later Edward III., then a youth of but eighteen, seized the reins of government, arrested Mortimer with his own hand in the castle of Nottingham, and summarily brought him to the block. Thus within three short years of storm, insurrection, and rebellion the manor or Sutton had seen three of its lords and masters attainted and beheaded. And three times in as many years the manor was forfeited to the Crown. It is no wonder that its value appears to diminish, the messuages to get more and more ruinous, and the very cocks and hens of Roger Bigod to disappear.

Edward III. was now well seated on the throne, which

he occupied for fifty years; and one of his first cares was to undo the infamous work of the favourites of his father and of his mother. Edmund, Earl of Kent, the son of Edward I., lay in a traitor's headless grave; but his sons Edmund, and then John, were restored in blood, in honours, and in estate, and were successively Earls of Kent.[1] Edmund, John, and John's widow became entitled to the manor, and peacefully enjoyed it; but on the death of John, in 1352, subject to the dower of John's widow, the inheritance passed to his sister Joan, commonly known as the "Fair Maid of Kent." Joan was the wife, first, of Sir Thomas Holland, one of the original Knights of the Garter, by whom she left a family, then of William, Earl of Salisbury, and then of Edward, the Black Prince, by whom she became the mother of Richard II. From Joan the estate passed through a succession of Earls of Kent and Earls of Somerset, all her lineal descendants, to Margaret, Countess of Richmond, and thence to her grandson, Henry VIII. But though during 150 years the estate descended in the same blood, this period includes the tremendous struggle of the Roses; so that attainder, executions, and forfeitures are for this period even more frequent in the annals of the manor than they had been in the 150 years preceding.

When in 1352 the estate came to Joan, the Fair Maid of Kent, its annual value had sunk to £8 : 1 : 6; "the ruinous Messuage" and "the Dovecote, intirely ruined," were valued at £0 : 0 : 0. The 300 acres of arable of the Conqueror's Survey were shrunk to 130; the pannage, or right of turning pigs to feed in the wood, was worth

---

[1] For the genealogies of York and Lancaster, Beauforts, Hollands, and Staffords consult the tables in Sir James Ramsay's valuable work, *Lancaster and York*, Oxford Clarendon Press, 2 vols., 1892, Tables I., II., III., IV.

5s.; and there is another wood "whose pasture is worth nothing" at £0 : 0 : 0. The Fair Maid, the great heiress and principal *parti* of her time, must have had more profitable estates than Sutton before she won the Black Prince, her chivalrous, ferocious, and splendid cousin. The fact was that Elizabeth, daughter of John, Marquis of Juliers, and widow of John, Earl of Kent, Joan's brother, had a settlement of these estates by way of dower, and she kept actual possession of them till her death in 1411. In the meantime the inheritance or feudal lordship continued to pass through the descendants of Joan.

Joan had a son, Thomas, by Sir Thomas Holland, who was created Earl of Kent after the extinction of that title in the person of Edmund of Woodstock; and Thomas the second in due time became Earl of Kent. He died in 1397, when Thomas, his son, who succeeded as Earl of Kent, was created Duke of Surrey. "He was one of those," writes the patient historian of the county, "who in the very beginning of the next reign (Henry IV.) entered into a conspiracy for seizing the King's person; but failing in the attempt, was taken prisoner at *Cirencester*, whither he had fled, and according to the custom of the times beheaded the day following without further ceremony. An attainder and forfeiture of his estates was the consequence."[1] The next year, 1400, Bolingbroke, for reasons of his own, restored the estate to the mother of the Duke, Alice, daughter of Richard Fitzalan, the tenth Earl of Arundel, and Earl of Surrey, the great seaman, who himself, after a stormy career, lost his head on the scaffold in the later days of Richard II., 1397.[2]

Manning and Bray, *Surrey*, i. 121.
[2] Stubbs, ii. 495.

The surviving son of Alice Fitzalan was Edmund, Earl of Kent, to which title he succeeded on the execution of his elder brother, Thomas, Duke of Surrey, in 1400. But as he died a few years after his unhappy brother without issue the inheritance next descended on their sisters. One of these was Margaret Holland (afterwards wife of that Duke of Clarence who was killed in his brother's wars in France), previously the wife of John Beaufort, Earl of Somerset, eldest son of John of Gaunt by Catherine Swynford, his mistress, and then his third wife.

Here we come, in 1408, into the times of the Beauforts, in which family the estate remained until its alienation by the Crown. It remained, indeed, but with wild vicissitudes, deaths, attainders, and constant revolutions. John Beaufort, Earl of Somerset, died, strange as it may seem, in his bed about 1410. His eldest son, Henry, Earl of Somerset, died a minor, and without issue, in 1418. John, Earl and Duke of Somerset, the next brother, his heir, assigned the estate to his younger brother, Edmund, eventually Earl and Duke of Somerset, who was killed in the first battle of St. Albans in 1455. His eldest son, Henry, Duke of Somerset, who succeeded, founder of the ducal house of Beaufort, was taken, after the battle of Hexham in 1464, and promptly beheaded on the field. The second and third sons were slain at Tewkesbury, 1471, without issue, and thereupon, the male issue of John of Gaunt being extinct, the manor of Sutton at last devolved on Margaret, Countess of Richmond, the famous mother of Henry VII.

One need hardly say that the manor of Sutton was not the only inheritance which the whirligig of civil war, battles, attainders, and executions had cast into the lap of Margaret Beaufort. As the only child of John Beaufort, third Earl of Somerset, she represented the family of John of Gaunt by his third wife. One part of the inheritance aforesaid was the claim to the throne of England. Henry VIII., as every one knows, at last combined the claims of the Red and White Rose; and it is indeed no wonder that the house built on the Wey by Henry's minister should be covered with the symbolic emblems of Red and White Rose in union; for the knight there received from his master a manor which for 120 years had belonged to the Red Rose, but which the White Rose had been so constantly confiscating, seizing, and occupying all through the grand tussle.

The succession to the manor of Sutton, which from the time of Edward I. really follows the lines of the succession to royal titles and the control of the State, is, as every lawyer would perceive, a legal, and not a possessory interest. The heirs-at-law were very far from being always in possession. Widows were very real powers in feudal times, and dower was a fact and not a conveyancing conundrum. In truth, Elizabeth, daughter of the Marquis of Juliers, and Alice Fitzalan, the daughter of the Earl of Arundel, both kept possession of the estate by right of their dower. And furthermore, when the estate did devolve on the Beauforts, their actual enjoyment of it not a little depended on the issue of the battles and the ups and downs of war and intrigue.

On the attainder of Henry, Duke of Somerset, after the battle of Hexham, the estate was forfeited to King Edward IV. He and his brother, Richard III., kept possession of the forfeited estates during their reigns. Edward IV. resided not seldom in his manor of Woking, which, as we saw, was conjoined to that of Sutton throughout the whole fourteenth and fifteenth centuries. In the hall of Sutton to this day stands the blazon of Richard when Duke of Gloucester. No doubt as king he held possession of the estate; but it was only on the battle of Bosworth, in 1485, that Henry VII. could put his mother in effective possession of estates which, confiscation and attainder apart, had been her property for the 20 years since the battle of Hexham, and which Margaret Holland had first brought to the Beauforts just 80 years before. Here, with Bosworth field, ends the whirligig of escheat and forfeiture which had swept round continually since the death of the great Edward Longshanks. During that period of 178 years the estate had been forfeited eight times on the attainder, execution, or death in civil war of the legal owner. There is nothing exceptional in this. It is a fair average specimen from a southern English county in the fourteenth and fifteenth centuries. There is much to learn by observing feudalism at home in its own manor-house and its "ruinous messuage."

We need not here rehearse the virtues, piety, dignities, and beneficence of Margaret Beaufort, sole remnant and hope of the Red Rose, Countess of Richmond, and then of Derby, who lies in so noble a monument in the south aisle of Henry VII.'s Chapel at Westminster.[1] She married first, at the age of sixteen, Edmund Tudor, Earl of Richmond, a son of Catherine of France, widow of Henry V., and thus she became the mother of Henry

---

[1] She "whose merit exceeds the highest commendation that can be given," as the laborious Camden declares. Her Latin epitaph was written by Erasmus.—Brayley, *Westminster Abbey*, i. 70. For Margaret Beaufort's title to the Crown see Mr. Alfred Bailey's excellent book, *The Succession to the English Crown*, 1879.

VII. Then she married Sir H. Stafford, son of the Duke of Buckingham; and thirdly she married Thomas, Lord Stanley, the hero of Bosworth, and first Earl of Derby. Great ladies in those days, as we see in the little story of our manor, married early and married often; and as their lords and masters soon came to untimely ends in the field or on the scaffold, they carried their hands and their possessions through half the feudal nobility. Lady Margaret, the saintly princess of whom Gray sings—

"Foremost and leaning from her golden cloud,
   The venerable Margaret"—

has perpetuated her name by the foundation of St. John's College and Christ's College at Cambridge, and the divinity professorships at both universities which bear her name. She was a learned and pious woman, as is fully told in Halsted's *Life*, and she herself translated from the Latin the *Imitation* and other books of devotion.[1] And as engaged in religious vows, she is represented in the well-known picture, belonging to Mr. Milner Gibson, exhibited at the Tudor Exhibition in 1890, in the habit of a nun. She died in 1509, at the age of sixty-eight, having lived to see her grandson crowned as Henry VIII.

Margaret Beaufort lived much at Woking from the battle of Bosworth till her death, and the manor of Sutton was practically a part of her home estate. She often received in it her son, Henry VII., many of his Acts being there signed. Woking and Sutton were both included in the settlement which Margaret made on the marriage with the Earl of Derby, and were appointed to the Earl for life after her decease. But

---

[1] C. A. Halsted, *Life of Margaret Beaufort*, 1839, p. 195.

as she survived him, the two manors, with much else, passed by her will to her grandson, now Henry VIII.

Henry VIII., when possessed of the manor and mansion of Woking, used it as a summer residence all through his reign. "In the middle of September 1515," we are told by Grafton, "he came to his Maner of Okyng, and thether came to him the Archebishop of Yorke, whom he hartily welcommed, and shewed him great pleasures," and there "a Letter was brought to the Archebishop from Rome, certifying him howe he was elected to be a Cardinall."[1] As Richard Weston was already attached to the King's person, and held various offices, there is every probability that he was often with the Court at Woking; and he may well have been one of those who congratulated Wolsey on the coveted Red Hat. During these visits he must have had occasion to notice the obvious advantages that the manor of Sutton would offer as the site of a mansion. Woking remained a royal manor and the residence of the sovereign all through the reigns of the Tudors; and in 1621 James I. granted it to Sir Edward Zouch. But a hundred years before this the manor of Sutton was granted to Sir Richard Weston in May 1521.

King Henry VIII., by Letters Patent, dated at Westminster 17th May 1521, in the thirteenth year of his reign, granted the manor of Sutton with its appurtenances and all the knights' fees thereto belonging, villains, goods and services, waifs and strays, wardships and rights, woods, meadows, pastures, fisheries, water, vineyards, ponds, rents, reliefs, escheats, courtleets, weirs, with all the profits of the same and free warren within the forest, in consideration of good and

[1] Grafton, *Chron.* p. 1016.

faithful service, "to his noble and well-beloved Privy Councillor, Sir Richard Weston, Knight, his heirs and assigns."[1]

Nine years later Sir Richard Weston received a further grant, dated 25th May 1530, which gave him license to impark 600 acres of land and pasture, 50 acres of wood, and 400 acres of heath and furze, in the parishes of Merrow and Clandon, with free warren and fishery.[2] This made him lord of the lands lying south of the manor of Woking, across both banks of the Wey, as far up as the top of Merrow Downs. The dates of these grants deserve notice. The first grant was during the zenith of the power of Cardinal Wolsey, when he had just negotiated a league between Henry VIII., the Emperor Charles V., and the Pope, at the time when Wolsey was aspiring to the Papacy, and when the English Government was straining every nerve to carry on the war with France. The grant of Sutton followed close on the visit of Charles V. to Henry VIII. at Dover and Canterbury. Sir Richard Weston had been one of the witnesses to the treaty with the Emperor, and one of the noblemen and knights appointed to receive and attend him at Dover. The second grant was made after the fall of Wolsey and the trial for the divorce of Catherine of Aragon.

From the date of the grant in Wolsey's time the manor has been held by the Westons, descendants of Sir Richard, and since 1782 by Westons from an allied branch of the same family. The present owner, F. H.

---

[1] The grant is abstracted in the *Calendar of State Papers*, Rolls Series (Brewer), iii., 1519-23, Record Office, No. 1324, 17, marked S.B., pat., p. 2, m. 18. An ancient copy of the patent is in possession of the owner of the estate, F. H. Salvin, Esq.   [2] Manning and Bray, iii. p. 60.

Salvin, is the sixth son of Thomas Salvin of Croxdale, in Durham, by Mary Ann Weston, eldest daughter of John Webbe-Weston, the devisee of the estate on failure of the issue of Sir Richard. It is somewhat remarkable that an estate which, from the Conquest to the battle of Bosworth, had been so often forfeited to the Crown should never since have passed out of the same family, although the only son of the grantee was attainted and executed fifteen years after the grant, although the grandson of the grantee was a notorious Catholic all through the penal laws of Elizabeth, and although its owners were Catholics and Royalists, malignants of the deepest dye, all through the times of the Civil War, the Commonwealth, and Protectorate, though they were non-jurors and obstinate Jacobites under the Dutch and Hanoverian dynasties.

From the day when Henry VIII. granted the estate to his favourite knight and to Wolsey's "most humble servant," "through whose goodnes and medyacion all that I have now proceded and came," as Sir Richard wrote to "my lorde legate's grace" in 1527, down to this day the manor of Sutton ceases to have any connection with the history of England, and becomes a mere private estate and unobserved country mansion. Henry VIII. was frequently there: indeed he constantly resided at Woking and at Guildford, and he could only pass from one to the other across the manor of Sutton. Elizabeth was often there too; for she, too, was constantly passing it on the way to Woking, Pirford, Guildford, and Loseley. From that day to the present time the owners of Sutton had little trust in princes, and small favour to expect at Court. They were Catholics, non-jurors, disaffected Jacobites, and deeply alien to all Protestant settlements. Henceforth the history of the manor concerns no one but the owners and their family.

It may be partly by chance, and possibly by some removal of painted glass from the old manor-house at Woking, but it is singular that to-day we find in the windows and quarries of the hall arms, emblems, and devices of a great number of historic persons and families, all of whom had some connection with the past history of the manor, who had owned it, or had been visitors in it, or were friends and colleagues of its owners. Amongst these may be mentioned the Beauforts, Edward IV. and Richard III., Henry VII. and Henry VIII., the Earls of Arundel, Earls of Derby, and Dukes of Norfolk, Archbishop Bourchier, Catherine of Aragon, Sir Reginald Bray, Edward VI., Mary Tudor, Philip of Spain, Queen Elizabeth, Bishop Gardiner, Paulet, Marquess of Winchester, Charles II., and the Earls of Onslow. There is no reason to suppose that Sir Richard Weston when he built his house was deeply versed in the history of his manor; but when he came to place in his hall the coats, crests, and devices of men of historic name with whom he had served, or who had visited his hall, he was really placing there the same emblems which centuries before had been borne on the pennons of the lords of the manor before him.

CHAPTER III

PART I.—BEFORE THE REFORMATION

SIR RICHARD WESTON THE ELDER—BUILDER OF THE HOUSE

SIR RICHARD WESTON, who built Sutton Place and there founded a family, was one of those typical men, at once soldiers, diplomatists, and statesmen, by whose arms and brains Henry VII. and Henry VIII. consolidated the great Tudor monarchy of the sixteenth century. In following up his life and story, we are struck with the vast change in social and political life which this monarchy introduced, and with the flexible, versatile, Italian character of the agents by whom these masterful kings were served. Ordinary history does not say much of Sir Richard Weston. But the State papers are full of his name. There is hardly a single State ceremony or event during the eighth Henry's reign in which he is not recorded to have part. A bare list of the offices he held would fill some pages. He is a soldier, seaman, ambassador, governor, treasurer, privy councillor, judge of the Court of Wards, courtier, the amasser of great possessions, a munificent patron of art, a wary, adroit, and successful man of affairs.

Sir Richard Weston was just such a man as was Sir Richard Cromwell, founder of the Hinchinbroke family, great-grandfather of the Protector, or such as Sir Henry Marney, Sir Edward Seymour, Sir Thomas Boleyn, and Sir John Fitzwilliam. He served his royal master for more than thirty-two years, from the first year of the reign until his own death at a great age; and there is almost complete evidence that he never lost the King's favour or resigned a single office till his last illness. He saw out all the changes of policy and religion, the book against Luther, the Reformation, and the Six Articles; he did homage to five of Henry's queens, he saw scores of his colleagues and his own son beheaded on charges of treason, and yet he retained to the last the confidence of the King. It gives one a new idea of Henry's character, to see the unbroken loyalty which he could show to an old and tried servant. Sir Richard seems to have been indeed a servant after Henry's own heart: brave, discreet, wary, magnificent, artistic, cosmopolitan, without troublesome scruples or feelings, either in Church or State; a man without any feudal connections or instincts, and with no dangerous ambition; devoted to his master, body and soul, essentially one of the "new men."[1] He rose into

---

[1] See Henry's own view of his councillors, in the answer to the rebels of Yorkshire, 1537. "In the beginning of our raigne, where it is said that so many noblemen were councillors, we doe not forget who were these council-

royal favour under Archbishop Warham long before Wolsey; he retained it under Wolsey, and after Wolsey's fall, after that of More, and after that of Thomas Cromwell. He served them all, and he outlived them all.

There is nothing about him of the old feudal nobility. He belongs to an ancient family of knights and squires, soldiers and crusaders, men of good blood, but not noble in the legal sense of the word. In the splendid pedigree of the family, the work of Garter-King-at-Arms in 1632, long preserved at Sutton Place, and now in the British Museum,[1] the family of Weston is traced from the time of Henry I.; but with its galaxy of Norman and feudal chivalry there is not a single alliance of a Weston with any of the greater houses or titled nobility. Sir Richard was evidently one of the able men, of courage, brains, and culture, on whom the Tudors relied to break the teeth of the barons and such remnants of them as the Wars of the Roses had left, and to build up a modern king-craft of a civilised, organised, rich, artistic, intellectual order, such as was the dream of Francis I., Charles V., and afterwards of Elizabeth of England and Henry IV. of France. Sir Richard Weston was evidently one of the men who helped on this work; after his kind, personally unscrupulous, grasping, time-serving, and self-seeking, but withal of

---

lors, for of the Temporalty there were but two worthy to be called noble— the one the Treasurer of England, the other the Lord High Steward of our Household; others as the Lords Marney and Darcy, but scant, wel-born gentlemen, and yet of no great lands till they were promoted by us, and so made Knights and Lords" (Speed, p. 776, bk. ix.) Howard of Norfolk was Treasurer; the High Steward was Talbot, fourth Earl of Shrewsbury (Brewer, i. 54). Weston was exactly one of Henry's scant, well-born gentlemen, of no great lands till promoted. Consult Paul Friedmann, *Anne Boleyn*, vol. i. pp. 26-29.   [1] Addit. MS. 31, 890.

unblemished credit, and staunchly faithful to his master and to his friends.

According to the pedigree made by Garter, one may suppose in anticipation of the famous Copley alliance of 1637, the Westons of Sutton are descended from a very ancient family seated in Lincolnshire in the time of Henry I. The judicious historian of the nineteenth century will as little guarantee as he will dispute the accuracy of a family genealogy of such absolute heraldic authority, and blazoned in so splendid and scientific a form as is the Roll which is now one of the prizes of the British Museum.[1] In that gorgeous family tree the race starts from Hayleric of Weston in Holland, County Lincoln, temp. Henry I., and descends through a succession of Nigels and Lamberts, who witness charters and otherwise prove their reality, if not their relationship, down to one Humphrey of Prested Hall, in Essex, 13 Richard II. (1390). Humphrey Weston, by his first wife, Catherine, widow of John de Beauchamp, was the father of John de Weston of Boston, 38 Henry VI. (1460), from whom descend in right line the Westons of Sutton. By his second wife, Joan, he was the father of the Robert de Weston, the ancestor of the Westons of Prested Hall, Essex,[2] from whom descended Richard Weston, Earl of Portland, 1632, temp. Charles I., and also John Webbe-Weston (the

---

[1] See Friedmann's *Anne Boleyn*, i. 37. "Nowhere has the making of false pedigrees been so extensively practised as it was in England during the sixteenth century. Every man or woman who rose into the royal favour had but to apply to the herald to have—for a consideration—some genealogical tree made out, the root of which was a fabulous Saxon chieftain, or an equally imaginary Norman knight." But then judicial Mr. Friedmann is a foreigner, of a somewhat sceptical turn, and a cruel judge of Henry and of Anne. Besides Segar's pedigree was made in the reign of Charles I.

[2] See Morant's *Essex*, ii. 70, 171.

devisee of the estates from the last male descendant of Sir Richard), who was grandfather of the present owner.

John, the eldest son of Humphrey aforesaid, was settled at Boston, in Lincolnshire. It is proudly recorded by Garter that he received four yards of scarlet cloth at the coronation of Henry V. in 1413. His son Peter (temp. Edward IV.), likewise of Boston, had by Agnes, daughter of John Daunay of Escrick, in the county of York, three sons, Edmund, John, and William. John, the second son, was Lord Prior of the Knights of St. John in England, 1476, and died in 1489. William, the third brother, was a Knight of St. John's at Rhodes. Edmund, the eldest, also of Boston, was the father of Sir Richard Weston and of Sir William Weston, last Prior of St. John's in England.

This Edmund Weston married Catherine, daughter and ultimately heir of John Camell of Shapwick, in the county of Dorset, by whom he had two sons and two daughters.[1] William, the younger son, became a Knight of St. John's, took part in the heroic defence of Rhodes against Solyman, and, after a life of great services in arms and in diplomacy, was, as his uncle had been, Lord Prior of St. John's in England, and died of grief, 1540, on the day of the dissolution of his order in England. The elder daughter, Mabel, married Sir John Dingley of the Isle of Wight, and was mother of Sir Thomas Dingley or Dyneley, who served at Malta in 1531, and who was executed in 1539. Ann, the younger, married Sir Ralph Verney of Bucks. The eldest son of Edmund Weston of Boston was Sir Richard Weston, the builder of the house.

Boston was at this time one of the great ports of the

---

[1] For the pedigree of Catherine (or Anne) Camell (or Cammell), traced from Sir John de Plecy, temp. Edward I., see Manning and Bray, ii. 638, and Hutchins, *Hist. of Dorset*, iii. 166.

kingdom, and it carried on a large trade with the Levant.[1] The Westons were great seamen as well as soldiers; Sir John Weston, 1474, and also Sir William, the Prior, 1520, served as Admirals of the Fleet of the Knights of Rhodes; and it is possible that the family assisted Richmond in his landing at Milford Haven before Bosworth. The services of three Westons, Knights of St. John, the brother and two uncles of Sir Richard, in the heroic crusade against the Turk, will be spoken of later. There seems some ground for thinking that the Westons had materially contributed to the successful venture of Henry Tudor, which eventually placed the crown on his head on Bosworth field.

Within a month of the coronation of Henry VII. in Westminster Abbey by Archbishop Bourchier,[2] we find Edmund Weston, the father of Sir Richard, promoted by the King. On 28th November 1485 a grant is made to Edmund Weston and Thomas Saintmartyn, Esquires, in survivorship ("in consideration of good and gratuitous services performed by them with great labour and great personal cost to themselves") of the office of Captain, Keeper, and Governor of the island of Guernsey, and castle of Cornet, and of the other islands and places in those parts, and the castles and fortresses within the same, and the revenues, without rendering any account thereof.[3]

What were these "good and gratuitous services" per-

---

[1] See Pishey Thompson, *History of Boston in Lincolnshire*, 1856, p. 184, tomb of a Weston, Knight of St. John. Sir W. Weston of Boston is mentioned 1333 and in 1377 (pp. 467, 469).

[2] Emblems of the King and the arms and mitre of the Archbishop are represented in the painted glass of the hall of Sutton; see chap. xii. "The Painted Glass Windows" (I. 6; II. 5).

[3] *Calendar*, Henry VII., i. pp. 186, 372, Public Records, Record Office, P.S. No. 514, pat., p. 2, m. 20.

formed at "great labour and great cost"? Doubtless the use of money or ships; possibly a contingent that fought at Bosworth. The extreme haste of the reward, within three months of the great battle, suggests it; and that the service was great is shown by the nature and value of the gift. Edmund Weston proved to be the survivor, or the more successful, for four months later, on 8th March 1486, there is a grant for life to Edmund Weston, now Esquire of the King's Body ("in consideration of various services in which he had expended large sums of money"), of the office of Captain, Keeper, and Governor of the island of Guernsey. The office became almost hereditary in the family. The year of the accession of Henry VIII., Richard Weston, the son of Edmund, was appointed to the same office, 22nd May 1509, and he held it for thirty-two years.[1]

The Westons were evidently of a family which had rendered signal service to the Tudors, and were high in favour with Henry VII. Edmund twice received a lucrative and important government, and was named Esquire of the King's Body in the first year of the reign. His younger brother, John, had been appointed by Peter d'Aubusson, then Grand Master of the Order, Lord Prior of St. John's in England; and Edward IV., in a letter to Pope Sixtus IV., accepts the nomination of the Grand Master and the Pope.[2] The elder prior, as afterwards was the second prior, his nephew, was employed in

---

[1] See W. Berry, *History of Guernsey*, 4to ed., 1815, p. 205. The office of Governor of the Island is one of great antiquity, and in the fourteenth and fifteenth centuries had been often held by royal princes. The Westons held the post continuously from 1488 to 1541.

[2] *Calendar of State Papers*, Venetian, 1202-1509 (Archives of Venetian Library), No. 452. Letter of Edward IV. to Pope Sixtus IV., 25th February 1476.

embassies by the King. In 1486 we find him one of the Commissioners to arrange a treaty between Henry VII. and James III., King of Scotland; and in 1488 he is one of the ambassadors to treat for peace with Ferdinand and Isabella of Spain.[1] He himself died in 1489.

Richard Weston, accordingly, in the reign of Henry VII. was the eldest son of an officer high in favour with the King, and heir of a family which had rendered him conspicuous services in peace and war. It does not appear whether Richard had any part in Bosworth field and the campaign which it ended. As he was probably born about 1465 or 1466, he would be under age at the time of the battle, but may well have taken part in it. He would be early introduced to the King and the Prince; and he certainly held office in Berkshire under Henry VII.[2]

The very first year of the young king, Henry VIII., we find Richard Weston receiving promotion and grants, just as his father Edmund had received them in the first year of Henry VII.; and in such hot haste that it would seem as if the splendid young prince (he was then but

---

[1] *Materials for History of Henry VII.*, Rolls Series (Campbell), vol. i. p. 480, vol. ii. p. 273. He is there called "Friar John Westoun, prior of the order of St. John Jerusalem in England."

[2] *Calendar of State Papers*, Henry VIII., i. 1505. In the *Privy Purse Expenses of Elizabeth of York, Queen of Henry VII.*, we find in 1502 that £4 : 10s. was paid to Richard Weston for "certain harnesses of gyrdelles by him brought for the Queen beyond the sea." And in 1502 and 1503 (pp. 23, 99) wages (£6 : 12 : 4) are paid to "Mrs. Anne Weston," a lady in attendance on the Queen. This was obviously Sir Richard's wife. Thus both he and his wife were in the service of Henry VII. as well as that of Henry VIII.; and in all probability Anne, afterwards Lady Weston, was in attendance at the death of the Queen, Elizabeth of York. There is also mention of money paid to Weston for "the kinges losse at disse opon Shrove Monday, £1 : 13 : 4," 18th February 1502; and again, "to Weston for the king to play at Cheke, £2."—*Excerpta Historica*, p. 127.

eighteen) thought that Weston, who was then more than forty, had not been duly recompensed. Henry VIII. had not been king a month, and had not yet been crowned, when three patents were signed in favour of Richard Weston. He was made Keeper of Hanworth Park and of the manor of Cold Kennington, Steward of Marlowe, Cokeham, and Bray, and finally he was appointed Captain, Keeper, and Governor of Guernsey, of the castle of Cornet, and the isles of Alderney, Sark, etc., as held by Edmund Weston, etc. All this on 21st to 22nd May 1509, before the King had been crowned.[1]

May, we shall find, is a critical month to the Westons. The day of the coronation Weston is appointed Steward of the Lordship of Flamsted ; two months later he has the custody and wardship of a young heir ; his wife, Anne Weston, "gentlewoman with the Queen," has the wardship of another young heir ; the next year he is in the Commission for Berkshire ; the security for a loan to him by the King of £100 is cancelled ; he has the grant of the manor of Upton Pole, Berkshire, forfeited by the attainder of Francis, Lord Lovell ; he has license to freight a ship with wools, skins, etc., to carry them to foreign parts through the Straits of Marrok (Morocco) ; and the next year he is appointed Lieutenant of the Castle and Forest of Windsor, with lodgings in the Lieutenant's Tower, and perquisites as held by Sir John Williams or Sir John Norres (2nd June 1511).

There is no doubt that he married some years before Anne, the daughter of Oliver Sands or Sandys of Shere who died on the 7th November 1515. His son Francis

---

[1] *Calendar of State Papers*, Henry VIII., i. 92, 93, 94, 231, etc. *N.B.*—This was six years before the rise of Wolsey, whilst the Great Seals were held by Archbishop Warham.

appears to have been born in 1511. Mrs. Weston is mentioned as gentlewoman of the Queen in 1509, as she no doubt was to Queen Elizabeth of York, who died 1503.[1] The King has only been on the throne two years when Richard had two noble governorships, lands, wardships, stewardships, and a mercantile patent. Truly this is a man bent on amassing a great fortune, the destined architect of a broad and stately career.[2]

Every few months during the earlier part of Henry's reign the State Papers record some appointment in favour of the Westons. In 1510 (*Calendar*, Henry VIII., i. 1262) we have a letter from the Grand Master of Rhodes, Emery d'Amboise, to the King, notifying receipt of the King's letter on behalf of William Weston of the preceptory of Badislay. The Grand Master has given him an annuity.[3]

In the following year a Weston is sent with the force under Lord Darcy to assist Ferdinand, King of Spain, in the campaign against the Moors.[4] Ferdinand had asked of Henry 1000 English archers. These were sent under the command of Lord Darcy. "There were appointed to go with the Lord Darcie, Lord Anthony Grey, brother to the Marquis Dorset, Henry Guildeford, Weston, Broune, William Sydney, Esquires of the King's Horse."[5]

---

[1] Manning and Bray, i. 524. For pedigree of Anne Sandys see Manning and Bray, ii. 671, where she is said to be the sister of Oliver Sandys of Shere, and daughter of William Sandes of Rotenby, St. Bees, in Cumberland. So Berry, *Genealogies of the Surrey Families*—Westons of Sutton Place.

[2] *Calendar of State Papers*, Henry VIII., i. Nos. 231, 424, 867, 885, 1006, 1207, 1208, 1707.

[3] Brit. Mus., Otho, ix. 4, 6.

[4] The history of this expedition may be read in the historians Brewer, i. 18; Rapin, i. 710; Rymer, *Fœd.* xiii. 297; Hall, *Chron.* p. 522; Stow, p. 488; *State Papers*, Henry VIII., i. 297, 1566.

[5] See Hall, p. 520.

Nothing came of the expedition, but Weston at any rate did not disgrace himself or lose favour. Shortly afterwards the King makes him a loan of £250.[1] According to Hall (*Chron.* p. 522), Weston and other young and lusty esquires had leave to visit the Court of Spain, where they were handsomely received. The King dubbed them all knights, "and gave to Sir Weston and Browne an eagle of Sicily on a chief to the augmentation of their arms."[2] If this were Richard Weston, he was too prudent to avail himself of this foreign knighthood and honour, for no trace of it ever appears in his house or his own history.

Richard Weston was made knight by Henry VIII. in 1514, and thenceforth his fortunes grew apace. He is present at the marriage of Mary, the King's sister, to Louis XII. of France, 14th October 1514.[3] In 1516 he is appointed Knight of the Body; he is made Keeper of Hanworth Park, of Le Mote Park in Windsor Forest, of the Swans on the Thames, of the Chase at Cranbourne, Steward of the Lordship of Caversham, and then of the Lordship of Marlowe, all of these, with salaries and dues. As Knight of the Body, he is in personal attendance on the King, and is associated with many of Henry's knights and ministers, with whom Weston became connected— Sir T. Arundell, Sir J. Russell, Sir C. Pickering, Sir W. Sandys, Sir W. Dennys.[4]

---

[1] *Calendar*, Henry VIII., i. 1455.

[2] This was no doubt the eagle displayed as borne by the Emperor Frederick II. See an example in Westminster Abbey (Boutell, *English Heraldry*, No. 200), and also as borne in the arms of the Emperor Charles V. The *Ordinary of British Armorials* (Papworth and Morant, i. 301) gives the arms of Frederick II., Emperor, as—*Or*, an eagle displayed, wings downwards, *sable*. So Sandford, *Genealogical History*, fol. 1707, p. 87. These were the arms granted by Segar in 1628 to Weston of Rugely, County Stafford.

[3] *Calendar*, Henry VIII., i. 5483.   [4] *Ibid.* iv. 2735.

One cannot here follow the shifting European policy of Henry and of his tortuous minister, the Cardinal. But whatever it may be, the King finds in Weston an ever-obsequious agent. On 2nd October 1518 Henry signed his solemn and short-lived treaty of peace[1] "between the Confederated Kings of France and England," and amongst the witnesses stands the name of *Richard Weyston* (sic). Others who sign the stately but worthless roll are Wolsey, Dorset, Surrey, T. Boleyn, Maurice Berkeley, Sir T. More, William Fitzwilliam; and on the 4th October 1518 is signed by the same personages the treaty of marriage between the Princess Mary and the Dauphin of France.[2] This was the vain and short-lived project of an alliance between Mary Tudor, afterwards our Queen Mary, and the eldest son of Francis I. He was then a baby of six months, and she was three; and, as we all know, she in the end married Philip II. of Spain. Had the ill-starred project of Wolsey succeeded, and the royal children of France and England lived to become husband and wife, a good many things might have gone differently. But, though the project resulted in nothing so far as the history of England is concerned, it perhaps had no small effect on the house of Sutton; for during his embassy in France Sir Richard Weston must have seen, envied, and determined to imitate the châteaux of the Loire.

In the autumn of 1518, tenth year of Henry VIII., a solemn embassy was sent over to Francis to obtain ratification of this treaty. The ambassadors named are the Lord Chamberlain, the Earl of Worcester, the Earl of Surrey, the Lord Admiral, West, the Bishop of

---

[1] Brit. Mus., Vit., bk. xx. 92; *Calendar*, Henry VIII., ii. 4469.
[2] Brit. Mus., Vit., chap. xi. 169; Brewer, Henry VIII., i. 194.

Ely, Dockwra, the Lord Prior of St. John's, Sir Thomas Boleyn, accompanied by seventy knights, with whom Sir Richard Weston, Sir W. Fitzwilliam, Sir Maurice Berkeley, and others were named.[1] They were abroad fifty days, and the expenses allowed to the Lord Chamberlain are £166, to the Bishop of Ely, £133, to the Prior of St. John's, £100, to Lord E. Howard, Lord Ferrers, Sir R. Weston, and other knights, £66 each.[2]

The ambassadors, with a train of about 500 persons, came by Calais to Paris. They were treated by Francis with great magnificence; and, desiring to display his wealth and taste, he induced a separate embassy, of which the Bishop of Ely, Sir T. Boleyn, the Lord Prior, and Sir Richard Weston were members, to visit the baby prince, who was then at Cognac, in Angoulême, the ancestral castle of Francis. The ambassadors were taken with much pomp along the Loire, where the châteaux of this glorious period of French art were just risen, or were rising, in all their fantastic grace.[3]

Sir Richard remained in France five months, at a time when the Court of Francis was at its zenith of pride and beauty. A letter to Wolsey[4] speaks of him and Fitzwilliam as still in France in January 1519; and a letter of Sir T. Boleyn, then permanent resident, to

---

[1] *Calendar*, Henry VIII., 4409; Brewer, i. 202.

[2] An interesting account of the embassy will be found in Hall's *Chronicle* (p. 596), and in Holinshed, vol. iii. (pp. 634 and 1519).

[3] According to Hall, *Chron.* p. 396, Henry VIII. (1519), "After divers feasts, jousts, and banquets made to the English ambassadors, the Bishop of Ely, with Sir Thomas Boleyn and Sir Richard Weston, were sent by the French King to Konyack, to see the Dolphyn, where they were well received, and to them was shown a fair young child; and when they had seen him they departed." The fair young child unfortunately died soon after, and his younger brother became Henry II.

[4] Brit. Mus., Calig. D. vii. 73; *Calendar*, Henry VIII., iii. 9 and 57.

Wolsey from Paris, 2nd February, informs the Cardinal that the Bishop, Sir R. Weston, and Fitzwilliam had left for England. Immediately on his return Weston received the important advancement which he retained for the rest of his life.

He was already Knight of the Bath. In a beautiful blazoned MS. in the British Museum (Claudius CIII. XIV. E.) is a list of the Knights Commanders of the Bath from the time of Henry VII. We there find that, 3rd January, anno nono, Henry VIII. (1518), Sir Richard Weston was "dubbed at Wyndesor the same time." His arms are blazoned precisely as they are seen in the glass of the hall of Sutton to-day: *Quarterly*, 1 and 4, *Ermine*, on a chief azure, five bezants; 2 and 3, *Argent*, three camels, *sable*. *Crest*, a Saracen's head langued, *sable*. Further in the same MS. book are the names of Sir Richard's son and grandson. "Sir Francys Weston" is knighted at the coronation of Anne Boleyn, 31st May 1533; and Sir Henry Weston is knighted at the coronation of Queen Elizabeth, 15th January 1558. The arms of Sir Francis are blazoned as those of his father. Sir Henry, in right of his mother, Ann Pickering, quarters *Pickering, Lascelles, Moresby, and Fenwick*.

A revolution in the palace was effected in 1519, an account of which we read in Hall's *Chronicle*, Henry VIII., 4to, 598. In that year "young men, Lord Carew and other the *King's minions*, were discharged at the request of the Council, and four sad and ancient knights were put into the King's privy chamber." They were Sir Richard Wingfield, Sir Richard Jerningham, Sir William Kingston, and Sir Richard Weston. All of them, we are told, were upwards of fifty years old.

In the British Museum is a letter from Sir T. Boleyn, ambassador in Paris, to Wolsey,[1] requesting information as to the effect of this appointment. Every man's tongue in Paris, he says, is full of it.[2] The King was now just twenty-eight. He had been on the throne and he had been married exactly ten years. He was in the heyday of his activity and splendour. Sir Richard, like all the sad and ancient knights, was upwards of fifty. He did not owe the friendship of Henry to any subserviency to the King's pleasures. Weston retained this office, that of Knight of the Privy Chamber, till his death, and as Knight of the Body he had a salary of £100. All the four ancient knights served the King long and steadily; there were several of them Captains of the Guard, Governors of the Tower, and the like. Sir W. Kingston was the jailor of Anne Boleyn and of young Francis Weston in 1536; it was from a report of Kingston to Wolsey that Francis Weston was arrested. Jerningham and Wingfield were both envoys of Henry in foreign courts.[3]

Sir Richard Weston, it is clear, was occupied with things more solid than Court gaieties. He now seems

[1] Calig. D. vii. 118.   [2] *Calendar*, Henry VIII., iii. 246.
[3] In this year there is an amusing passage recorded by Hall, *Chron.* p. 599, where Sir Richard Weston figures before Queen Catherine and her ladies in an unwonted part. A banquet was given at *Beaulieu*, a royal palace at Newhall, in Essex. After the feast "eight maskers entered the chamber and danced with the ladies sadly, and communed not with the ladies after the fashion of maskers, but behaved themselves sadly. Wherefore the Queen plucked off their visors, and there appeared the Duke of Suffolk, the Earl of Essex, the Marquis of Dorset, Lord Burgavenny, Sir Richard Wingfield, Sir Robert Wingfield, *Sir Richard Weston*, Sir W. Kingston; all of these were somewhat aged, the youngest man of fifty at the least. The ladies had good sport to see these ancient persons maskers." The Queen was now thirty-four, the King twenty-eight, and the dark years of their lives had not begun.

to have turned his mind very seriously to duties that involved trust, care, and profit—the wardships of heirs of tender years. In the very year 1519 he has several such grants, amongst others that of William Lytton, of Knebworth, Herts, with custody of the profits of the manor of Knebworth and a reversion of part of the manor. He has a grant of the wardship of Ann, daughter and heiress of Sir Christopher Pickering, deceased, 11th July 1519.[1] Now the prudent knight eventually married this girl, heiress of immense possessions in Cumberland, to his only son, Francis, in 1530, and they became the ancestors of the Westons of Sutton Place. The knight nursed the young lady and her estates for eleven years, and the husband he found her was only about nineteen at the wedding, and must have been cutting his teeth when the knight secured the wardship. In the same year Sir Richard is mentioned as associated with Sir Thomas Lovell, the Master of the King's Wards, with a salary of £100 a year. He had also a salary of £100 a year as Knight of the Body, and he gets a grant of £79 for a new lodge in Windsor Forest. And in the following year (1520) Sir Richard Weston and Sir E. Belknap are appointed to be surveyors, governors, keepers, and sellers of wards and their possessions during pleasure, at a salary of £100.[2]

But Sir Richard Weston is not content with wardships and the care of infants and their possessions. He passes from soldier, diplomatist, official, to the place of judge. In 1519 "the following councillors, my Lord of Westminster, the Dean of St. Paul's, my Lord of St. John's, Sir Richard Weston, and four others, are appointed to hear the causes depending in the 'Sterred Chambre,' and will sit in the White Hall in Westminster, where

[1] *Calendar*, Henry VIII., iii. 405.   [2] *Ibid.* vol. iii. 1121, 10.

the said suitors shall resort."[1] In the following year took place the meeting of Henry and Francis, known as the "Field of the Cloth of Gold." Sir R. Weston is one of the knights selected for Hampshire, along with Sir W. Sandys, Sir W. Fitzwilliam, and Sir W. Dennys.[2] Doubtless we have the portrait of the knight himself in one of the pictures of the scene now in Hampton Court; but there is no means of identifying him; his banner is not visible, and beyond his name as one of the knights in the King's retinue we have no record of his part.[3]

The alliance with Francis, as history relates, was short indeed. In spite of the efforts of Wolsey, Henry in his self-will flung himself into the arms of his young nephew, the astute Charles V., and within a few months he signed with him a treaty of alliance. Weston, as before, was one of the witnesses (Brit. Mus., Galba, bk. vi. 144).[4]

---

[1] *Calendar*, Henry VIII., vol. iii. 571. This is, of course, the famous Star Chamber, finally suppressed in 1641 by the Long Parliament.

[2] *Ibid.* iii. 703.

[3] In the College of Arms is an exemplification of the standard of Sir Richard Weston, thus blazoned: "*Or* and *Vert*. A. on a wreath *Argent* and *Sable*, a Saracen's head *affronté*, with a band round the neck, *Or*, couped at the neck proper, wreathed about the temples *Argent* and *Azure*. Motto on each side of the two bands, *Ani boro*." The arms are the same as before described (*Excerpta Historica*, p. 183). As to this motto, a long and apparently undecided battle has raged amongst the heralds as to the origin of this motto, its correct form, and whether it belongs to the family of *Weston* or to the Order of St. John; see the *Herald and Genealogist*, v. 530; vi. 369; viii. 182. It is said that it is derived from the Syriac *Ani buroh*, meaning "I go," "I am sped," "I am killed." The story is that Sir Hugh de Weston, having killed a Saracen emir in hand-to-hand conflict and taken a Moslem standard, took as his crest and motto the head and last cry of the emir. Other authorities have found *Sane Baro* as a motto of the priors of St. John, and declare that the motto is not a family motto at all. Certain it is that in the College of Arms this motto is attributed to Sir R. Weston in the sixteenth, and also to J. Webbe-Weston in the eighteenth century.

[4] *Calendar*, Henry VIII., iii. 739; Rymer, *Fœd.* xiii. 714.

In July followed the meeting of Henry and the Emperor, and again, with Boleyn, Berkeley, Fitzwilliam, and others, Sir Richard Weston attends the King.

In the dark tragedy carried out by the insatiable ambition of Wolsey and the remorseless jealousy of his master — the judicial murder of Stafford, Duke of Buckingham, — Sir Richard Weston has a part. In April 1521 there is a highly significant passage in a letter from Pace to Wolsey.[1] Pace, who was then at Greenwich with the King, and was his secretary, informs Wolsey, who was then in London, under date (16th April), that "Sir Richard Weston signifieth unto your Grace that the King doth well approve such things as you communed with him this morning." What were these things?[2] The letter refers just above to the examination of the Duke's serving-men. It is not precisely so stated, but one remembers that the trial of the Duke began on 8th May, just twenty-two days after this letter.

Wolsey stood at the head of the French party, Buckingham of the Spanish. The Duke, the son of Richard III.'s Buckingham, beheaded in 1483, was at the head of the English aristocracy, and claimed descent both from John of Gaunt and also from Thomas of Woodstock, sons both of Edward III. The Duke had openly sworn to have Wolsey's head, if both survived the King, and Wolsey had sworn (less openly) to have the head of Buckingham. As Shakespeare makes the Duke say (*Henry VIII.*, Act I., Scene 1):—

---

[1] *Calendar*, Henry VIII., vol. iii. 1233; see Vit., bk. iv. 96, and Ellis, *Letters*, etc., 2nd series, i. 286.

[2] Brewer, i. chap. iii.

> "The net has fall'n upon me! I shall perish
> Under device and practice....
> ... It will help me nothing
> To plead mine innocence."

Wolsey triumphed. On 16th April the Duke was arrested—the very day of Weston's message to the Cardinal. On 8th May the indictment was found.[1] The jury who found the indictment were the Lord Mayor (Sir John Brugge) and fourteen others. Amongst them are Boleyn, Fitzwilliam, William Shelley, Marney, Lovell, Sir J. More, and *Sir Richard Weston*.[2] Weston is thus one of Henry's creatures in the judicial assassination of the next most eminent representative of the royal house; and the Duke died the death of a traitor, as his father had done in 1483, as his grandfather had done in 1455, as his great-grandfather had done in 1460, as his great-uncles in 1464 and 1471, and his mother's great-grandfather in 1455.

The unlucky Duke was executed on 17*th May* 1521, and it is most significant that the grant of the manor of Sutton was sealed *on that very day* to Sir Richard Weston, one of the jury on the indictment of the Duke.[3] On that day was made the grant in fee simple to Sir Richard Weston, Knight of the Body, Knight Councillor, etc., of

---

[1] *Calendar of State Papers*, iii. 1284, R. O. Rep., iii., App. II. 230; *State Trials*, i. 287.

[2] Every one of these were closely associated with Weston through life. Fitzwilliam built Cowdray Castle, and More's son built Loseley Hall. Lovell was Sir Richard's colleague in custody of the wards; William Shelley was an ancestor of Mary Copley, who married the sixth owner of Sutton in 1630, and Boleyn's son and daughter were executed together with Sir Richard Weston's son in 1536.

[3] See *State Papers*, Henry VIII., iii. 1324, 17, Record Office, S.B. pat., p. 2, m. 18.

the manor of Sutton, in Surrey, found by inquisition at Southampton to have been held by Margaret, Countess of Richmond, on whose death it descended to the King. For a full account of this grant see note above, chap. ii. Was this grant the price of blood? Who now can say? If it were, the sins of the father were visited unto the third and fourth generation. Exactly sixteen years later, on 17th May 1537, young Weston was beheaded on the same charge and on the same spot.

Honours continue to pour in upon Sir Richard. In the next year, 1522, he is made one of the cup-bearers to the King along with Brian, Jerningham, Lord Herbert, and Lord Roos. In the year following he is Sheriff for Berkshire. In the same year the bubble of the French alliance broke down; and, in spite of Wolsey, the King received the Emperor with great state. Sir Richard Weston, along with Boleyn, Fitzwilliam, Kingston, Marney, and the Prior of St. John's, is ordered to attend the King at Canterbury, 27th May 1522;[1] and in one of the attendances on the King, Weston received a grant of £100.[2] On New Year's Day 1522 he receives "twelve pairs of shoes."[3]

In 1523 followed the foolish and useless war with France, and here Sir Richard Weston raised a contingent and served under the Duke of Suffolk.[4] The force consisted of 13,000 or 14,000 men, and a further foreign contingent of 7000 men. It was the largest army, as Wolsey said, that had ever left these shores for a hundred years.[5] It proved a miserable failure, owing to the incapacity of Brandon and the petty jealousies of the

---

[1] See *State Papers*, Henry VIII., iii. 2288. [2] *Ibid*. iii. 2483.
[3] *Ibid*. iii. 2585. [4] *Ibid*. 3288.
[5] Brewer, i. 504; ii. 1; Hall, p. 662.

allied princes. Suffolk sailed in great pomp in August, and returned crestfallen in December 1523.

Hall relates that "the Duke and his captains came not to the King's presence in a long season, to their great heaviness and displeasure. But at the last all things were taken in good part, and they well received and in great love, favour, and familiarity with the King."[1]

But though Sir Richard earned no glory in a war ill-planned and shamefully mismanaged by Brandon, the coarse and stupid commander-in-chief, the martial honour of the Westons was sustained by his brother Sir William. He took part in the heroic defence of Rhodes, June to December 1522, under the immortal type of the true Crusader, Villiers de Lisle-Adam. A graphic account of this magnificent exploit, where 300 knights, with about 1000 soldiers and 4000 townsmen, for six months kept at bay the whole forces of Solyman the Magnificent, at the height of the Turkish power, may be read in a report in our *State Papers* by Sir Nicholas Roberts, one of the survivors.[2] Sir William Weston bore his share in this great struggle, was wounded, and lived to be appointed by his noble chief the Head of the Order in England.

In 1525 Sir Richard obtained the important and lucrative appointment which he long retained. This was evidently the gift of Wolsey; for Wolsey asks Henry VIII. to give to Sir R. Weston the office of the Duchy of Lancaster in lieu of that of Master of the Wards, or his annuity of £100 per annum (1525). In the Record Office is a Bill signed by Wolsey appointing Sir R. Weston, Knight of the Body, to be Treasurer of the

---

[1] Hall, p. 972; in Brewer, ii. 2.
[2] *Calendar III.* 1272; see the story in Brewer, i. 581, and in Porter's *History of the Knights of St. John* (ed. 1883, p. 360).

Town and Marches of Calais, surrendered by Sir W. Sandys.[1] Sir W. Sandys, who in 1523 was made a peer by Wolsey,[2] was subsequently Comptroller of the Household. It was this Sir W. Sandys who built the Vyne in Hampshire about 1509. He was a valiant soldier and a staunch Catholic, the exact contemporary of Sir R. Weston, dying in 1540, two years before him, and was closely associated with the knight during his whole career. Compare the *History of the Vyne*, by Chaloner W. Chute, late owner of the Vyne, 1888. The arms, badges, and devices of Sandys do not appear at Sutton, but many of the devices given in Mr. Chute's work may be seen at Sutton, and the inventory taken at the Vyne, 1541, should be compared with that of Sutton, 1542, preserved at Loseley.

This year, 1525, was that of the battle of Pavia, in which Francis I. was taken prisoner, the year in which Sir Thomas Boleyn was created Viscount Rochford. Henry made peace with France soon after, and entered into an alliance against the Emperor in the year following.

Sir Richard appears to have resided much in Calais in discharge of his duties. On various local grounds it seems more probable that the house was at least partially built in the years between the grant of the estate, in May 1521, and the appointment of the knight to his treasurership in Calais, 1525. There is frequent mention of him in the *Chronicles of Calais*.[3]

Nor was Sir Richard content with obtaining office for himself. The very next year, 1526, we have an entry

---

[1] *Calendar IV.* 58. The salary appears to have been £140 per annum.
[2] *Calendar III.* 2982.
[3] Camden Society's publications, *Chron. of Calais* to 1540, edited by J. Gough Nichols, 1846.

that "young Weston" is to be the King's page.[1] From that day the spoiled lad lived mainly at Court till his worthless young life was cut short on Tower Hill. An account of him is reserved for the next chapter. And again, in 1527, we have Sir Richard interceding with Wolsey to promote his brother, Sir W. Weston, "the Turkopolyer" of the Order, to the office of Prior of St. John's in England. The letter is dated 12th April 1527, and is written from Calais. It may be seen in the Record Office.[2]

As the letter is one of the two which have been traced in the handwriting and with the signature of Sir Richard, it is here set forth verbatim.

"Pleaseth yo' good grace to be advertyzed That where as I am credebly enfourmed that my lorde of Sainct John's is veary sore sick, and lyeth at the mercy of God—In cas God do call hym out of this transytory lyff, I beseche yo' grace as my singular good and gracious lorde and refuge in all my peticions and affaires (through whose goodnes and medyacion all that I have is proceded and com), That it may please yo' grace the rather at the contemplacion of this my poore instance and supplycacion to be bening and gracious lorde unto my brother Sr Willm. Weston, Turkepolyer, in the preferrement, and promocion of him unto the foresaide lorde of Sainct John's rome; Reducing unto your grace's rememberaunce the consyderacion, that by auncyen custume and good congruence The Turkepolyer hath evermore bene wont to succede the master of Sainct Johns in his rome. Wherefor eftsones I humbly beseche yo' grace to be good and gracious lorde unto my said brother in the premisses. And I trust yo' grace shall allways fynde him in arredynes to do yo' grace as acceptable servyce to his power as ever any other in that rome

[1] *Calendar IV.* p. 861.   [2] *Ibid.* No. 3035.

hath done. And during his lyff and myn yoʳ grace shall bynde us from much to more, to contynue yoʳ grace's servauntes and bedemen, At the toune of Caleys the xii day of Aprel.

"Yoʳ most humble servᵗ

"RYCHARD WESTON."

"Endorsed—To my Lorde Legate's grace."

Whether owing to the importunity of Sir Richard, the influence of Wolsey, or rather, let us trust, his own fame and character, Sir William Weston was on 27th June 1527 appointed by the Grand Master Lord Prior of England. This put him at the head of the titular Roll of the Barons, made him a member of the Upper House, and gave him rank as one of the great officers of State. The letter of Sir Richard calls for little comment. It shows him as the almost menial "bedeman" of Wolsey. But such language was the ordinary form of all solicitations in that age. The rhythm of the words almost recalls the collects of Cranmer in the phrase "through whose goodnes and medyacion all that I have is proceded and com." The spelling is much superior to the time, and the language is that of a practised penman. It is probable that the letter is in the handwriting of the knight, but hardly that it is his own composition. It is a somewhat fulsome letter to be addressed to the Cardinal in 1527 by one of Brandon's captains, and by one who in 1530-36 was in high favour with the Boleyns and Cromwell. Such was the way of the times!

In this year, 1527, and in the very month in which this letter was written (April), the Records reveal that Henry first stirred with his advisers the possibility of obtaining a divorce from Catherine. In the great fireplace of the hall at Sutton, and in that of the panelled parlour, is still to be seen, in contemporary terra-cotta castings, the pomegranate, the special badge of Catherine of Aragon.[1] Would a Knight of the King's Chamber, an obsequious follower of Wolsey, put up in his fireside the personal badge of the Queen at any date later than April 1527? In the July following Wolsey went to France, passing by Calais, and he must have there seen the Treasurer.

In the following year we have a second letter of Sir Richard to Wolsey "written at the Kinges towne of Calays the XXXth day of October" 1528. The letter is in the Record Office. It is entered in the *Calendar*, vol. iv., No. 4887. It is a business letter of no great importance, and is without any special character or interest.

It begins thus:—

"Pleaseth your grace to be advertyzed that I have receyved by the handes of my Lorde Chamberlayne, the lettres which it hath pleased your grace to send unto me, whereby your grace wolleth me to make undylaid payment unto the said Lorde Chamberlain Captain of Guysnes."

It ends thus:—

"Wherefore I beseche yo' grace that I may be advertyzed of yo' pleasure in the premisses. And I shall endeavour myself to accomplisshe the same to the best of my power; humbly beseching your grace to be good and gracious lorde unto the Kinges poor servauntes here in this toune, who suffre great necessyte for lacke of payment of their wages."

The whole letter is an urgent appeal to Wolsey to permit the first payments made into the Treasury of

---

[1] This badge was also placed in his house by Lord Sandys, and is still to be seen there.—*Hist. of the Vyne*, C. Chute, p. 135.

Calais—the Company of the Staple being in arrear of their dues—to be paid to the "Kinges poor servauntes in Calays," of course including Sir Richard Weston himself. He insists that his own salary was payable from the day of his patent.

The Lord Chamberlain mentioned above is Lord Sandys, whom Weston succeeded at Calais. It will be noted that the spelling, writing, and phraseology of these two letters agree in the main. They are certainly signed and probably written by Weston. The handwriting of both letters is the same, and the name *Weston* in the first letter seems to coincide with the signature.

The signature, strangely enough, varies in spelling. The letter of 1527 is signed Rychard Weston. The letter of 1528 is signed Rychard Weyston, as was the Treaty of 1518. The knight, like every one in that age, had no settled mode of spelling his own name. In 1532 he again wrote *Rychard Weston*.

The two letters above are the only pieces of Sir Richard's own correspondence of any interest now in the Public Records, though his name occurs in many hundreds of papers. There is nothing singular in this. Letters of any importance were in those days instantly destroyed, and private correspondence, as Friedmann tells us (Preface 6), hardly ever alluded to public affairs.

The better to understand the man we have to deal with, we must take some note of the momentous change which now began in the history of England.

PART II.—AFTER THE REFORMATION

It was in July 1528 that Wolsey first received his great rebuff from Anne Boleyn and his first formal reprimand from the King. In July 1529 he was practically superseded, and his fall began. In October following he was deprived of the seals and was a ruined man. In November 1530 he was arrested, and he died a few weeks later.[1] Thomas Cromwell took his place. In this very year Cromwell became the King's secretary and chief adviser. He actively allies himself with Anne and her party; he suggests an attack on the Churchmen as a means of securing the divorce. In 1531 Catherine is expelled from the palace; in 1533 Henry VIII. is married to Anne Boleyn, and the train of events is prepared which brought about the Reformation.[2]

Through all these stirring times Sir Richard Weston, as a practical man, kept on undisturbed the even tenor of

---

[1] See Friedmann, i. chap. iii. [2] Friedmann, i. chaps. iv., v., vi.

his way; and before the fall of Wolsey, "through whose goodnes and medyacion all that he has proceded and came," Sir Richard is high in favour with Wolsey's successor and Wolsey's enemy, Anne Boleyn, in whose goodness he appears to have found another mediator, we can suppose "his singular good and gracious lady and refuge in all his petitions and affairs." No doubt the stout old knight (he was now upwards of sixty-five) said to Wolsey in the words of Cromwell (Shakespeare's *Henry VIII.*, Act III., Scene 2):—

> "O my lord,
> Must I, then, leave you? must I needs forgo,
> So good, so noble and so true a master?
> Bear witness, all that have not hearts of iron,
> With what a sorrow Cromwell leaves his lord.
> The king shall have my service; but my prayers
> For ever and for ever shall be yours."

The King certainly had the old knight's service, and so did the Queen, and three queens after her. The Treasurer of Calais parted from Cromwell as easily as he had parted from Wolsey. And the knight had his reward, and also his retribution. That is to come; in the meantime Sir Richard and his house thrive exceedingly.

Three years after his appointment as Treasurer of Calais Sir Richard was made Under-Treasurer of England —Michaelmas 1528 (20 Henry VIII., Rot. 24, memoranda in the Rolls, sub voc. *Sub-Thesaurarius*). This office, though not of great authority or value, was one that could only be then held by a trusty and devoted servant of the King, who was ready to execute any order whatever with silent precision. Gardiner had been made Chief Secretary to the King in July 1529, and Anne's influence was now paramount. The office of Under-Treasurer was held by Sir Richard for twelve years more. He surrendered it at the time of his last illness (he must have been then about seventy-five), in the thirty-second year of Henry VIII., 1541, Hilary Term, as is testified by a memorandum in the Record Office, Rot. 7. It is there stated that he surrendered this office to the King, and Sir John Baker was appointed in his place, Sir John Baker paying to Sir Richard £100 a year for his life. Sir Richard withdrew from office with grace and profit; £100 was the salary of the Speaker of the House of Commons, half the salary of the Lord Chancellor, and is equal, at least, to £1200 of our money.

All this while the records of the Exchequer are full of the bounties of the King to "young Weston," who had been made page in 1526. And it must have been one of the duties of the Under-Treasurer to pay out or countersign the orders for young Weston's hose and shirts, and for the monstrous sums which the King suffered him win at "dyce," tennis, and "imperiall." But after four years of these high jinks at Court, the prudent old knight thought it time for the lad to settle. Accordingly in May 1530 Francis Weston was married to Ann, the daughter and heiress of Sir Christopher Pickering, the great heiress of Cumberland, whose wardship the old knight had secured in 1519, eleven years before. The marriage was a splendid alliance, for Ann was one of the great *partis* of her age, and brought to the Westons of Sutton Place undoubted quarterings and indisputable estates. Nor was the marriage at all unfavourably viewed at Court. The King gave him as a wedding present £6 : 13 : 4, a sum equivalent to about £80 to-day, and one wonders if it was the fashion of those times to send wedding presents in specie or by draft. The wedding was hardly over when "young Weston" continues the same gambling games with his sovereign, beats him at tennis at 40s. a game (that is £24!), and wins at a sitting at dyce £46 (*i.e.* £550!).

Sir Richard, however, as became his years, steadily kept his eye on the main chance. In the very month in which his son is married, May 1530, he received a new grant of lands, a license to impark more than 1000 acres of land and heath at Merrow and Clandon, the present Clandon estates of the Onslows, and in 1533 he obtained a renewal of his patent as Captain, Warder, and Governor of Guernsey, which he had now held for twenty-four years, since the King's accession, and it is regranted to Sir Richard and his son in survivorship. The office was thus made hereditary in the third generation[1] (*State Papers*, Calendar VI., p. 596, No. 1481).

This last grant was in the full tide of the ascendency of Anne Boleyn. She was crowned 1st June 1533. Francis Weston, now become, in right of his wife, an illustrious and broad-acred squire, was made Knight of the Bath at the coronation, and soon became one of the Queen's personal courtiers and gentleman of her chamber. The coronation of Anne was received somewhat coldly by the mass of the English nation, and by all but the party of the Court. But the two Westons were foremost in testifying their devotion. Within two months of the coronation Henry made a state visit to Sutton Place.

In two letters preserved at the Record Office we hear of this visit. On the 4th of August 1533 Lord

---

[1] There is in the Record Office a letter of Sir R. Weston to Cromwell, 1st September 1532, relating to the seizure of some Guernseymen's goods, to the value of £1500 (*Calendar V.*, No. 1276).

Sandys, writing "at the Vyn" to Lord Lisle at Calais says :—

"Concernyng newis here be non wourthe the writing, saving that God be thanckid the Kinges highnes is in prossperous astate at this present tyme at Sir Richard Westons" (*Calendar VI.*, No. 936).

And on the 6th of August we have a letter, written and dated from Sutton by Sir John Russell to Lord Lisle, in which we read :—

"My Lord, newes here ys none but that thankyd be God, the kynges Highnes ys mery and in good helth and I never saw hym meryer of a great while then he is now. And the best pastyme in huntyng the redd dere that I have sene. And for chere what at my lord Marques of Exetours Mr Treasourers and at Mr Weston's, I never saw more dylicates nor better chere in my lyff. The kyng was myndyd to go to Fernham, and from thens to Est Hampstede and so to Wyndsour. And now he commyth not ther by cause of the Sweatt. And he was fayne to remove from Guyldford to Sutton, Mr Weston's howsse, by cause of the sweatt lykewise. And now within these viii days he commyth from hence to Wyndsour, and sone after the Quene removyth from thens to Grenewich, wher Her Grace takith her Chambre."[1]

Lord Sandys, the writer of the first of these letters, was Sir Richard's old colleague, whom he had succeeded as Treasurer at Calais. Sandys was now Lord Chamberlain of the Household, and one of the commissioners and judges by whom Anne was done to death. His place, the Vyne, in Hampshire, is within a ride of Sutton.[2]

[1] *Calendar VI.*, No. 948.
[2] *History of the Vyne*, by Chaloner Chute, 1888.

He was presumably a connection of Weston's wife, *née* Anne Sandys.

Lord Lisle, to whom both letters are addressed, was Deputy of Calais. He was Sir Arthur Plantagenet, one of the official group called to the Upper House by Wolsey, along with Sir William Sandys, in 1523.

Sir John Russell was afterwards Lord Russell, founder of the ducal house, and a tried envoy and minister of Henry.

The Treasurer was Sir William Fitzwilliam, a firm friend and neighbour of Weston's, afterwards known as the Earl of Southampton, who had recently received the adjacent manor of Pirbright, etc.[1] He and Lord Russell were two of Weston's executors. Thus all the persons mentioned in these letters were closely associated and belong to the innermost circle of Henry's confidants.

The news, or no news, which Sir John Russell conveys to the Deputy of Calais was not a little disingenuous. There was indeed great news at that crisis, and no one knew it better than Sir John. A few weeks before, the Pope and cardinals in open consistory had annulled the pretended marriage with Anne, and on the 28th of July Lord Rochford, her brother, reached the King with the news. The Court had left London and gone to Hampton Court. The King was restless and anxious; the Queen was expecting her confinement, and she and the King were frantically hoping for a son. Elizabeth was born at Greenwich, 7th September, whither the King and Queen had returned on 28th August. When the King

---

[1] Sir William Fitzwilliam had a grant of the manor of Pirbright, 19th December 1520, a little before the grant of Sutton to Weston, and Sir William died seized of it, 14th October 1542.—Manning and Bray, *Surrey*, i. 148. He was created Earl of Southampton, October 1537.

was at Sutton, three weeks previously, things were almost desperate with him, and he was trying to conceal his anxiety from the expectant mother. His "pastimes in huntyng the redd deer" were often at this time expedients to meet his council secretly; and it is not improbable that the old roof of Sutton Hall has covered many a gloomy council board and caught the murmur of whispered plans in one of the great crises of Henry's reign—the real turning-point in the Reformation. The following year Fisher and More were committed to the Tower, and the convocation of York declared that the Pope had no power in England. It is most doubtful that Anne, within one month of her expected delivery, on which so much turned, was then at Sutton with the King. She was carefully nursed, whilst he travelled about, angry, restless, and violent.

In 1534, the year following, Cromwell sends to Weston a patent that had been granted to him (*Calendar VII.* No. 73).

A little later we find him still Steward of Cokeham and Bray. And in the same year are two memoranda in the voluminous and curious document known as Cromwell's *Remembrancer*.[1] In that year Cromwell was made Master of the Rolls, and Henry was declared, by Act of Parliament, head of the Church. It must have been a terrible dilemma to the old knight, the brother of the Lord Prior of St. John's. Did Cromwell mean by these lists to remind Weston that he owed all to the King?

If hint were given at all, Sir Richard acted on it, for

---

[1] *Calendar VII.* No. 923, i. vii. "Item, a paper of the names of the offices of Sir Richard Weston." "Item, a paper of offices and fees granted by the King's Hygnes unto Sir Richard Weston, knight." Repeated search has failed to discover these lists.

he never swerved from his duty to his sovereign nor lost the favour of those in power. The tremendous drama unfolds itself with rapid revolutions year by year. In 1535 Fisher and More are executed. In 1536 Catherine died and Henry fell in love with Jane Seymour. In April, with Cromwell's assistance, he determines on the destruction of Anne. Cromwell himself, Lord Sandys, Sir Wm. Fitzwilliam, and others are amongst the commissioners and judges. On 2nd May Anne is arrested. Two days later Francis Weston is arrested. On the 17th of May he is executed. Two days later the Queen is executed. On the third day after Henry marries Jane Seymour, the mother of our most Protestant sovereign, Edward VI., Defender of the Faith, and founder of the Established Church of England.

Sir Richard held on to his King, whose passion and lust had just cut off his only son. There is abundant evidence that the execution was regarded by himself, by the King, and by others as a melancholy incident which in no way affected his public position any more than if his heir had died by any ordinary accident. There is extant, in a fragmentary state, a letter from a trusty agent of Cromwell and Cranmer, an old friend of Sir Richard's, who says: "I lament extremely the evil sort of young Wes[ton, because of the] amity which I had with his father a man of great [? favour with?] the King's Majesty, a prudent and most gentle Knight" (Edmund Harvell to Thomas Starkey, 15th June 1536; B. M., Vit., bk. xiv. 228; *Calendar XI*. No. 1142). This is the only contemporary character of Sir Richard Weston that we have. Every one, and especially the King and his ministers, were friendly to the "prudent and most gentle knight." In September of this year Sir W. Weston writes two letters from Sutton to Cromwell, remonstrating with him in matters relating to the Priory of St. John's. In October we have a list of the noblemen and gentlemen to attend the King's own person. For Surrey there are Sir Richard Weston, with 150 men-at-arms, and he and his brother, the Lord of St. John's, are named to attend the Queen's Grace.[1] Queen Anne brought the son to Tower Hill; Queen Jane must be served by the father.

In June of the next year the governorship of Guernsey, etc., had to be filled up, as a vacancy had been caused by the death of Sir F. Weston, who had held it since 1533. Accordingly, by patent 26th June 1537, "the office of Captain, Keeper, and Governor of Guernesey and the island of Cornet is granted to Sir N. Carewe, K.G., in reversion from Sir R. Weston, now holding it, in lieu of Sir F. Weston, attainted and executed."[2] About this time Cromwell seems to have resided at Sutton. On 11th July Sir J. Russell, writing apparently by the King's order from Guildford to Cromwell, says, as he, Cromwell, has a servant ill of the plague, the King suggests that not to frighten the Queen, then with child (Edward VI.), Cromwell might lie at Mr. Weston's, Mr. Browne's, the Lord Marquis's, or other good fellows' houses and meet the King by day.[3] Cromwell evidently chose Sutton and went there. We hear of him there on 17th July and on 26th August.[4]

At the splendid pageant of the christening of the young Prince, who became Edward VI., 15th October 1537, a scene preserved to us by Holbein, we find Sir Richard Weston present as usual.[5] And when a few weeks later

---

[1] *Calendar XI.* No. 579. [2] *Calendar XII.* pt. ii. 191 (46).
[3] *Ibid.* pt. ii. No. 242. [4] *Ibid.* pt. ii. Nos. 267, 583.
[5] *Ibid.* pt. ii. No. 911 (ii.).

Queen Jane Seymour is buried (12th November), we have him there at the pompous funeral.[1] Births, marriages, and deaths come all alike to the veteran courtier.

Jane Seymour died in October 1537. The Six Acts were passed in 1539; in 1536 the Lesser Monasteries were suppressed; in 1539 the Greater Monasteries. In 1540 Henry married Anne of Cleves, repudiated her, had Cromwell executed, and married Catherine Howard.

The year 1540 was one of importance for Sir Richard Weston. He was of great age, and had served the King more than thirty years. At the marriage of Anne of Cleves, in January 1540, Sir Richard, who had figured in the pageants of three queens already, was sent to meet the fourth queen on her landing in England. He is there with Sir Walter Dennys, his own son-in-law, and Sir T. Arundell, whose daughter married Sir Richard's grandson. The odious marriage enraged Henry against Cromwell, its adviser; and in July the great contriver of the Reformation, Thomas Cromwell, now Earl of Essex, lost his King's favour and his own head.

But the fall of Cromwell no more shook the credit of Sir Richard than did that of Wolsey. In the very year of it the old knight is appointed Master of the New Court of Wards.[2] It was a new office created by 32 Henry VIII.,

---

[1] *Calendar XII.* pt. ii. No. 1060.

[2] Appended to Ley's Reports, folio 1659, by Sir James Ley, afterwards Earl of Marlborough, is a *Treatise concerning Wards and Liveries*. "The Master of the Wards," runs the patent, "shall dispose of all our wards, idiots, lunatics, and their lands, tenements, and hereditaments." There had always been an officer to deal with the estates of tenants *in capite* dying with heirs under age as Master of the Wards. Sir Richard Weston had held this office since 1519. But after twenty years it was found necessary to create a Court of Wards, in which, under statute, were consolidated the equitable authority and powers of the Crown over all estates where the legal owners were under any incapacity. Such an office was practically that of Chancellor, and must

c. 46; enlarged by 33 Henry VIII., c. 22; and abolished by the Long Parliament, confirmed at the Restoration by 12 Car. II., c. 24. And it was natural that Sir Richard Weston, who in 1519 had been appointed with Sir Thomas Lovell Master of the King's Wards, and in 1520 had been named with Sir E. Belknap to be surveyor, governor, and seller of wards and their possessions, should now be appointed Master of the New Court.

He seems to have held office until his death. But a new disaster was on him. The Greater Monasteries were suppressed in 1539; but the illustrious Order of St. John still remained at its house in Clerkenwell. The old prior, Sir William Weston, who had been relieved of his duties through the infirmity of old age four years before, died on Ascension Day, 7th May 1540, the very day of the Dissolution of the Order in England. He was treated by the King with great honour, for he received a pension of £1000 a year.[1]

This month of May seems strangely big with weal and woe to the house of *Weston*. The first batch of offices and honours fell to Sir Richard 21st May 1509. On the 17th of May 1520 Sir Richard Weston has the grant of Sutton, the very day of the execution of Stafford, Duke of Buckingham. In May 1530 he had a grant of Merrow and Clandon, and in May of that year, too, his only son is married to a great heiress. In May 1533 Sir Francis is made Knight of the Bath. On the 17th of May 1536 that son is beheaded as a traitor on the very

have opened unlimited opportunities for jobbery and malversation to unscrupulous men.

[1] An enormous sum, five times the salary of the Lord Chancellor, perhaps equivalent to £12,000. The entire revenue of the house at the Dissolution was only £282.

day of the same month as the Duke in the same place. And now in May 1540 the Order of St. John, of which Sir William Weston is the English head, is suppressed, and he himself dies of grief on the same day.

Within two years Sir Richard had to follow his noble brother. In 1541 Sir Richard's infirmities compel him to surrender to Sir John Baker his office of Under-Treasurer of England,[1] 20th January 1541-42. It is remembered before Thomas, Duke of Norfolk, that Sir R. Weston, Sub-Treasurer of England, *ob senectutem debilitatam et continuam infirmitatem*, resigns his office with a pension of £100 a year, payable to him by Sir John.[2]

In the year following, his long and busy life was over. He died 7th August 1542, it would appear about the age of seventy-five. His will was proved in November of that year, and in the *Inquisitiones Post Mortem* (34 Henry VIII.) he was found to hold lands in Somerset, in Surrey, in Hampshire, in Dorset, and in Berkshire.

He was buried in the family vault in the Parish Church of the Trinity in Guildford, in the chapel which he built for the purpose; but all traces of his burial and his tomb have perished in the destruction and rebuilding of the church. By his will, made the 16th day of May 1541 (always the month of May is an epoch in the Weston calendar), he describes himself as Sir Richard Weston of Sutton, in the County of Surrey, Knight. He appoints as his executors "my Lorde Pryve Seale," that is, Lord Southampton, formerly Sir W. Fitzwilliam, his old col-

---

[1] Record Office, 32 Henry VIII., Rot. 7.
[2] Hilary Term, 32 Henry VIII., R. O. Memoranda Roll, Recorda, L. Treasurer Remiss., L.T.R. Sir Richard's style in Latin runs thus—"Miles pro corpore, Magister Wardorum, Thesaurarius Calisiæ, et Sub-Thesaurarius Angliæ."

league, and the builder of Cowdray Castle, "my Lorde Admirall, Lorde Russell," *i.e.* Sir John Russell, the founder of the ducal house, his wife Anne, and Sir Christopher More, Knight, the founder of the house of Loseley, to be overseer, with legacies of £20 to each of those named.

Sir Richard dies as a good Catholic.[1] He bequeaths "his soul to Almighty God and to his blessed mother our Lady Saint Mary and to all the holy company of Heaven"; and he wills that "there may be said immediately after his decease fifteen trentals of masses for his soul and his father's soul and his mother's soul." He bequeaths to Lady Kingston "the Pownse Cupp with the cover which Mr. Wyngfield gave me."[2] Lady Kingston was the widow of Sir W. Kingston, the Constable of the Tower, who had been the jailor of Anne Boleyn and of Francis Weston. It was, as we now know, solely through the report made by Kingston to Cromwell that young Weston had been implicated. No doubt both kept their own counsel, and the father never knew the whole story. Sir W. Kingston and Sir R. Wyngfield were two of the four "sad and ancient Knights" who entered the King's Privy Chamber in 1519 along with Weston and Jerningham.

The will of Sir Richard is short and simple. He bequeaths to Anne, his wife, all his lands for life, and then to Henry Weston, his grandson, the only child of Sir Francis (then aged six years), in default of which the lands were to go to the sons of his daughters, Lady Dennys

---

[1] Lady Weston, the widow, seems to have been in 1542 and 1543 an adherent of the Princess Mary.—*Privy Purse Expenses of Princess Mary*, by Sir Harris Nicolas, pp. 33, 34, 110.

[2] *Pounce* cup was a cup with holes to sprinkle pounded sugar, said to come from *pumex*, pumice, *quasi spumex*, pouncet box, box with holes for scent.

and Lady Rogers. To his wife he bequeaths his personal goods, furniture, and household stuff for her life, and then to Henry Weston. And after some gifts to servants, he gives the residue of his estate to Anne, his wife, to dispose of "for the health of our souls and our friends' souls and of all Christian souls." Truly the venerable knight made a pious end of his life. If there were no recording angel, he was indeed an honourable man.

The will was proved 22nd November 1542, A.D. MD "quadragesimo secundo." For the proof of the will an inventory was prepared which remained in the archives of Loseley Hall until it was recently presented by the late Mr. More-Molyneux to F. H. Salvin, the owner of Sutton Place. It will be described when we are speaking of the house (chap. viii.) The executors deposited with Sir W. Gresham as banker the sum of £363 : 5s. in specie and gold chain. "The cheyne of fyne gold with a cross," weighing 68 ounces, was valued at £107 : 6s. This must have been a grand jewel, as it would now amount to £1280 alone.

The inventory gives a list of furniture, stores, and goods suitable for a house of the kind, tapestries for the great hall, "and a grete carpet to the table there"; "a gret carpet in the parlour agreable to the table there : a turkey carpet in the wadrobe : a grete carpete to lay under the kyngs fete : also xxv carpetts for wyndows in sundry chambers (no doubt carpets for the oriels), besyds the seyd xxv carpetts iii verder peces to lay in wyndows." This profuse use of carpets was unusual luxury in 1530. Verdures were tapestries of scenery.

There is the priest's chamber, and the fool's chamber, and the lads of the kitchen, Sir John Rogers's chamber (his son-in-law), a chapel, and chapel stuff. In the armoury are 102 pairs of harness, 102 sallats[1] and gorgeats,[2] 88 paire of "spleatts,"[3] 38 bows, and 54 sheaves of arrows with their cases, 25 bills and 1 battle-axe, and a pavilion (tent) and a hall. Of plate there are two gilt basons and ewers, 2 white silver basons and 2 ewers parcel gilt, 8 silver pots and 4 silver flagons, 18 chased goblets, 4 standing cups and 7 cruises, 6 dishes of silver, 24 trencher plates of silver, "18 silver spoons of the apostles upon the knobs." Let us trust these were real "antique" and not made up at Birmingham or Antwerp. There are also 8 silver spoons of another sort, a chafing bason, and chafing dish, etc. In all, the plate is priced at £164 : 2 : 6 = about £2000. There are 400 sheep, 100 beasts, and 60 horses. It must have been a stately mansion, well stocked and mounted.

So Sir Richard Weston was gathered to his fathers, and little Henry Weston, his grandson, became his heir and successor.

Lady Weston, his wife, survived him at least a few years, though she must have been of venerable age. A Mrs. Weston, most probably the same, had been a lady in the service of Queen Elizabeth of York in 1502; and in 1510, thirty-two years before her husband's death, she was gentlewoman to the Queen, Catherine of Aragon, was the wife of Sir Richard, and guardian of a young ward. Her family of Sandys or Sands was a branch of the family of Rotenby, St. Bees, in Cumberland, whence her father, William Sandys, came. Her brother was

---

[1] *Sallats* or *sellats* were *helmets*, engraved or chased, said to come from *cælata*, chased. So Shakespeare: "But for a sallet, my brain-pan had been cleft with a brown bill" (2 *Henry VI.*, Act IV., Scene 10).

[2] Pieces for the throat.

[3] "*Spleats*"=*splents* were little plates which protected the arm, *garde de bras*, Palsgrave (Halliwell, *Dict. of Archaic Words*, ii. 786).

Oliver Sandys of Shere, in Dorking, and she was doubtless of the family of William, Lord Sandys.[1] She proved the will of Sir Richard, and possibly had much to do with the bringing up of the young heir of Sutton Place, then a boy of seven or eight. She seems to have attached herself to the party of Mary and her Catholic friends. We have frequent notices of her in the *Privy Purse Expenses of Princess Mary*, ed. Sir H. Nicolas.[2]

During the years from 1537 until 1544 money is entered for the servants of Lady Weston for bringing presents of pudding and artichokes for the Princess Mary when at Guildford; and again we have her sending to the Princess "Peacocks, herons, and swete baggs" (sachets). Mary was born in 1516, and Lady Weston may have been gentlewoman to the Queen Catherine at her birth.

Besides the only son, Francis, Sir Richard and Lady Weston had two daughters.

Margaret, the wife of Sir Walter Dennys, the eldest son of Sir William Dennys, of Dyrham, County of Gloucester, by Anne, daughter and co-heiress of Maurice, Lord Berkeley. There is in the painted glass in the hall (lower north bay, No. 7) an emblem or *rebus* for her— a Marguerite growing out of a tun; and in the lower south-west window (No. X. 3) is a magnificent coat of arms of Sir Walter Dennys, quartering the coat of Berkeley in right of his mother. She afterwards married Richard Stafferton.

The second daughter, Katherine, named, of course, after the Queen (her mother being Lady of the Chamber), was married to Sir John Rogers, son of Sir John Rogers of Brianston, Dorset (see Hutchins' *Dorset*, i. 250, 3rd ed., 1861). One of the rooms at Sutton was called in

---

[1] Manning and Bray, ii. 671.   [2] Pp. 33, 34, 110.

the inventory "Sir John Rogers's room." In the time of James I. the Herald's Visitation for Surrey records as being in the hall the arms of Rogers; but they are no longer visible.[1] Both Lady Dennys and Lady Rogers had sons named Richard, after their grandfather. They are mentioned in the old knight's will on failure of heirs of Sir Henry Weston.

[1] On the tomb of Sir John Rogers of Brianston the arms are given thus —1 and 4, *Argent* on a chief *or*, a fleur-de-lys *gules*, in base a mullet, pierced *sable*. 2 and 3, *Argent, fretty sable*, a chief *gules*.

Sir Richard Rogers, grandson of Sir Richard Weston, married Cecilia Lutterel, and died 1604. Their grandchild, Elizabeth Rogers, in the fifth generation, married Charles Stuart, sixth Duke of Lennox and third Duke of Richmond. He died September 1672.—Burke, *Dormant Peerages*, p. 513.

PART III.—WESTONS, KNIGHTS OF ST. JOHN

As the Lord Prior of St. John's Order in England, Sir William Weston, the brother of Sir Richard, was so closely associated with him throughout life, some account must here be given of the Westons of St. John.

The Westons had a long connection with the martial order, whose true style is—The Knights Hospitallers of the Order of St. John of Jerusalem, commonly called the Knights of Malta, after their establishment there in the year 1530, or the Knights of Rhodes, down to the capture of the island by the Turks in 1522.[1]

[1] There are various histories of this Order by Sutherland and others, one of the more recent being that by Major-General W. Porter, revised edition, 1883. It contains lists of the priors, and a full account of the glorious defence of Rhodes. Other information has been supplied from the Records of the Order by Mr. E. Waterton, in a paper communicated to F. H. Salvin, Esq.

CH. III   SIR RICHARD WESTON THE ELDER   83

The illustrious Order of St. John, founded in 1118, never shone so nobly as during the sixteenth century, when they, almost unaided, maintained the honour of Christendom against the Turks. They were established at Rhodes in 1311; and on the loss of that island they were settled by the Emperor Charles V. at Malta, which they held down to the present century. They had various houses in England, of which that of St. John's at Clerkenwell was the centre. The Order was governed by a Grand Master, who usually resided at Rhodes, or afterwards at Malta. The head of the English branch was called Lord Prior of St. John's in England, and his headquarters were at the house in Clerkenwell, suppressed at the Reformation in 1540, remains of which existed until our own day. The Lord Prior of St. John's was entered as first of the lay barons in the Roll of Peers, coming next after viscounts. Selden, in his *Table Talk*, says—"The Prior of St. John's was *primus Baro Angliæ*, because, being last of the spiritual barons, he chose to be the first of the temporal. He was a kind of otter, a knight half spiritual, half temporal."

Not to speak of a certain *William Weston* who, as Knight of the Order, witnessed two charters in 1280 and 1281, or of a Thomas Weston who was made Commander of the Commanderies of Dingley and of Copmanthorpe in 1420 and 1422, we have two uncles of Sir Richard and Sir William Weston mentioned as knights in the fifteenth century. Sir William Weston, the elder, was brother of Sir John Weston, the prior, and was Knight of the Order in 1471.

His brother, Sir John Weston, was the son of Peter Weston of Boston, in Lincolnshire, by Agnes, daughter of John Daunay of Eskrigg, County York, and she was a sister of Sir William Daunay, the Turkopolier of the Order, an official usually regarded as lieutenant, and second to the Grand Master. Peter Weston was grandfather of Sir Richard, who thus had four Knights of St. John amongst his near relations—viz. three uncles and a brother, his brother and one uncle being Lords Prior, and two of his uncles Turkopoliers of the Order.

Sir John Weston, the uncle, was at one time General of the Galleys of the Order, and was Turkopolier in 1471; and in 1476 (24th July), by a Bull of the Grand Master, Peter d'Aubusson, dated from Rhodes, Sir John Weston, Turkopolier and Commander of Balsal and Newland, was appointed Lord Prior in England.

It was the custom of the first Tudors often to employ the Lord Prior of St. John's on embassies; and as we have already seen above, he was named as Commissioner on Embassies to the King of Scotland in 1486, and to the King of Spain in 1488. He died in 1489, having lived to see his elder brother, Edmund, Governor of Guernsey, and Edmund's sons, afterwards Sir Richard and Sir William, young men of promise and ambition.

The third Weston, Knight of St. John, of this particular house, was Sir William Weston, the brother of Sir Richard. He was the second son of Edmund Weston of Boston, of whom we have spoken above (p. 43). On 27th September 1510 certain rights of *ancienneté* were granted to him in Rhodes. The knight was then about forty; his brother Richard was already high in favour at Court, and Governor of Guernsey, as their father Edmund had been. Sir William is summoned to a chapter at Rhodes in June 1515. (Sir Richard, the brother, was then Knight of the Bath, and attending Mary Tudor on her marriage to the King of France.) He was appointed

Turkopolier, apparently before the great siege of Rhodes (July to December 1522). At this he distinguished himself greatly, was wounded, and for his services he received the next year special honours. In July 1523 a Bull from Baiæ, near Naples, granted to Sir William Weston, Turkopolier, with the universal consent of the English knights, right of *ancienneté* and succession to the priories of England and Ireland. The defence of Rhodes against Solyman is one of the most glorious and moving episodes in modern history, as Villiers de Lisle-Adam, the Grand Master, who conducted it, was one of the most perfect types of the hero—in courage, piety, endurance, and dignity of nature fit to stand beside even Godfrey de Bouillon. To have earned the trust of such a man was the glory of a life.

On 27th June 1527 a Bull of the Grand Master, Villiers de Lisle-Adam, from Corneto, appoints Sir William Lord Prior of England, and three days later Sir William notifies his appointment to the King. He shortly after returned to England and took his seat in the House of Lords as Premier Lay Baron. In 1532 it seems that, as Prior of St. John's, he exchanged the Manor of Hampton Court for the Priory of Stanesgate, in Essex (*Calendar V.* No. 627, xviii.) He spells badly, and like a German, for *joint patentee* becomes *jund pattend* (*Calendar V.* No. 417).

There is evidence that the Lord Prior did not belong to the party of Thomas Cromwell and the Boleyns. He was not employed by Henry VIII. On the contrary, there is every evidence that he opposed the Reformation and the anti-papal policy of Henry, and held by the claims of Mary Tudor. Morette, the ambassador of Francis I. in England, then actively opposing the party of Anne, "gave a great dinner party, at which the Dukes of Norfolk and Suffolk, Sir William Weston, Prior of St. John's, Lord Abergavenny, and other influential adherents of the papacy were present. Palamede Gontier told them of the *auto da fé* at Paris lately, when Francis himself with his sons had marched in the procession and had watched the torturing and burning of a good number of Protestants. The English lords were delighted to hear of this, and praised Francis for what he had done."[1]

Sir William Weston was apparently in opposition, and soon withdrew from public life. The *Calendars* contain a few letters from him to Lord Lisle, Cromwell, etc., and various references. From the *Journals of the House of Lords*, vol. i. 103, the name of the Prior of St. John of Jerusalem appears regularly as a daily attendant at Parliament in the 25 Henry VIII., 1533. He comes next after Viscount Lisle, the junior viscount, and above Lord Burgavenny, the senior baron, ancestor of the Marquis of Abergavenny. The Lord Prior also appears as a regular attendant in the Parliament of 28 Henry VIII., 1536. He does not appear in the Parliament of 31 Henry VIII., 1539, although the abbots of the great monasteries do; and his name never occurs again in the Roll of Parliament. We have a letter of the Prior, written in French, 7th September 1537, from Sutton, superscribed "to me neve Sir Thomas Dyngle." This is his nephew, Sir T. Dingley, a Catholic martyr, who was executed for denying the supremacy in 1539. In the year 1539 Sir William Weston, *continuis devexatus infirmitatibus*, appoints Lord Latymer and Lord Windsor as his proctors.

---

[1] Friedmann, ii. 54, citing a despatch of Gontier himself. See the despatch abstracted, *Calendar IX.* (1535), No. 174, Gontier to Chabot, where the name is spelt *Ovaston*.

The old knight was borne down by illness and yet more by grief.

On 7th May 1540 his Order was dissolved in England. By the Act of Dissolution he was secured a pension of £1000 a year. "But," says Weever, "he never received a penny of it; for it so fortuned that upon the seventh day of May 1540, being Ascension Day, and the same day of the Dissolution of the House, he was dissolved by death, which strooke him to the heart at the first time when he heard of the Dissolution of the Order."[1] And Fuller quaintly remarks, "His Hospital and earthly tabernacle were buried together, and gold, though a great cordial, could not cure a broken heart."[2]

The venerable knight was buried with great state and laid in a noble tomb in the Church of St. James, at Clerkenwell. An account of this tomb, now destroyed, may be seen in the *History of Clerkenwell*, by W. I. Pinks, London, 8vo, 1865; new edition by Edward J. Wood, London, 1881, from which the following notes are taken.

The Priory of the Knights of St. John was retained by Henry VIII. in his own hand, and was preserved from destruction by being used as a royal store. The church was destroyed by the Protector Somerset. In the reign of James I. what remained of the priory became private property. It was destroyed in the last century (1788). John Weever, who was buried in the church, describes the monument of Weston as he saw it about 1640. "In the North wall of the Chancel is a fair marble tomb, with the portraiture of a dead man lying upon his shroud, the most artificially cut in stone that ever man beheld."[3]

---

[1] J. Weever, *Funeral Monuments*, 1631, p. 430.
[2] Fuller, *Memoirs*, folio, p. 574.
[3] Weever, *Funeral Monuments*, p. 430.

Above it was a canopy with escutcheons, arms, and crests, and above the recumbent figure, apparently, were two kneeling figures and the objects of their adoration. In the centre of the canopy was the achievement of the Lord Prior in stone, above which, on a helmet, is the Saracen's head, *affronté* or full-faced, wreathed *argent* and *azure*. The arms are the same as those of Sir Richard at Sutton, quarterly, *Weston* and *Camell*, with the Cross of St. John in chief. Underneath is the motto, which seems to read ANY BORO.

When the old church was removed in 1788 this noble monument was destroyed. The skeleton measured exactly 5 feet 11 inches, and Pennant, in 1793, saw fragments of it in the garden. The effigy remained in the church, and was afterwards removed to the gatehouse. That is the last remnant of a gallant man.

Sir William was a great seaman as well as soldier, and commanded the first ironclad recorded in history. She was called the *Great Carrack*. She was sheathed with metal and perfectly cannon-proof. She had room for 500 men and provisions for six months. A picture of this famous ship is in the Royal Collections at Windsor.

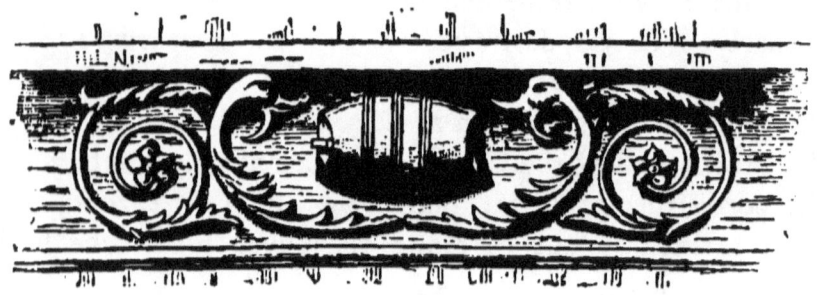

CHAPTER IV

SIR FRANCIS WESTON, THE SON AND HEIR

THE only son of Sir Richard Weston, the founder of Sutton, must have been a boy when his father received his grant of the manor and built the house. He entered the King's service as page in his teens, was a spoiled favourite, first of Henry, and then of Anne Boleyn, and was suddenly beheaded about his twenty-fifth year in the lifetime of his father. It does not appear in what year precisely he was born; but he did not obtain livery of the lands to which he was entitled in right of his wife until 24th June 1532,[1] although he was married to her in 1530. It is highly probable that this gives the date of his majority, as his father would certainly have secured him in possession of the vast estates he had obtained by marriage at the earliest possible moment.

Again, in 1533, Sir Richard procured the grant of the office of Governor of

[1] *Calendar*, Henry VIII., v. No. 1207 (4).

Guernsey in survivorship to himself and his son Francis.[1] In the same year Anne Boleyn was married, and Francis Weston was created Knight of the Bath during the ceremonies, 31st May 1533. It is hardly conceivable that such an office as the governorship of Guernsey, or such an honour as the knightship of the Bath, could have been conferred on a youth still under age; and it is almost as unlikely that, in his position, livery of the lands of his wife should have been withheld from him after he was of age.

The only circumstances on the other side are, first, his name Francis, and his being treated as a child, found in clothes, and mentioned with Patch, the Fool, down to his marriage, and always spoken of as "young Weston." Francis is a name that never occurs in the Weston pedigree either before or since;[2] it is not the name of any royal or eminent Englishman of that age, and until 1515, we may say, was a most uncommon name in England.[3] Francis, Duke of Angoulême, and heir-presumptive under Louis XII., did not come to the French throne until 1st January 1515. After that date there was every reason why a courtier of Henry VIII. who attended the marriage of Mary Tudor to Louis XII. and followed his king to the Field of the Cloth of Gold should have named his son after the French king. But before 1st January 1515 it was a most uncourtierlike thing to do. But it must be remembered that the Westons were a family with wide foreign connections. In 1502 Richard Weston is paid £4: 10s. for "gyrdelles" "brought for the Queen beyond the sea," and in 1510 he had license to freight a

---

[1] *Calendar V.* No. 1481, p. 596.
[2] The present owner of the house is *Francis* H. Salvin.
[3] Miss Yonge, *Christian Names* (*Francis*), vol. ii. p. 198.

ship to trade through the straits of "Marrok." Francis was a name common enough in Italy and France. However, if Francis Weston were not born until 1515, he must have been married at fifteen, and made governor and knight at eighteen, and executed at twenty-one.

The more probable view is that he was born in 1511, and named Francis after the Duke or some other foreign prince. His father was then about forty-five, was high in favour, had served in Spain, and held several offices. Even then Francis Weston would be a most precocious youth; but the dates of his career are intelligible enough. He was brought to Court and made page (*ætat.* fifteen). He beats the King at tennis, playing for heavy stakes (*ætat.* nineteen). He could hardly have beaten Henry, who was so great a tennis player, until about that age, and had he been some years older, an ambitious courtier would hardly have been so ill-advised as to beat his king at all. The spoiled lad is married (*ætat.* nineteen); comes of age, and is made Knight of the Bath (*ætat.* twenty-one); is made Governor of Guernsey and Gentleman of the Queen's Chamber (*ætat.* twenty-two); his only son is born (*ætat.* twenty-four); he is executed for high treason (*ætat.* twenty-five). Truly a brief, rapid, and brilliant career, even in those days.

The name of Francis Weston first occurs in 1526, when the Records inform us that "young Weston" was appointed to be the King's page.[1] In the *Chronicles of Calais*[2] and the *Privy Purse Expenses of Henry VIII*.[3] we have constant mention of young Weston as a spoiled minion of the King and reckless gambler. In May 1530 (*ætat.* nineteen) 3s. are paid for Master Weston's shirts,

---
[1] *Calendar IV.* p. 861.   [2] *Chronicles of Calais*, edited by J. Gough Nichols.
[3] *Privy Purse Expenses*, edited by Sir Harris Nicolas.

15s. for three pair of hosen, 20s., "the King's reward at Easter" (equivalent say to £12). Then we have £6 paid to Lord Rochford for Weston for four games of tennis which he won of the King at 4 angels apiece. This is high play, £72 for four games.

In May 1530 the sum of £6 : 13 : 4 is paid to Master Weston at his marriage.[1] In the same year is an entry for "hose for Master Weston, Mark, and Patche, the King's fool." Mark, of course, is Mark Smeaton, Anne Boleyn's musician, who was executed along with Weston and the rest. In 1531 the King's "reward" has risen to £2=£24, for the minion is now a married man and has a wife to keep, and is not let into possession of her estates. The King loses £4 to Weston at tennis at 40s. a game; he loses £4 : 10s. to Weston at Eltham at bowls at 4 angels the game. The King lends "young Weston" £20; that is £240. He pays him £46 (=£550), "for that he wonne of the King at Dyce at Langley, C C (200) corons" (crowns), and soon after £6 : 3s. (=£75), "wonne of the King at Imperiall." In 1532 £46 : 1 : 4 (=£560) is paid to Master Weston, "wyune of the King at Dyce at Calys"; again £18 was lost by the King to Weston "at popes July's game"; then £3 at the same; then 50 crowns (£150) is lost at cards and dyce to Bryan and Weston; 4s. is paid to a servant "who brings brawn and pudding from Lady Weston (his mother) to the King"; and 4s. for a present of wild fowl. "Tips" and "vails" were in those days substantial things. Fifty shillings "to drink y^r honour's health" to the footman who brings a parcel of brawn and pudding is a truly royal *pourboire*. In 1532 "young Weston's" reward against Christmas has risen to £5 (=£60);

[1] *Calendar V.* pp. 750, 757, 759.

Henry did things handsomely, even if he did cut off heads.[1]

But young Weston is now of age; and in 1532[2] he is appointed as Gentleman of the Privy Chamber, the office with which his father began his career, twenty years before, and he is ordered to serve six weeks in the Privy Chamber along with Sir N. Carew, Sir John Russell, Browne, Page, Bryan, and Knevitt. These men, who live on the canvas or cartoons of Holbein, are all members of the innermost circle of Henry's favourites. Browne is the half-brother and successor of Fitzwilliam, Earl of Southampton. Sir Nicholas Carew was a constant agent of Henry, a Knight of the Garter, and one of Anne Boleyn's enemies. Sir John Russell, afterwards Lord Russell, was one of Sir Richard Weston's executors. Sir Richard Page was arrested with Francis Weston in 1536, but allowed to escape. Sir Francis Bryan was a frequent envoy of Henry; he was cousin of Anne Boleyn, and brought news of her condemnation to Jane Seymour. Gardiner called Bryan "the vicar of Hell."[3] The gentlemen of the King's Privy Chamber in 1532 were not burdened with scruples or indifferent to promotion.

Henry had privately married Anne Boleyn on 25th

---

[1] Among various entries in the *Privy Purse Expenses of Henry VIII. from 1529-32*, edited by Sir Harris Nicolas (1527), are the following—"Hose for Weston, 15s.," p. 15; "£6 at Tennis," p. 37; "20s. reward at Easter," p. 37; "reward for keeping a young hound, 15s." (no doubt at Sutton Place), p. 50. "A servant for bringing two bucks, 6s. 8d."; in 1532 "the Kyng lost at Pope Julius game to my lady marques, master Bryan, and Master Weston, £9 : 6 : 8." Again at Greenwich, the same game and same players, £18 : 12 : 4; again, the same game and same players without Bryan, £3 : 12 : 8. The "lady marques" here is obviously Anne Boleyn, created in 1532 Marchioness of Pembroke. Weston, a lad barely of age, is one of the royal minions at the intimate parties of play.

[2] *Calendar V.* No. 927.   [3] Friedmann, ii. 185, 302-9.

January 1533, and in April he publicly appeared with her as his wife. The coronation in Westminster Abbey took place on 1st June following; on 31st May she went in state from the Tower to Westminster, according to the custom at coronations down to James II. On that day Francis Weston was made Knight of the Bath, and his name and arms are enrolled accordingly in the MS. already cited as in the British Museum (Claudius CIII. XIV. E.)

At the coronation of Anne, says the historian,[1] "The people remained silent. There was none of the enthusiasm with which in all ages Englishmen have greeted a popular queen." It was not easy to find her an adequate escort. So it appears that the young Court favourite, now just twenty-two, was promoted to be Knight of the Bath. "Among the friends of Anne there was a young courtier named Sir Francis Weston, the son of Richard Weston, Under-Treasurer of the Exchequer. He had first been a royal page, but had risen to the rank of Groom of the Privy Chamber, and was now one of the gentlemen of it. For the last eighteen years, by reason of his office, he had resided constantly at Court, and he had obtained a good many grants and pensions.[2] In May 1530 he had married Ann, the daughter and heiress of Sir Christopher Pickering, and having thus become a man of considerable property, he was created at the coronation of Anne a Knight of the Bath."[3]

An account of the family of Pickering of Westmor-

---

[1] Friedmann, i. 205.

[2] This is a slip of the very accurate Mr. Friedmann. Francis Weston had been seven years only at Court, 1526-33 (*ætat*. fifteen to twenty-two); he does not seem to have had any pension but his salary. He is apparently confused with his father. [3] Friedmann, ii. 248.

IV SIR FRANCIS WESTON, THE SON & HEIR

land and Cumberland proves that the heiress was of ancient race and large possessions.[1] The estate of Killington, in Kirby Kendal, had been granted to William de Pickering, 44 Henry III. (1259). His descendant, Sir James Pickering, married the heiress of Moresby, Cumberland. Sir James's son, Sir Christopher Pickering, had an only daughter, Ann, who ultimately inherited the Pickering and Moresby estates. She was made the ward of Sir Richard Weston on the death of her father, Sir Christopher, in 1519; and eleven years later she was married by her judicious guardian to his son, Francis, then apparently about nineteen. She brought into his family shield the quarterings of Pickering, Threlkeld, Lassels of Eskrigg, Moresby, Fenwick, Tyliol, Longuevilliers, Etton, and Lewkenor.[2]

Their son (and only child), afterwards Sir Henry Weston, was born in 1535. The next year Ann was a widow. She then married Sir Henry Knyvett of East Horsley, Surrey; and her third husband (for heiresses then never long remained single) was John Vaughan, whom she outlived. She died in 1582, fifty-two years after her first marriage, and nearly fifty years after the great tragedy of her life. She is not mentioned in Sir Richard's will, as she was then Lady Knyvett. By her will she directed that her body should be buried, not near that of any of her three husbands, but beside that of her father-in-law, Sir Richard Weston, who had been laid in Trinity Church, Guildford, just forty years before.[3]

---

[1] Nicholson and Burn, *Westmorland*, 4to, 1777, vol. i. p. 261.

[2] The arms of Pickering: *Ermine*, a lion rampant *sable*, crowned *or*, are given by Benolt in the *Visitation of Surrey*, collection of arms with their quarterings. They can no longer be seen at Sutton Place.

[3] Manning and Bray, ii. 640.

History knows nothing more serious of Sir Francis Weston than his gambling escapades and tennis-playing until the great tragedy in which he had a brief, humble, but cruel share. This is not the place wherein to tell again the oft-told tale of the judicial murder of Anne Boleyn. It has lately been restudied and written afresh by a learned student, who has ransacked the archives of this and of foreign countries with great success.[1]

So far as Weston was concerned the story is this. It was in April 1536 that the first steps were taken towards the execution of Anne Boleyn. On the 24th the King signed a secret Commission authorising certain persons named and nine judges to inquire into every kind of treason and to try the offenders. Besides certain great officials there were named Lord Sandys, Thomas Cromwell, Fitzwilliam, and Paulet. The Commission met avowedly to find evidence which might convict Anne of guilt. "Her courtiers," we are told, "soon found out that the surest road to her favour was either to tell her that other men were in love with her, or to pretend that they were in love with her themselves. She was extremely coarse, and lived at a most dissolute court; so that the flattery she asked for was offered in no very modest terms."[2]

On the 30th April Mark Smeaton, a Groom of the Chamber and player on the lute, was arrested, and either torture, fear, or hope led him to confess that he had been guilty of criminal acts. On 1st May Noreys was arrested; on 2nd May Anne was taken to the Tower,

---

[1] *Anne Boleyn, a Chapter of English History*, 1527-36, by Paul Friedmann, 2 vols., 8vo, Macmillan, 1884. It has also been told by Mr. Froude in his slipshod and partisan style, *Divorce of Catherine of Aragon*, 1891.

[2] Friedmann, ii. 247.

and her brother, Lord Rochford, followed. The Queen was put into the custody of Sir William Kingston, the Constable (one of the "sad and ancient Knights" with Sir Richard Weston in 1519), and of Lady Kingston, to whom the old knight by his will bequeathed "the Pownse Cupp with the cover." Fitzwilliam, Paulet, and the Kingstons, with Lord Sandys, were foremost amongst the enemies of the Queen. They were also all old friends and colleagues of Sir Richard Weston.

In the Tower Anne began to talk to her attendants in a state of hysterical excitement, and every word she uttered was carried to Kingston and his wife. The Queen talked of Noreys and then of Francis Weston. Noreys was engaged to Margaret Shelton, Anne's cousin, and one of her attendants. The Queen thought Francis Weston was making love to the girl, neglecting his young wife, who remained away from Court. She had upbraided him, she said, with making love to Margaret and for not loving his wife. The young man, perhaps knowing her appetite for flattery, had answered that he loved someone in her house more than either his wife or Madge. Anne asked who was that, and Weston replied it was herself. She professed to be very angry, it is said slapped his face, rebuked him for his impudence, and told him to go home to his own wife. Weston continued his flirtation, and said that Noreys, like himself, came to her chamber more for her sake than that of Madge. The original account runs thus:—

Sir William Kingston to Cromwell—"Sir, syns the makynge of thys letter the Quene spake of Wes[ton, saying that she] had spoke to hym bycause he did love hyr kynswoman (Mrs. Shelton and) said he loved not hys wyf, and he made ansere to hyr [again that h]e loved wone in hyr howse better then them bothe. And [the Queen said—who is] that? It ys yourself. And then she defyed hym, as [she said to me].

"WILL'M KYNGSTON."

All this pitiful cackle the half-crazy Queen repeated in the silly strain of the courts in which she had lived from childhood, and under the influence of unnerved anxiety and excitement. Every word of it was repeated to Lady Kingston, and reported by Sir William to Cromwell. An old copy of his report may be read to-day in the British Museum.[1] That day Sir Francis Weston was arrested and placed in the Tower.

The prisoners of the Queen's household were tried on 12th May, the Duke of Norfolk presiding, Henry and Cromwell in secret arranging every detail. Smeaton pleaded guilty, Weston and the rest not guilty, to all the charges. For the grand jury twelve knights were sworn. They were all officials, justices, sheriffs, and men trusted by the Crown. A verdict of guilty was pronounced, and they were all condemned to the horrible punishment reserved by the old law for the crime of high treason. "An attempt was made to save Sir Francis Weston, whose family was powerful and rich, and had generally sided with the Boleyns."[2] He was a very beautiful young man, another historian relates, and his mother and wife had offered a sum of 100,000 crowns for his life.[3] Even

---

[1] Kingston to Cromwell, 3rd May 1536, Cotton MSS., Otho, C. x. fol. 225, British Museum; Ellis, 1st series, ii. 53; Singer's *Cavendish*, ii. 217; *Calendar X.* No. 882.

[2] Friedmann, ii. 283.

[3] Miss Strickland, *Lives of the Queens of England*, vol. iv. 264. Mr. Hepworth Dixon boldly says (*Two Queens*, iv. 321), "The young man's mother, dressed in the deepest mourning, flung herself at the King's feet and prayed for a reprieve. His young wife offered to give up everything they had in the world—land, houses, and manorial rights, the appanage of a baron—if

the French king, whose name he bore, and perhaps whose godson he was, seems to have interceded on his behalf. "Quelque instance quaye faicte levesque de Tarbes ambassadeur ordinaire de France et le Seigneur de Tinteville lequel arryva yci avant hier pour en saulver ung nomme Vaston."[1] He is also called "Master Ubaston who used to lie with the king." On 16th May the condemned were told to prepare for execution. They confessed, made out lists of their debts, wrote farewell letters to their families, whom they were not suffered to see. The letter of Sir Francis may be seen in the Record Office.[2]

"Father and mother and wyfe, I shall humbly desyre you for the salvacyon of my sowle to dyschardge me of thys byll, and for to forgyve me of all the offences that I have done to you. And in especyall to my wyfe, whiche I desyre for the love of God to forgive me, and to pray for me, for I beleve prayer wyll do me good. Goddys blessing have my chylderne and meyne. By me a great offender to God.

"Endorsed—detts to divers by Sr Francis Weston."

The poor lad saw the truth at last.

The list of his debts at the end of which his letter was written amounts to the sum of £925 : 7 : 2, owing to about fifty different persons.

the King would spare his life. But Henry wanted a confession, not a sum of money, and he answered the broken-hearted women, 'Let him hang, let him hang!'" But Mr. Dixon gives no authority for this somewhat melodramatic scene; nor does he give any for his assertion (p. 253) that Weston was near or kin to the Queen. We can hardly take either statement on the authority of *MSS. penes Dixon.—Two Queens*, iii. 360; iv. 253, 321, and *Tower of London.* J. Husee to Lord Lisle, letter of 13th May, "If any escape, it will be young Weston, for whom importunate suit is made."—*Calendar X.* No. 865.

[1] Chapuis to Charles V., 19th May 1536, *Calendar X.* No. 908; also quoted by Friedmann. It may be noted that Dinteville is no doubt the ambassador in Holbein's famous picture lately added to the National Gallery.

[2] Henry VIII., 1536-37, x. No. 869.

The lad owes "my cousin Dingley with my father" £30. He owes £6 to "Barnarde my father's Coke"; to "Browne, the draper," £50; to "Genenes, the page of the chamber," £6:13:4; to "my lorde of Wylshyre," Anne Boleyn's father, and one of his own judges, £40 in angels; to "Bridges, my taylor," £26; to "parson Robynson" £66; "item to a pooer woman at the Tennes play for bawles I cannot tell howe muche!" to Mr. Bryan, "the vicar of Hell" aforesaid, £76 in angels; to the Kynges Hyghnes £46; and to Marke Smeaton £73:6:7. These of course are gambling debts. But as the King had the boy's head, he would hardly ask for the £46. He owes his shoemaker £46 (=£552); to Sir Richard Gresham £41; to "Lady Mosgrave" £56, for which she held a pledge of plate; and to *Secheper* (? Shakespeare) that pleythe at the dyce, 30 crowns.

The total of the debt (£925) might amount, say roughly, to about £12,000 of our money, and was equal to about ten times his yearly salary as Gentleman of the Chamber.[1] It was a goodly list for a young man of twenty-five. It was nearly three times the amount at which, five years later, his father's whole personal estate was proved by the executors.

By royal order the scaffold was prepared, not at Tyburn, but on Tower Hill; and instead of being hanged, disembowelled, and quartered, the prisoners were simply beheaded. They were allowed to address the people who had come in great numbers to witness their execution. They did not confess their guilt; but as was usual, and indeed necessary for the sake of their families and possessions, they made no vehement protestations of

---

[1] The salary of the Lord Chancellor was £200, and the revenues of the Priory of St. John at the Dissolution were £282.

innocence. It was part of the terrible game that was played by courtiers and politicians that if they spoke at all they would not attack the government or their judges, for ample means remained of bringing them to retribution.[1] So Weston, like the others, confessed that he was a sinner, but said nothing which could be tortured into evidence against the Queen. According to Constantine, in his letter to Cromwell, Weston said: "I had thought to live in abomination yet this twenty and thirty years, and then to have made amends; I little thought I would have come to this."[2]

So on Wednesday, the 17th of May, Sir Francis Weston was executed on Tower Hill; and all the eye-witnesses relate that he died with courage. "They died very charitably," writes John Husee to Lord Lisle, 19th May (*Calendar X.* No. 919).

Nothing in life became him like the leaving it; but like the sovereign whom his great-grandson served in the next century—

> "He nothing common did or mean
> Upon that memorable scene,
>   But with his keener eye
>   The axe's edge did try;
> Nor called the Gods, with vulgar spite,
> To vindicate his helpless right;
>   But bowed his comely head
>   Down, as upon a bed."[3]

---

[1] In the *Excerpta Historica*, p. 260, is given a translation of a letter from a Portuguese gentleman, probably an eye-witness of the execution of Anne Boleyn and Weston, whom he calls *Monsire Nestorn*, "the which said no more than that they besought the bystanders to pray for them, and that they yielded themselves to death with joy and exceeding gladness of heart."

[2] Friedmann, ii. 285; *State Trials*, i. 425; Wriothesley, *Chron.* Camden Soc. 1875, pp. 36, 39; Hall, *Henry VIII.*, 214.

[3] A. Marvell, *Horatian Ode*.

The body with the head was placed in a simple shell, and thrown into a grave with that of Noreys in the churchyard of St. Peter's in the Tower.[1]

The Queen was beheaded within the Tower on 19th May. She had undoubtedly caused the death of the poor lad by her frenzied talk, as she had encouraged him to continue with her a coarse and unmeaning flirtation. There is not the slightest reason to assume any kind of criminality between them worse than gross folly and shameless indecorum. Anne was now a woman of thirty-four, who had lost her health, her looks, and her spirit, already on the verge of disgrace and repudiation, and known to be surrounded by deadly enemies and unscrupulous rivals. The wild lad was merely a butterfly casually crushed between the fierce millstones of ambitious intrigue; and clearly he was a mere accidental object of Cromwell's plot. The whole thing was as sudden as lightning. Sir Francis, a gay and popular courtier, was arrested suddenly on the 4th of May, and on the 17th he was a headless corpse. This 17th of May was the same day of the same month on which his father had helped in the execution of Buckingham, and also that on which he had received the princely gift of Sutton.

The judicial murder of his only son does not appear to have made any difference in the official position of Sir Richard Weston. The son was attainted, and all his goods and estates were confiscated to the King, the list of debts and request that they might be paid was an ordinary and necessary form. The father's estate, offices, and favour

---

[1] Camden Soc., Wriothesley's *Chron.* vol. i. p. 36; Hep. Dixon, *Story of Two Queens*; *Tower of London*; Doyne-Bell, *The Tower*; Miss Strickland, *Life of Anne Boleyn*; Weever, *Memorials*, p. 514; Froude, *Divorce of Catherine of Aragon*, 1891.

were not touched by this disaster. In the days when desperate games were played at Court, wherein the stakes were heads, it was a point of honour with the gamblers to pay the forfeit with a good grace and bear no malice. The Earl of Wiltshire (Sir Thomas Boleyn) was duly summoned to the Court which condemned his own son and daughter to death; and the Duke of Norfolk, the hero of Flodden, with tears in his eyes condemned the Duke of Buckingham to the scaffold.

Sir Richard bore his bereavement like a man, retained the King's good graces, saw the childhood of the grandson who survived to inherit Sutton, and was appointed by Henry and by Cromwell, the two murderers of his only son, to attend the ceremonies and funeral of Jane Seymour, the baptism of Edward VI., and the state reception of Anne of Cleves, Henry's fourth wife.

The young widow in due course married Sir Henry Knyvett, one of the comrades and fellow-courtiers of her first husband, and doubtless forgot her brilliant young spouse, of whom she had seen so little.

There is a curious and interesting account of Francis Weston and his execution in Crapelet's *Lettres de Henri VIII.* (2nd ed., Paris, 1835, p. 185). It is in the form of a poem, in French, composed in London, 2nd June 1536. Weston, it says, was young, of high and ancient lineage, of good manners, and exceeding all in elegance; in jousts, in the dance, and in leaping a perfect athlete, and in tennis excelling the most skilful players of the nation. None dared intercede for him but his mother, who, oppressed with grief, humbly petitioned the King, and his wife, who offered freely rents and goods (*i.e.* lands and chattels) for his deliverance. But the King resolves that the sentence passed at their trial should be carried out. And if money had had any avail for him, the fine would have been 100,000 crowns.

The French is :—

> "Pauvre Waston qui estoit de jeune aage
> Yssu de hault et très ancien lignage
> De bonnes meurs et graces tous passant,
> En lisse, en bal, à saulter, effaçant
> En jeu de paulme en grand perfection
> Les plus adroitz de cette nation.
> Et de tous biens en luy tant abondait,
> Que le pays tout honoré rendoit.
> Nul pour luy n'en osa faire instance
> Sinon sa mère, en grand dueil oppressée,
> Qui humblement au Roy s'est adressée ;
> Sa femme aussi, offrant entièrement
> Rentes et biens pour son delivrement.
> Mais le Roi veult que soit exécutée
> De leur procès la sentence arrestée,
> Et si l'argent pour luy eust eu puissance
> D'escuz cent mil eust fixé la chevance."

Out of this plain tale Mr. Hepworth Dixon and Mr. Froude have elaborated melodramatic romances of their own. Mr. Dixon tells us that the "mother, dressed in the deepest mourning, flung herself at the King's feet." All we know is that she was "oppressed with grief," and humbly addressed the King, possibly by petition. Mr. Froude says the mother and young wife "appeared in court," meaning before the judge and jury. That would have startled even a Tudor judge, and was quite impossible even in that age. Mr. Dixon tells us that Henry answered the broken-hearted women, "Let him hang, let him hang!" Mr. Froude tells us that Weston was well known in Paris, and had been much liked there. We have not a word recorded of Henry, nor is there a trace of the lad having ever gone to Paris. Next we are told that M. Dinteville came over as his friend. But M. Dinteville was a special ambassador of Francis. And then Mr. Froude quotes the lad's last letter (see above, p. 99), in which, by the way, he inserts three errors of copying, as proof of young Weston's guilt. It is well known that discreet silence in prison and at the scaffold was the price that one paid for being spared torture and confiscation. Mr. Froude's argument would excuse every judicial murder by any Tudor or Stuart sovereign. The idea of Weston's self-proven guilt is as gratuitous an invention as Mr. Dixon's "deepest mourning," "the appanage of a baron," and the King's "Let him hang!" or Mr. Froude's own introduction of the wife and mother at the trial offering bribes to judge and jury, Weston's Parisian popularity, and M. Dinteville's friendship.

Assuredly Francis Weston was not a man to be remembered long. The doggerel of the Rhyming Chronicle in Cavendish's *Life of Wolsey*[1] puts the truth when it runs thus:—

> "Weston the wanton, ye shall understand,
> That wantonly lyved without feare or dreade.
>
> .   .   .   .   .   .
>
> Beyng but young, and skant out of the shell,
> I was dayntely noryshed under the king's wyng,
> Who highly favored me and loved me so well
> That I had all my will and lust in everything."

[1] Cavendish, *Life of Wolsey*, by Singer, vol. ii. p. 30.

A wanton and a worthless youth! But youth, beauty, high courage, and splendid station, suddenly cut off in blood amidst the whirl of a great historical tragedy, command our sympathies, we know not why, and however little reason for sorrow that we find in sober reflection.

CHAPTER V

SIR HENRY WESTON

HENRY WESTON, the only child of Francis, who was the only son of Sir Richard, was an infant in his first year at the date of his father's bloody death, and a boy of seven when by the death of his grandfather he succeeded under the *will* as devisee of all Sir Richard's lands. He could not of course *inherit* through his father, whose attainder involved "corruption of blood." It appears by the inquisition taken after the death of Sir Richard[1] that Henry, the only son of the attainted Sir Francis, was born in 1535, and that his aunts, Margaret, Lady Dennys, and Catherine, Lady Rogers, were alive.

Young Henry was bred to arms, not to courts.

[1] R. Off. *Inquisit. Post Mortem*, 33-34 Henry VIII., Berkshire.

During the stormy times which closed the reign of Henry VIII., and which followed on the reigns of young Edward and Mary, the heir of Sutton was a youth in his teens. He came of age in the fourth year of Mary's reign, in the height of her effort to restore the Catholic faith by force.

The young soldier distinguished himself in the war with France, which broke out when he was but twenty-two; and at the age of twenty-three he was greatly honoured for the gallant stand he made when Calais was lost for ever to the English crown, to the inexpressible grief of Queen Mary, as we all know, and the incalculable advantage of the English people. Mary, as we are told, died of grief within a few months of this memorable feat of arms.

At the accession of Elizabeth, in 1558, the young hero of Calais stood high in favour. As a minor he had taken no part in politics or in the great religious revolutions of the last twenty years. His father died on the scaffold during the judicial murder of Elizabeth's mother, and had undoubtedly fallen a sacrifice to her mother's imprudent conduct, and to the bitter animosity of her mother's enemies. He himself had married a lady of the noblest blood, who was a cousin of Elizabeth herself, and who, like her husband, had lost a father on the scaffold.

Accordingly, at the coronation of Elizabeth, January 1559, Sir Henry Weston was created Knight of the Bath, and his name and arms are duly entered in the MS. volume already cited,[1] as had been those of his father and grandfather.

---

[1] Cotton MSS., Claudius CIII. XIV. E. The arms given are quarterly of six—1. *Weston.* 2. *Camell,* as before, chap. iii. 3. *Pickering: Ermine,* a lion rampant *sable,* armed *gules,* ducally crowned *or.* 4. *Lascelles of Eskrigg:*

In the year 1550, second to third year of Edward VI. cap. 6, by Act of Parliament, he had obtained restitution in blood after the attainder of his father, and possession of all estates which he had inherited through his father. And in the same year the estates at Clandon were confirmed to him which had been leased for sixty years to Sir Richard in 1532 (Pat. 2 Eliz., Treas. Remembr.) Sir Henry was thus a man of large possessions, being in enjoyment of the lands of his grandfather, Sir Richard, and entitled in remainder to the lands of his mother, the heiress of Pickering. She died in 1582.

Sir Henry Weston married in 1559 Dorothy,[1] daughter of Sir Thomas Arundell of Wardour, also, like Sir Francis Weston, one of the Knights of the Bath at the coronation of Anne Boleyn, and also beheaded for treason (1552) as one of the partisans of the Protector Somerset, on the fall of the haughty Seymour. Her mother, Margaret Howard, sister of Catherine Howard, the fifth wife of Henry VIII., was the elder daughter of Lord Edmund Howard, Marshal of the Horse at the battle of Flodden, and granddaughter of the second Duke of Norfolk, the famous commander in that battle.

Argent, three chaplets gules. 5. *Moresby* (Cumberland): *Sable*, a cross argent, in the first quarter a cinquefoil *or*. 6. *Fenwick* (Northumberland): Perfesse, *gules* and *argent*, six martlets counter-changed. Crest: A camel *sable*, spotted *argent*, collared and hoofed *or*.

[1] This lady is named Margaret in Segar's great pedigree of Weston in the British Museum, and this has been followed by Manning, Hoare, Collins, and others. It appears from a very fine old pedigree of the Arundells and from family deeds, now in the possession of Lord Arundell and Wardour at Wardour Castle, Wilts, that her only name was Dorothy. So also in the parish register of West Clandon, Surrey, the birth of her sons is thus registered, *e.g.* "1561, 13th October, was baptized Henry, son of Sir H. Weston, knight, and Dorothy, his wife." It throws some suspicion over the accuracy of Segar's pompous pedigree, with its roots traced back to Adam, when we find him in error on so important a name.

Through her mother, Margaret Howard, Lady Weston was thus allied to the royal house and to the noblest families of the age. Her family history is so characteristic of the times, and is stained with bloodshed so often and so continuously, that it may be of interest to follow it.

Lady Weston's father, Sir Thomas Arundell, of an ancient family in the west, obtained from his father, Sir John Arundell, the grant of Wardour Castle, in Wiltshire, formerly a royal possession. His mother was Eleanor, youngest daughter of Thomas Grey, second Marquis of Dorset. Her three brothers, Henry, Duke of Suffolk, Thomas, and Leonard, were all beheaded. Eleanor's nieces were Lady Jane Grey, who married Guildford Dudley, and Catherine, who married Lord Hertford, and died of her cruel confinement in the Tower in 1567. Henry, Duke of Suffolk, who was beheaded in 1554, married Frances, eldest daughter and co-heiress of Charles Brandon, Duke of Suffolk, by Mary, sister of Henry VIII. Sir Thomas Arundell, by his wife, Margaret Howard, became the grandfather of Sir Thomas Arundell, the hero of the battle of Gran, Count of the Holy Roman Empire, 1595, and first Baron Arundell, 1605.

Sir Thomas Arundell, father of Lady Weston, and his wife, Margaret Howard, were both committed to the Tower, and he was executed in the desperate duel between the Protector Somerset and Dudley, Duke of Northumberland, in 1552.[1]

Margaret Howard, mother of Dorothy, Lady Weston (temp. Queen Elizabeth), was by her father's side granddaughter of the second Duke of Norfolk, attainted in

---

[1] Machyn's Diary, pp. 10, 15.

1485, but eventually restored, and great-granddaughter of the first Duke of Norfolk, the Jockey of Norfolk, who lost his life on the field of Bosworth. Her uncle, the third Duke of Norfolk, was attainted in 1546; her cousin, the Earl of Surrey, was beheaded in 1547; the Earl's son, fourth Duke of Norfolk, was beheaded in 1572; and his son Philip, Earl of Arundel, was attainted and died in the Tower, 1594. Margaret Howard's sister was Catherine Howard, whom, on sufficient proof of her adultery and vice, Henry beheaded in 1542. Margaret Howard's aunt was Elizabeth, the wife of Thomas Boleyn, Lord Rochford and Earl of Wiltshire, whose daughter was Anne Boleyn, and whose son was Lord Rochford, both beheaded in 1536, as was also Lady Rochford in 1542.

Dorothy Arundell, Lady Weston, whose portrait smiles so gracefully from the walls of the hall where she entertained Elizabeth, was thus a lady endowed with a somewhat interesting family tree, full of splendid alliances and of blood-stained records. She was the cousin of four queens, of Catherine Howard, Anne Boleyn, Elizabeth, and Lady Jane Grey. Her father's uncle, her mother's sister and cousin, had all three married into the royal house of Tudor, the first being the husband of Henry VIII.'s niece, and the two latter being wives of Henry himself. The heralds must have drawn up her genealogical tree with unusual expectation of reward and no little professional unction; for it is freely studded with dukes, duchesses, princesses, kings, and queens. And as these illustrious personages really have a place in the history of England, the tree is not nearly so imaginative as is too often the case with the heraldic glories of that age.

But if the tree is full of splendid alliances, it is also as full of bloody memories. It is at once comical and shocking to note how a person of distinguished lineage in that sixteenth century could make out a list of relations by blood or marriage who had all suffered death on the scaffold or had been attainted as "traitors." In fact, in Tudor times to be attainted as traitor was nearly equivalent to the modern phrase of "going out of office"; and to be gently born at all, it was almost essential that at least one member of your family should have been condemned to be hanged, drawn, and quartered.

The following chronological table may represent the havoc which politics had made in the family of Dorothy Weston *née* Arundell :—

ATTAINTED RELATIONS OF DOROTHY ARUNDELL, WIFE OF SIR HENRY WESTON, 1560.

Father's side.

1. Her father, Sir T. Arundell . . beheaded 1552
2. Father-in-law, Sir Francis Weston . „ 1536
3. Father's uncle, Henry, Duke of Suffolk „ 1554
4. „ „ Thomas, Lord Grey . „ 1554
5. „ „ Leonard, Lord Grey . „ 1541
6. Father's first cousin, Lady Jane Grey . „ 1554
7. Lady Jane's husband, Guildford Dudley „ 1554
8. Lady Jane's brother-in-law, Francis Dudley „ 1554
9. Lady Jane's father-in-law, Duke of Northumberland, beheaded 1554
10. Father's first cousin, Catherine Seymour, died prisoner in the Tower 1567

Mother's side.

11. Her mother, Lady Arundell, attainted but not beheaded 1552
12. Mother's sister, Catherine Howard, beheaded . 1542
13. Mother's first cousin, Anne Boleyn, beheaded . 1536
14. Mother's first cousin, Earl of Surrey, beheaded . 1547
15. Mother's first cousin by marriage, Lady Rochford, beheaded 1542
16. Mother's cousin, fourth Duke of Norfolk, beheaded 1572
17. Mother's sister-in-law, Ann Howard, attainted . 1542
18. Uncle, third Duke of Norfolk, attainted . . 1546
19. Grandfather, second Duke of Norfolk, attainted . 1485
20. Great-grandfather, first Duke of Norfolk, killed in civil war 1485
21. Cousin, Earl of Arundel, died in the Tower, attainted 1594
22. Great-uncle, Lord Thomas Howard, attainted, died in the Tower 1536

She must have been a fine lady. The noble portrait in the hall reputed to be by Federigo Zucchero represents her as she stood there in the heyday of her dignity and grace. She is attired in the Venetian laces and brocades, with frill, ruff, head-dress, in the style so familiar to us as that of Elizabeth. The embroideries are superb, and she is covered with jewels, in the fashion of that time, holding a feather fan in her hand. The picture was exhibited at the Royal Academy in Burlington House in 1884, and was described as by Zucchero, full length, canvas 71 by 40 inches. Zucchero, who was born in 1543, and worked much in Flanders, came to England in 1574, where he stayed until 1578, painting the Queen, her courtiers, and ministers, amongst others Lord Howard of Effingham, who was at once a cousin and neighbour of Lady Weston. The date of the picture was about 1575, when she was about thirty-five. But, of course, the experts refer the portrait to some other hand. There is also a portrait of her about fifteen years later, in which we see the same features, somewhat dimmed by the advance of years.

Sir Henry Weston was Sheriff of Surrey in 1569 and in 1571, and he represented the county in the Parliament of 1571.[1] He entertained Elizabeth at Sutton Place on several occasions.[2] The first occasion was in the beginning of her reign, in her second year, when the Protestant religion was being officially re-established. Sir Henry, who had been recently knighted and married, was but twenty-five years of age, and was in the first spring of his youthful fame and splendour. On that occasion a fire took place in the house, the exact effect of which is not quite apparent. In Machyn's Diary (*Camden Society Publications*, p. 241) we read: "The vij day of August was Suttun bornyd, wher the Quen's grase dyd ly iij nyghtes afor, that was master Westun's plase." Again Elizabeth was certainly there in September 1591, on her way from Farnham to Richmond, and we have a letter of hers to Sir H. Unton, ambassador in France, "given under our signet at Sutton near Guildford," 11th November 1591.[3]

---

[1] Loseley MSS., by Rev. A. J. Kempe, 1835. In order to fill his public office of sheriff Sir Henry was compelled to conform to the Elizabethan regimen, and accordingly we find that he made a declaration of "obedience to the Act of Uniformity of Common Prayer and Observance of the Sacraments."—*Calendar*, Elizabeth, 1547-80, p. 348, the date being 28th November 1569.

[2] Nichols's *Progresses of Queen Elizabeth*, chap. i. p. 86, and chap. iii. p. 121.   [3] Rymer, *Fœd.* chap. xvi. p. 122.

At the second visit Sir Henry must have been a man of fifty-six, and Elizabeth was two years older. Many things had happened in the interval. Mary Queen of Scots had been executed just three years, and the Armada had been destroyed just two years before. The tremendous struggle between the two religions was at its height, and the times were dark and terrible, especially to Englishmen who were not willing to worship in the forms prescribed by the imperious daughter of the first Defender of the Faith. Sir Henry may have retained the personal goodwill of his sovereign, but he holds no office now. He is employed neither in war nor in peace. He no longer serves in Parliament; he receives neither grant nor honour. The Reformation is established, and the Westons of Sutton Place have henceforward no part with princes, courts, and office; and they drop quietly from the pages of English history, well content if they can preserve their heads, their liberty, and the remnant of their estates from the grasp of a government wherein they have no share.

Sir Henry Weston is frequently referred to in the Loseley papers abstracted by the *Historical Manuscripts Commission*, vol. vii. He is at Loseley (p. 649 *a*); Lord Howard of Effingham writes to Sir W. More (5th April 1591) begging Sir William's good offices to obtain election of Lord Howard's "cousin," Sir H. Weston, to the vacant office of Verderer of Windsor Forest. In another letter (p. 661 *b*) Lord Howard speaks of Sir Henry "as his good friend and kinsman." Sir Henry asks for the support of Sir W. More in his election, 1558-59. There is a letter (17th November 1569) from Thomas Copley to Sir H. Weston begging for reasonable time to consult his conscience (p. 622 *a*). In the *Calendars*, 1547-80, there are many notices of his acting as magistrate in formal matters.

It seems almost certain that Sir Henry Weston was a secret supporter of the old faith. In 1569 a letter is addressed to Sir Henry, then High-Sheriff for Surrey, by one Sir Thomas Copley of Gatton, who signs himself "your loving neighbour and assured pore friend,"[1] in which Sir Thomas begs his loving neighbour's protection and help under the persecution to which he was exposed. Now this Sir Thomas Copley was a "Popish recusant" of the most pronounced kind, most dangerous to Elizabeth's government; he retired to the Spanish Netherlands, and ultimately joining the Spanish arms, served in war against his country and Queen, and died in 1584. Letters of marque were granted to him by Requesens, Philip's viceroy, in which he is styled Don Thomas Copleus. It was the great-granddaughter of Sir Thomas, Mary Copley, who ultimately brought the estates of Gatton to the Westons, when she married, in 1637, John Weston, the great-grandson of Sir Henry.

It is melancholy that no evidence can be found that Sir Henry drew or offered his sword in the great struggle which Elizabeth waged with the foreign powers for her life and nation, 1584-88. There is rather evidence to the contrary. Sir Henry was not more than fifty, and had yet seven years of life. At the end of May 1584, whilst the murder of Elizabeth and invasion was imminent, just one month before the assassination of the great William of Orange, it was ordered, 31st May, that 1000 men should be raised in Surrey, and the following captains of 250 men each were named—Sir Henry Weston, Sir T. Carew, Sir T. Browne, Sir George

[1] Loseley MSS., 1835, pp. 241, 243.

More; but it is recorded that "Sir Henry Weston, having great occasion to be in the North this summer, *desires to be discharged as captain*, and W. Gresham was appointed in his room" (Manning, iii. p. 666). Sir H. Weston's name does not after this appear in the official records of Surrey, nor is he mentioned in the story of the Armada, 1588.

Again in 1591[1] there is recorded an order to search Sutton House for concealed priests, and to find one Morgan, believed to be there concealed under a false name.[2]

Sir Henry Weston died 11th April 1592, at the age of fifty-seven, having made his will the year preceding, which was duly proved, 16th May 1592. In it there is no trace of the Catholic profession so obvious in the will of Sir Richard. The Queen is named as Defender of the Faith. The knight is described as of Sutton, in the parish of Woking, and goes on: "First—I commend my soul to Almighty God and to His Son Jesus Christ, my Saviour and Redeemer, and to the Holy Ghost, Three Persons and one God; most humbly beseeching the most Holy and blessed Trinity to have mercy on my soul, and to pardon and forgive my sins and offences; that I may after this mutable life ende with the Elect, and have the life and fruition of the Godhead by the death and passion of our Lord and Saviour Jesus Christ." This is evidently the writing of a man who has before his eyes the Thirty-nine Articles of Religion and the service-book of Edward VI., as now by law was established. It is the language of the Judicious Hooker, nay, almost it might seem of Jeremy Taylor or John Milton.

[1] *Hist. MSS. Comm.* vii. 649.
[2] In the will of Sir Henry is the gift of a mourning ring to "his cozen Morgan."

There is not the slightest reason to suppose that this edifying and somewhat Calvinistic formula was at all the composition of the gallant knight himself. He is as little responsible for the sonorous benedictions as he is for the legal verbiage of the bequests that follow. In 1590 it would have been most dangerous to deny that the Queen was Defender of the Faith. And a man who was known as "the loving neighbour" of Sir Thomas Copley, the recusant, rebel, and traitor, and whose house had just been searched for a concealed priest, might naturally leave the drafting of his will to the learned doctors of the Court of Arches, whose business it was. His own last words can be as little taken literally as those of his father on the scaffold.

The will directed that the testator should be buried in the Chapel of the Holy Trinity, where his grandfather had been laid exactly fifty years before, which had opened for his own mother just ten years before. There were gifts to the poor of Guildford and Woking, West Clandon and Merrow, Send and Ockham.

He gives to his wife various chattels, sheep, cattle, horses, "and one coach which was my Lady, my mother's, with all the furniture therewith belonging," and two coach-horses, six feather beds, "whereof one of them to be the bed that I now lie on." He gives to his wife one half of his plate, and the jugs of ivory bound with ribs of silver, and the one half of his linen, and the furniture of the chamber "known as my Lord of Leicester's Chamber," and he gives to his wife for her life all the furniture of his house at Clandon. There are numerous gifts to servants, a gift of personalty at Sutton to his son Richard, legacies to his half-brothers, Sir Henry Knyvett and Thomas Knyvett, and to his half-sister Lady Dacres.

He gives to his daughter Jane the residue of the personalty at Pirford and Ockham, and he appoints his daughter Jane sole executrix. There are legacies to Sir W. More (of Loseley), his cousin Morgan, E. Slyfield, his cousin Stoughton ; and then he directs that the estates, manors, lands, tenements, and hereditaments shall go according to the terms of a series of settlements made in the same year, John Weston the younger being therein described as of Ockham.

So the gallant Sir Henry, having made his disposition of his goods, and having commended his soul to God, was buried in Trinity Church, Guildford, and was succeeded in the estate of Sutton by his son, Richard.

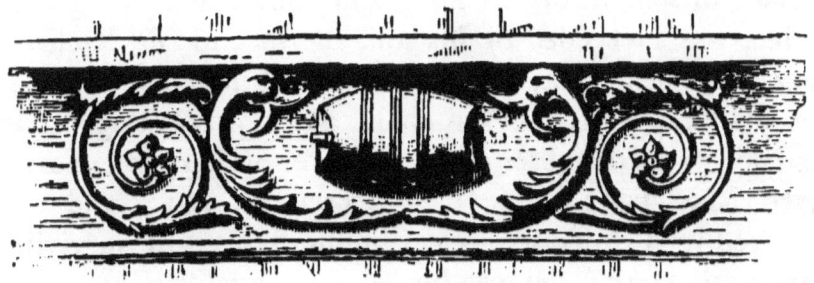

CHAPTER VI

SIR RICHARD WESTON, THE AGRICULTURIST, 1613-52

SIR HENRY WESTON, the heroic knight and defender of Calais, in which fortress his grandfather had so long held office, was succeeded by his son, the second Sir Richard, who was born 1564, and who was knighted by James I. on his accession at Whitehall, 23rd July 1603.[1] He married Jane, daughter of John Dister of Bergholt, Essex, 27th May 1583.[2] He died September 1613, and was interred in Trinity Church, Guildford, his wife surviving him until 1625; she was buried at West Clandon. His life seems to have been absolutely uneventful, both in the history of his country and of his own family. He was succeeded by his eldest son, the third Richard, fourth in

---

[1] Nichols's *Progresses of James I.*, vol. i. 215. As is well known, James I. made knighthood compulsory on all gentlemen of an adequate estate; and in his canny way treated it as a source of royal revenue.

[2] Parish Register of West Clandon, Surrey.

CH. VI SIR R. WESTON, THE AGRICULTURIST

descent from the founder, who was born in 1591, and was thus twenty-two on his accession to the estate.

The third Sir Richard was a man of enterprise, who passed much of his life abroad in Flanders, where it is said that, as a Catholic, he was educated. He introduced many agricultural and industrial improvements into England. In 1622 he was knighted at Guildford by James I.[1] In 1641, doubtless to carry on his canal scheme, he sold Temple Court Farm, at Merrow, with the mansion at West Clandon, to Sir Richard Onslow, M.P. for Surrey in the Long Parliament, and a stout Parliamentarian. This was the origin of the Clandon estates of the Earls of Onslow.[2]

In 1645, the year of the battle of Naseby, in the midst of the civil wars, Sir Richard Weston published anonymously a very remarkable book on agriculture, in which he detailed a system that effected a practical

[1] Manning and Bray, iii. p. 89.
[2] During the absence of Sir Richard Weston abroad it is said that Sutton Place was occupied by Ann, Countess of Arundel, widow of Philip Howard, eldest son of the fourth Duke of Norfolk, who was beheaded in 1572. Philip, Earl of Arundel, was attainted in 1590, and died in the Tower, it is thought by poison, in 1594. A few years ago, in making some alterations in Sutton Place, a deed was found concealed, executed by " Anne, Countesse Dowager of Arundell," dated 13th April 1621. The south bay window (light 3) has the arms of Fitzalan, seventeenth Earl of Arundel, quartering Widville, Clun, Maltravers. Obviously this is a simple coincidence, and was long before the time of Ann, widow of Philip Howard, in 1621. It appears from the Coke MSS., in the possession of Lord Cowper at Melbourne Hall, that in 1619 the Countess sent for a physician from London to attend her grandchild, Charles Howard, who was seized, as it would seem, with peritonitis, and who died at Sutton Place. The aged Countess wrote from thence: " I beseech you send with speed the best doctor may be had." The physician who came down, and who attended the child and conducted the *post-mortem*, was the illustrious William Harvey, then at the height of his reputation. We must count the immortal discoverer of the circulation of the blood as amongst the historical persons who have stayed in the house.

revolution in British farming. In the valuable historical sketch prefixed to the article on "Agriculture" in the *Encyclopædia Britannica*, vol. i. p. 297 (9th edition), Mr. J. Wilson, the eminent authority on farming, declares that Sir Richard's little volume marks "the dawn of the vast improvements which have since been effected in Britain." Mr. Wilson makes the natural mistake of confounding our Sir Richard with Sir Richard Weston, his kinsman, the ambassador, and afterwards minister as Earl of Portland; but he speaks of him as having the merit of being "the first to introduce the 'great clover,' as it was then called, into English agriculture about 1645, and, probably, turnips also. His directions for the cultivation of clover are better than was to be expected." The result was astonishing. In less than ten years after its introduction, says Mr. Wilson, "the cultivation of clover, exactly according to the present method, seems to have been well known in England." It is interesting to the present writer, as he pens these words, to note in the high "Manor Field," by the Chapel of St. Edward, one of the most magnificent crops of red clover in blossom to be seen in the county. After 400 years of stormy history the deserted and ruinous manor for which Roger Bigod and his peers had contended was to be the nursery of scientific agriculture in Great Britain.

Sir Richard introduced into England from his foreign experiences other grasses, and also the systematic cultivation of turnips. He was the first, we are told, to cultivate turnips as a cattle crop. The importance of this cannot be over-estimated. As Mr. Wilson says (*Ency. Brit.* i. 297), "the introduction of turnips *as a field crop* constitutes one of the most marked epochs in British agriculture." Sir Richard was an enthusiast for agriculture, and his little book has a curious bibliographical as well as historical interest. It was frequently reprinted, but remained without a name, and was never directly acknowledged or even published by its author. It is extremely rare; but it may be seen in various forms in the British Museum. It was first published in 1645, without name, by Samuel Hartlib, Milton's friend and correspondent, a busy Puritan pamphleteer and editor. In 1651 Hartlib published, in small quarto size, what he calls an *Enlargement of the Discourse of Husbandry used in Brabant and Flanders—Sir Richard Weston's Legacy to his Sons*. To that edition Hartlib prefixes a preface of his own, in which he says that the author of the discourse which he formerly published was unknown to him, but having lighted on a more perfect copy he offers it to the public in a second edition. Hartlib prints two letters of his own, dated 2nd May and 10th October 1651, to Sir Richard Weston, begging him to revise and republish the book, but he seems to have had no answer at all from the knight, who died in 1652, at the age of sixty-one. And then Hartlib published in 1652 an edition, corrected and enlarged, entitled *A Discourse of Husbandry used in Brabant and Flanders: showing the wonderful improvement of land there; and serving as a pattern for our practice in this commonwealth*. It is preceded by a long and flowery Scriptural appeal to the Council of State by Hartlib himself. The garrulous Puritan continued to publish other works on husbandry, to which he added little, having no practical knowledge of his own.

Sir Richard's own work is curious and instructive, and, as being exactly contemporary with Milton's famous tractates, it has a certain literary interest. The earnestness, the solemnity, the involved sentences, the occasional dignity of its rhythm remind one of a tiro whose ideal was the epistle to Mr. Hartlib on education. It is a real testament or last will. It opens thus: "My sonnes, I have left this short ensuing Treatise to you as a Legacy; if I shall not live my selfe, to show you (what therein is written) by examples, which I know instruct far more then precepts; yet precepts from a dying father, instructing of his children what he hath seen and known and received information of from witnesses free from all exceptions, should make such an impression on them, as at least to believe their father writ what he thought was true; and therefore suppose those things worthy to be put in practice by them, which he himself would have done, if it had pleased God to have granted him Life and Liberty"—and five or six lines more before the verbose old knight can end his sentence.

He then goes on to show how his method will improve barren and heathy land by ways commonly practised in Brabant and Flanders, but unknown in England, and lead to a noble augmentation of an estate. "That man is worthy of praise and honour, who being possessor of a large and barren demesne constrains it by his labour and industry to produce extraordinary fruit, which redounds not only to his own particular profit, but also to the public benefit. Cato saith, it is a great shame to a man, not to leave his inheritance greater to his successors than he received it from his predecessors."

He says the object of all men is to get land and to cultivate it. He waxes eloquent, if not extravagant, like all projectors, over the vast profits to be made by his system. "By this little Treatise you shall learn how to do more than treble your principal in one year's compass; and you shall see how an industrious man in Brabant and

Flanders would bring 500 acres of barren and heathy land that was not worth at the most about £5 a year to be worth £7000 a year in less time than seven years." Land worth £14 an acre, or at modern computation of money, about £70 per annum ! Truly the knight is an enthusiast. The estate of Sutton has no very rich soil at all: the water meadows are fairly good, but the upper lands are of the Bagshot sand, with patches of clay. Some of the land is exceedingly poor ; and it is interesting to find one of the great revolutions in British agriculture made on one of the poorer soils.

"You must not expect," says the knight, "either eloquence or method in this ensuing treatise, but a true story plainly set forth in the last will and testament of your father, which he would have you execute ; but before all things to be sure you lay the foundation of your husbandry upon the blessing of Almighty God, continually imploring His Divine aid and assistance in all your labours ; for it is God that gives the increase, and believing this as the quintessence and soul of Husbandry, *Primum quærite Regnum Dei, et postea hæc omnia adjicientur vobis:* These things being briefly premised, I will leave the rest to this short ensuing treatise, and commit you all with a father's blessing to the Protection and Providence of Almighty God." All this, except for the use of the Vulgate instead of the Authorised Version, might have come from Milton, Hartlib, or any other Puritan ; and it is curious as written in the height of the Civil War by a Catholic Royalist.

Sir Richard tells us that he went abroad, after thirty years' experience in husbandry (that is, in the first year of the Civil Wars), having improved his land as much as any man in this kingdom hath done both by fire and water, but found he was to learn a new lesson in Brabant and Flanders. This Arthur Young, or rather Coke of Holkham, of the seventeenth century, tells us how he landed at Dunkirk, went thence to Bridges (Bruges), a distance of 40 miles; thence to Gaunt (Ghent), 24 miles distant, and so to Antwerp. He found the cultivation of flax the wealth of Flanders, and he describes his talk with " the *Bores*, so they term their farmers " (Boers). " One acre of good flax," he says, " is worth four or five acres of the best corn." He carefully studies the raising of flax, clover-grass, and turnips. He declares that clover is worth £12 per acre, and he insists on the enormous profit to be made by cultivating clover-grass, turnips, and flax. "Regina Pecunia!" he cries to his children, "Monie is the Queen that commands all." This was no doubt the root idea of the founder of the Weston family; but what a change in the hundred years which separate the third Sir Richard from his grandfather, the gallant soldier of Calais, Sir Henry, and his great-grandfather, the wild courtier, Sir Francis!

But the knight is a genuine enthusiast; and he closes his testament thus: " Besides the excessive profit you will reap by sowing these commodities, imagine what a pleasure it will be to your eyes and scent to see the russet heath turned into greenest grass; which doth produce most sweet and pleasant Honeysuckles; and what praise and reputation you will gain by your examples, first introducing that into your country, which being followed by others, must needs redound to the general benefit of the whole commonwealth. I do by my Will command you for to execute no more than what I would myself to-morrow put in practice, if I had Liberty: you should then learn these things I have set down by examples, which I am enforced to leave to you as a father's precepts, and with a Father's blessing to you all, desiring God Almighty to guide you and direct you in all your actions, I will leave you to His Divine protection and providence." Then after this sonorous conclusion there follows, with delicious *naïveté*, a sort of codicil to his will in these words—" Note, that the Clover-grass seed will be ripe about a month after it appeareth in the husk."

The little treatise itself is only of twenty-seven small quarto pages, but it contains much careful practical advice, and is the work of a thorough man of business. No doubt Sir Richard's example was of far greater value than his book. It would seem indeed that his estate was seized and put under sequestration by the Commonwealth, which accounts for the form of his " Legacie." He lives seven years after its date, and does not seem to have been incapacitated by disease, nor is it clear why he should speak of himself as a dying father; but he was evidently not free to work his estate himself; and he seems to have pushed his industrial schemes with the aid of influential Puritans; nor is there in his little treatise one word that betrays any kind of political or religious party spirit. It gives us a new insight into English life to find that, in the ten years that separate the battle of Edgehill from the battle of Worcester, a Royalist gentleman of wealth and rank in Surrey could devote himself to an industrial revolution, and write very popular pamphlets, as Hartlib tells us, on agriculture.

Sir Richard Weston was not only the first to introduce into British farming the systematic culture of grasses and of roots, but he was also the first to popularise in England the method of canalisation by locks. These he studied in

Holland, where we are told that he travelled in his youth. He finally resolved to introduce the invention into his own property. He began by making a cut from the river Wey near Stoke Mill for the purpose of watering some of his meadows, and he carried it some 3 miles, greatly improving his property.[1] He made a lock at Stoke, and formed the idea of making the river navigable from Guildford to Weybridge. He entered into agreements with most of the proprietors through whose lands the canal was to pass ; and so early as 1635 he had been named one of the Royal Commissioners for the scheme.

Before the work had proceeded far the Civil War began (1642); and as Sir Richard Weston joined the Royalist party, his estate was seized, and he was not allowed to compound as many had been. Accordingly, he looked out for a coadjutor on the Parliamentary side, and he found him in James Pitson, a major in the Parliamentary army, and a Commissioner for Surrey in 1649. Pitson entered into an agreement to solicit the discharge of Sir Richard's sequestration, and to apply for an Act of Parliament to authorise the navigation. The petition was presented in the name of the Corporation of Guildford, Pitson, and another, and Acts were passed in 1650 and 1651 by the Long Parliament. The capital was £6000, of which Sir Richard found £3000.

Thereupon Sir Richard went to work with extraordinary energy. He employed 200 men at a time, and pressed on the operations with such rapidity that in nine months he had finished 10 out of 14 miles of the canalised river (the new cuttings do not exceed more than 1 or 2 miles). In doing this he expended £4000 of his own

---

[1] This account is abridged from Manning, iii. Appendices LIV.-LVI., who had access to documents and deeds in possession of the family.

money, and used timber of his own to the value of £2000. He had thus expended £6000 (which may be equal to about £30,000), and he agreed to raise another £1000. But in the midst of his labours he died, in May 1652, aged sixty-one. After the death of Sir Richard his younger son, George, finished it as far as the last lock, within 1 mile of its termination. But it was then taken out of their hands by Pitson, who finished the remaining part; and the navigation was opened in November 1653, just as the Protectorate of Oliver was about to succeed the Long Parliament.

The canalised Wey from Guildford to Weybridge was now open for some 14 miles. It had ten locks, four tumbling bays (weirs), and twelve bridges. Its utility was immediately proved, for it soon produced a revenue of £1500 per annum, which on a capital of £10,000 was 15 per cent. But the landowners were still unpaid, and a long course of litigation ensued, which lasted nearly twenty years, and practically ruined the family of the projector himself, although in 1662, at the Restoration, a Committee of the House decided that Sir Richard Weston was the designer of the navigation. In 1670 John Weston, the heir of Sir Richard, submitted to arbitration, and was released from the incumbrances created on his estate, and in 1671 a new Act was passed which settled the claims of the various litigants.

"Thus," says the historian of the county, "after all the labour, expense, and vexation incurred by Sir Richard Weston and his family, all the recompense they obtained was to be discharged of the incumbrances incurred in prosecuting the work, and the trifling privilege of lading and unlading their own goods on that land which they had dedicated to the public service." It is the usual fate of inventors. The canal proved of great public utility, and is still in use, the first of all the canals in our kingdom. Sir Richard's dreams of wealth were cruelly disappointed. The practical advices of his legacy were sounder than his cry of *Regina Pecunia!* He left his estate greatly reduced and burdened to his children; but he left to his country lessons in husbandry of priceless value, and the first-fruits of an industrial revolution which, down to the age of steam locomotives, was the source of untold wealth and progress.

According to Aubrey (*Surrey*, iii. p. 228), it was about 1643 that Sir Richard introduced the grass called *Nonesuch* into the parish of Worplesdon, part of the Sutton estate, along with the first clover-grass out of Brabant and Flanders, "at which time he also brought over the contrivance of locks, turnpikes, and tumbling bays for rivers. He began the making of the new river in 1650 or 1651, but he lived not to finish it, dying 7th May 1652." Sir Richard, indeed, appears to have been occupied for a large part of his life with the scheme of the canal, and it seriously encumbered his estates and impoverished himself. In 1635, during the ministry of Laud, he was named member of the Royal Commission for the consideration of the project, but the Act was not obtained until 1650, under the Commonwealth. A second Act was passed in 1651. By this, navigation was effected from London to Guildford. The canal was not completed in Sir Richard's lifetime. It is a singular example of devotion to industrial improvement that the knight, belonging to a Catholic and Royalist family, should have spent seventeen years in carrying through the Wey canalisation scheme, and should have had sufficient credit to obtain official sanction for it—first from Charles I. in the crisis of Strafford's policy, and then from the Commonwealth after the execution of the King.[1]

Sir Richard had as his contemporary another famous Sir Richard Weston, created Lord Weston of Neyland 1628, and Earl of Portland in 1632, the unpopular minister of Charles I., who died in 1635.[2] The Earl of Portland was descended from Humphrey Weston, a common ancestor of himself and of Sir Richard Weston, the founder. From Dorothy, the sister of the Earl, who married Sir Edward Pincheon of Writtle, the family of Webbe-Weston and of the present owner, F. H. Salvin, are descended. The last male descendant of the Earl of Portland died in 1688, when the title became extinct.

But though Sir Richard Weston of Sutton belonged to a Catholic and Royalist family, and was a cousin and neighbour of his namesake, the anti-popular minister of Charles and colleague of Strafford, the Westons of Sutton took no great part in the Civil War, nor does the house ever seem to have been the scene of any act whatever in the great struggle which tore England in pieces between 1640 and 1650. During all this time Sir Richard, now a man of between fifty and sixty, seems to have kept himself tolerably aloof from politics. He was denounced as a recusant, and apparently arrested. On 16th May 1650 an order was issued for Richard Weston to be sent in safe custody for holding correspondence with the

---

[1] The editor of Camden's *Britannia* (Suth-rey) says that the navigation of the Wey brings in great profits to this part of the country, and speaks of Sir R. Weston, "to whom the whole shire is obliged as for this, so for several other improvements, particularly clover and saintfoine."

[2] See Gardiner, *Hist. of England*, 1603-42 (1628-29). "Weston, the Lord Treasurer, was as unpopular at Court as he was in the country." Clarendon, in his trenchant way, calls him "a man of big looks and of a mean and abject spirit."

enemies of the Commonwealth; but he escaped absolute ruin after his sequestration, for which he did not compound.[1] But two of the family have their names mentioned in the records of the troubles; nor does the slightest injury seem to have befallen the house. The hall with its painted glass, crowded with crowns, mitres, and garters, and the devices of royal personages, Catholic bishops, and "malignant" peers, with the arms and quarterings of Fitzalans, Paulets, Howards, Stanleys, Copleys, and Bourchiers, the emblems of Catherine of Aragon and Bishop Gardiner, of Mary Tudor and Philip of Spain, and a portrait of a king, said to be Charles I., remains untouched, although it is within a day's ride of Basing House, and the scene of many a combat in Hampshire and Berkshire.

The account here given on the authority of Manning, who had access to family papers, may be supplemented by the recent *Calendar of the Committee for the Compounding*, 1643-60, Rolls Series, 5 vols., 1889-92. From the records of this Committee, now for the first time given to the world, it appears that the Westons of Sutton Place were obstinate delinquents. William Copley's estates were sequestered in 1650 as a recusant, as were those of his two daughters, his heirs, married to Sir R. Weston's two sons, also recusants. In 1651 Sir R. Weston is reported to be a Papist, a recusant, and delinquent. In June 1651 his whole estate is sequestered as a Papist and delinquent, allowing one-fifth to his wife and children. In 1652 an order was made to permit Sir Richard to enjoy two-thirds of his estate, if he can prove that he has

---

[1] *The Catalogue of the Lords, Knights, and Gentlemen who have compounded for their Estates*, Th. Dringe, London, 1655, and reprinted, Chester, 1733, does not give any Weston of Sutton Place.

committed no act of delinquency since 1648; and this he did in April of that year. But, 8th July 1652, it is certified that he is dead; and, his widow refusing the oath of abjuration, two-thirds of her jointure is to be sequestered. John Weston, the son, seems to have borne arms for the King, as also did his brother George, and to have been taken prisoner at Colchester.

The house was no doubt spared because, lying wholly within the sphere of the Parliament's power, and close to Guildford, a stronghold of the Puritan party, no opportunity was left to the owners of Sutton to raise the royal standard. Being an utterly indefensible private mansion, and not castellated, it could not be regarded by either side as a military post. Certain it is that during the whole of the Civil Wars the Westons of Sutton busied themselves with their estates, their improvements, canal navigation, and clover-grass; they sold broad acres and acquired broad acres; they were married and given in marriage; and never meddled or appeared in any public part whatever, whether civil or military, except as obstinate delinquents. Sir Richard Weston, the agriculturist and scientific landowner, was in possession of the estates for nearly forty years, and died quietly at the age of sixty-one, in 1652, during the crisis which led to the Protectorate of Oliver Cromwell, and was buried with his ancestors in Trinity Church, Guildford. His wife, Grace, daughter of John Harper of Cheshunt, Herts, survived him many years, and lived well into the Restoration of Charles II., until 1669. She was buried at Guildford, 28th February in that year. And at last the manor and hall of Sutton finally pass out of all touch with the history and progress of England, and sink into the simple routine of an ordinary county estate.

CHAPTER VII

FROM THE CIVIL WARS TO THE PRESENT TIME

THE 247 years which have glided by since the death of the famous agriculturist until to-day need not occupy many pages. They recount nothing but the even tenor of an ordinary Catholic family. As Richard, the fourth of that name, the eldest son of Sir Richard, the agriculturist, died in infancy, the estate was inherited by the second son, John, who in 1637 had married Mary, daughter and heiress of William Copley of Gatton, near Reigate, on whom with her sister Anne had descended the considerable estates of the Copleys in Surrey and Sussex, together with some very ancient quarterings in which the Copleys seem to have taken no small pride.[1]

---

[1] It was in anticipation of marriage, perhaps, that the portentous pedigree of the Westons, now in the British Museum, was prepared by Garter King

CH. VII FROM CIVIL WARS TO PRESENT TIME 135

The pedigree of the Copleys of Gatton, in Surrey, and of Roffey or Roughey, in Sussex, may be read in full in Berry's *Sussex Genealogies*, 296, and also in Horsfield's *Sussex*, ii. 263. William Copley was a grandson of Sir Thomas Copley, the exile and rebel in Elizabeth's time who had married Katherine, daughter and heiress of Sir Thomas Luttrell. Sir Thomas Copley was himself son and grandson of two successive Sir Roger Copleys, high-sheriffs of Surrey in 1529 and 1514, and traced his descent to Sir Geoffrey Boleyn, the Chief-Justice Sir William Shelley, Thomas, Lord Hoo of Hastings, Lord Beauchamp of Bletsoe, Sir R. Waterton, and Leo, Lord Welles.

Thus it comes that the hall and house are full of the arms of the Copleys and the families whom they claimed to quarter in their coats. Everywhere we observe *argent*, a cross moline *sable*, a crescent for difference, for *Copley*; *or*, a lion rampant double-queued *sable*, for *Welles*; *sable*, a fess engrailed between three whelk-shells, *or*, for *Shelley*; and so forth. In the west and east staircases are three painted escutcheons with the arms of Sir Thomas Copley dated 1567 and 1568. In these and in the windows may be seen the arms of *Welles, Hastings of Hoo, Waterton, Engaine, Shelley, Luttrell, Belknap, Havercamp*.

Mary Copley, who was apparently only seventeen at her marriage, brought wealth to the family; and she seems to have kept her husband and his kinsmen well out of civil war and treason, which had caused the ruin of her own great-grandfather. It may be assumed that much of the woodwork, panelling, etc., which we now

of Arms in 1632. The original vellum roll measures nearly 27 feet in length by 5 in breadth, and was imposing enough to convince even Copley of Gatton that Weston of Sutton was by no means *novus homo*.

see was executed about this time, or at least during the long possession of Sir Richard Weston, 1613-52; and in all probability the glasswork of the hall was repaired, renewed, and altered, and the numerous lights with Copley coats of arms were inserted. These were, no doubt, brought from Gatton or Roffey, for many of them, and also the escutcheons on panel, are obviously of sixteenth, and not of seventeenth century work. It is plain that the coat in the panelled hall over the fireplace there (see chap. x.), showing the arms of Weston impaling Copley, is of the date of the marriage, 1637. This was also, no doubt, the period of the building of the second or western quadrangle, which is certainly no part of the original design of 1521.

It is worth noting that during this period the royal mansion of Woking on the Wey was pulled down by the Zouch family, to whom it had been granted by James I. in 1620; and it has been suggested that some of the older fragments of painted glass, especially the royal devices in the two bays, may have been brought from Woking about this time. As to the coats of the Copleys with their quarterings, some of which are evidently fine early work (*e.g.* window VI. 2), it is quite as probable that they record some visit or other connection with Sir Roger Copley of Gatton, the sheriff of the county about the date of the foundation of the house. However, the three escutcheons on panel, with the monogram T.C., could only have been brought in after 1637 by the heiress of the Copleys, and some of the glass has doubtless the same origin. It will be noticed that there are in the hall windows alone no less than eight Copley coats with their quarterings.

With the Copley alliance, the sale of the estate and

mansion at Clandon, and the completion of the Wey canal, the Westons of Sutton seem to have taken a new departure. In 1654 John Weston and Mary his wife sold the estate of Gatton (Manning, ii. 231). The old house at Sutton became their only seat, and was completely renovated and altered. The eastern wing, which the destruction of the gatehouse by fire had made more or less inaccessible, except through the great hall, was probably abandoned as a residence. The western wing, in the original plan the offices, was now converted into the residential part of the quadrangle; and a new quadrangle was built out on the west of it, between the original house and the garden, to serve as offices. The coat of arms which Aubrey saw "in the parlor" about 1673 was till lately in the panelled hall, which was thus in the western wing of the house. It is now placed over the broad staircase; and perhaps the three crosses moline on the parapet of the south side of the house were of this date, and were rudely inserted in the Tudor ogee niche.

A portrait, stated to be that of John, the husband of Mary Copley, is in the hall, together with that of William Copley, his wife's grandfather, a picture dated "1620, *ætatis suæ*, 55." (William Copley, the elder, was born in 1565.) John, to judge by his portrait, was a very mild and inoffensive person, who looks as if he would rather not be asked to make up his mind. He was in possession of the estate, like his father before him, for nearly forty years, all through the Protectorates of Oliver and of Richard Cromwell, the Restoration of Charles II., the reign of James II., and the Revolution of 1689. Whatever John thought, history knows nothing of what John did. He paid his dues quietly, and kept his estate together. He was gathered to his fathers in

Trinity Church, Guildford, in the reign of William and Mary in 1690, as was his wife, Mary Copley, in 1694, she being seventy-four.

Thus in the 170 years since the grant of the estate there had been only five owners in possession, with an average tenure of thirty-four years. What tremendous changes had taken place in England in those 170 years: the change of religion, the disappearance of feudalism, new manners, fresh modes of life. In 1520 there were living men who had fought in the Wars of the Roses. In 1690 Newton, Addison, and Swift were in active career; and yet the old place of Sutton was scarcely changed, either within or without. The quadrangle stood untouched, just as the contemporaries of Holbein and Trevisano had fashioned it in the age of Francis I. The owners of Sutton clung to the old religion, and maintained the mass in their ancient chapel; and amidst the revolutionary fervour of Jacobites and Orangemen they gazed silently on the helmets, the halberds, and escutcheons in the hall, where Catherine, the daughter of Ferdinand, the Catholic, had been entertained, where Henry VIII. had conferred with Wolsey and Cromwell. The house and its belongings remained a solid bit of Catholic and feudal England in the midst of Protestant and Whig.

John's son by Mary Copley was Richard, fifth and last of that name, of whom we know even less than of John, his father. He married Melior, daughter of William Nevill of Holt, Leicestershire; and dying in 1701, after a tenure of only eleven years, was buried at Guildford, 25th April. He left the estate to his only son, John.

John, the second of that name, and the last heir male of the blood of the founder, was in possession for nearly thirty years, from 1701-30. He married Elizabeth, sister of Thomas, the first Viscount Gage. She was a daughter of Joseph Gage by Elizabeth Penruddock, heiress and great-granddaughter of Colonel Penruddock, who had attempted insurrection under the Protectorate, and was beheaded by Cromwell in 1655. John Weston himself was fined £939[1] for refusing to take the oaths to King George.

But John Weston managed to restore and repair the house. He refitted the upper part of the eastern wing, which had been in a dilapidated state since the fire of 1561, and, it is said, formed it into a long gallery. In the window (VIII. 3) is a rude memorandum cut with a diamond that John Weston "putt in this painted glass, August ye 28, 1724." This, then, may be taken as the date of the principal eighteenth-century restorations in the house, especially of the more recent insertions and confusions in the painted glass, the panelling in the dining-room, staircases, and part of the eastern long gallery.

It seems to be now at last ascertained that the lady on whose behalf Pope interested himself so fiercely in his youth, and out of whose case he invented the tragic story on which his famous lines *To an Unfortunate Lady* were based, was no other than Melior Gage, the wife of John Weston (2) of Sutton Place. This Mrs. Weston is evidently the lady to whom one of Pope's letters is addressed (Elwin and Courthope's *Pope's Works*, x. 259). See an account of her, vol. v. 132, and in *Athenæum*, 15th July 1854. Pope, in an undated letter, addresses the lady in grandiose and devoted language. "Your own guardian angels cannot be more constant, nor more silent." Pope

[1] J. Robinson, *Names of the Roman Catholic Non-jurors*, 1745.

writes to Caryll, 25th June 1711: "I am just informed that the tyrant [John Weston] is determined instantly to remove his daughter from the lady. I wish to God it could be put off by Sir W. G[oring]'s mediation, for I am heartily afraid it will prove of very ill consequence to her." The child was Melior Mary, the last descendant of the founder, then aged eight. Pope himself was only twenty-three when he rushed into this domestic quarrel. He tells Caryll, 2nd August 1711, that it was her "ill fate to be cast as a pearl before swine," *i.e.* John Weston. Pope writes frequently on Mrs. Weston's behalf, and even quarrelled with his own relations because they did not take up the lady's part with sufficient eagerness. The youthful poet met the proverbial fate of those who interfere in quarrels matrimonial. He writes to Caryll in the year following, 8th November 1712. "Mr. W[eston] is gloomy upon the matter—the tyrant meditates revenge; nay, the distressed dame herself has been taught to suspect I served her but by halves, and without prudence." Very likely, indeed! and one cannot but feel that the distressed dame may have been the more prudent of the two.

But Pope's passion seems to have outlived the lady's coolness. For, five years later, 13th September 1717, he writes to Martha Blount with this curious outburst of ill-humour. He speaks of a journey—"having fled from the face (I wish I could say the horned face) of Moses [in the original it stood—Mr. Weston], who dined that day at my brother's."

The young poet's devotion to the lady must have been one of the few romances of his life. We can hardly doubt that he had known the husband and wife before the quarrel, and there is every probability that he had been a visitor at Sutton Place. It is hardly fanciful to imagine that the author of *The Rape of the Lock* once meditated couplets in Lady Weston's Walk, where young Sir Francis once flirted with the beauties of Anne Boleyn's court, and where Elizabeth may have listened to the flatteries of Raleigh.

It seems clear from a note of Pope's appended to his letter to Mrs. Weston that she was the original of the *Unfortunate Lady*. The story of the poem was pure imagination. Mrs. Weston was separated from her husband, but she returned, and lived in peace. She did not die abroad, friendless, and by suicide, but in the bosom of her family, by natural causes, and in her own home. She was, in fact, buried in the family vault in Guildford in 1724, eleven years after Pope's outburst. But when we recall the tragedies that have befallen the Westons of Sutton Place, there is a new meaning in the curse which the poet pours out (verses 30-46)—

> "On all the line a sudden vengeance waits,—
> Thus unlamented pass the proud away."

Certain it is that Melior Mary, daughter and sole heir of John Weston, was the last of her race. She gave her ancestral estate to another family of Weston: they also are extinct in the male line.

John Weston died in June 1730, having lived well into the reign of George II.; his wife had died in 1724. Both were buried in Guildford. He left the estate to his daughter, Melior Mary, then aged twenty-seven. A very pleasing portrait of this lady at a rather earlier date hangs in the hall. Its date is 1723, when she was aged twenty. And, though she had beauty as well as acres, and, according to her monument, "superior understanding and distinguished virtues," she lived and died unmarried and in solitary possession of her ancient patrimony for fifty-two years. The lady, as masses of family papers testify, was a most energetic, industrious woman of business, and seems to have been constantly engaged in complicated litigation. She apparently did nothing to alter and hardly anything to repair her mansion, in which she seems to have lived in great retirement. She died in June 1782 at the age of seventy-nine, and was buried in Trinity Church, Guildford, where a monument with an elaborate record of her merits was placed by her grateful successor.

Melior Mary was the last survivor of the blood of the founder. Her aunt, Frances Weston, whose portrait, in the Lely style (about 1700), hangs in the hall, had married William Wolffe of Great Haseley, who was a son of John Wolffe of Great Haseley by Ann, daughter and co-heiress of John, son of Sir Edward Pincheon of Writtle, by his wife, Dorothy, sister of the first Earl of Portland. The Wolffes of Great Haseley were thus descended from Sir Richard Weston, the founder, through Frances, the sister of John Weston, the last male Weston of Sutton;[1] and they were also descended from the Westons of Essex, the senior branch of the Westons of Prested Hall, both families, like the Westons of Sutton, claiming descent from Hamon de Weston of Weston under Lizzard, temp. Henry II.

The Wolffes, then, during the middle of the last

[1] Frances, the youngest sister of John Weston, married William Wolffe about 1700. It is curious that T. Benolt, Clarencieux King of Arms, found at an earlier date the arms of *Wolffe* in the hall of Sutton—all the more that they are not the arms of Wolffe as quartered by John Webbe-Weston (H. 7, College of Arms, Suthery and Isle of Wight). As given by Benolt, the arms display neither wolves nor wolves' heads erased, as all the many variations of *Wolffe* do; but are quarterly, first and fourth (without tinctures), six mullets, three, two, and one.

century were evidently regarded as the eventual heirs of Sutton, since Melior Mary was now a confirmed old maid. And portraits of William Wolffe by Hussey, and also of John Wolffe, his grandson, also by Hussey, and dated 1754 (*ætat.* eleven), may be seen in the hall. But William Wolffe died in 1739, and his grandsons, John Wolffe, in 1758, Charles Wolffe, in 1768, and William Cosmos Wolffe, in 1766. Whatever females there were of the house were nuns. Thus, at the decease of Melior Mary Weston in 1782, the blood of the founder, both in the male and female lines, was exhausted. As her tombstone records, Miss Weston was "the last immediate descendant of an illustrious Family which flourished in this county for many successive generations." She stood, in fact, in the eighth generation from Sir Richard, the grantee of 1521. Melior Mary at her death had the absolute disposition of all her estates, and was without any blood relations whatever nearer than her mother's nephew, the second Viscount Gage, and John Webbe, third in descent from John Wolffe of Great Haseley, whose son had married Frances Weston, and fifth in descent from Dorothy Weston, sister of the first Earl of Portland.

Accordingly, Melior Mary Weston, very naturally passing over her cousins, the Gages, on her mother's side, resolved to devise her estates to John Webbe as descended from the sister of William Wolffe, the husband of her paternal aunt, Frances, and also as descended from the Westons of Prested Hall, Essex, and of West Horsley, in Surrey. By her will, then, Melior Mary devised her Sutton estate to John Webbe, on the condition of his taking the name and arms of Weston.[1]

---

[1] In Trinity Church, Guildford, may be seen a handsome monument to Melior Mary Weston. It reads thus—

This within a few weeks he did; and on 6th July 1782 a proper license was granted and duly recorded by Garter and the rest of his *posse comitatus*, authorising John Webbe to take and bear the name and arms of Weston. He was thenceforward styled John Webbe-Weston of Sutton Place; the arms of Weston being thus blazoned—"Arms: *Ermine*, on a chief *azure*, five bezants. Crest: on a wreath of the colours, a Saracen's head couped at the shoulder, the tongue hanging out proper, wreathed about the temples, *argent* and *azure*, to be borne singly or quarterly with Webbe; being *gules*, a cross between four falcons, *or*. Motto: *Ani boro*" (College of Arms, *Norfolk*, i. 124).

John Webbe-Weston possessed the estate for forty-one years; and during his tenure many changes were made

> To the Memory
> of
> Melior Mary Weston
> of Sutton Place in the county of Surrey, Spinster
> This Marble was erected
> as a tribute of sincere respect and gratitude by
> John Webbe Weston
> of Sarnesfield Court in the county of Hereford, Esq.
> Who
> in pursuance of her last will and bequest
> succeeded to her name and estates
> She
> was the last immediate descendant
> of an illustrious Family
> which flourished in this county
> for many successive generations, and
> with the ample possessions of their ancestors
> inherited
> their superior understanding
> and distinguished virtues
> obiit, 10 Junii, MDCCLXXXII, æt. 79.
> R.I.P.

VII   FROM CIVIL WARS TO PRESENT TIME   145

in the house, but fortunately many others which he had projected were abandoned. Mr. Weston at once proceeded to pull down the ruinous gatehouse and the whole building that connected the east with the west wing on the north side of the quadrangle. This was accomplished in 1782, as the bills of the contractor, William Brooks of London,[1] show. There can be no question that the house gains in comfort by opening the quadrangle to the north. A quadrangle only 81 feet square and 35 feet high, with a tower of about 50 or 60 feet on one side and a vast roof on the other, never could have been quite airy or light.[2] The removal of the north tower and wing greatly improved the comfort and convenience of the house; though there is a tradition in the family that George III., when returning from a stag-hunt, was shown over the house in the absence of the owner, and then said, "Very bad, very bad! tell Mr. Weston the King says he must build it up again!" If

---

[1] Voluminous bills, documents, specifications, and estimates relating to the works are still in the possession of F. H. Salvin.

[2] The elevation of the north wing and gatehouse as seen from within is exactly reproduced in a careful architectural drawing, signed and dated—"Front of Sutton in com. Surry as it stood, Jan. 22, 1750, John Wolffe delin. 17 Feb. 1750." "Front of Sutton towards the Court as it stood Jan. 22, 1750, the little pillars $67\frac{1}{2}$ high, 5 ft. diam. The Court 81.3 square exclusive of the base." These drawings show that the quadrangle was perfectly symmetrical; one gives the northern (outside) view of the gatehouse, and one gives the southern (inside) view of the same. The hexagonal turrets were precisely the same as those now standing on the south wing, which are also $67\frac{1}{2}$ feet high, 5 feet diameter. The arch of the gateway into the court seems circular. The gatehouse had three stories, the lower window of eight lights, the two upper windows of four lights. On each side of the gateway were three windows uniform with the east and west wings. The drawing is evidently by John Wolffe, first cousin of Melior Mary, the then owner, who may have been contemplating the removal of the ruined wing.

L

His Majesty saw the gatehouse in course of demolition, his remark was natural; but if he meant that the gatehouse and north wing added convenience to the house, we cannot admire the royal taste. Mr. Weston spent between £2000 and £3000 in repairs, restorations, and renewal of the house; and these were finished in 1784. Fortunately he did not carry out the monstrous proposal of Bonomi, an Italian architect of repute in the last century, who prepared a design to transmute the house in a modern bastard Italian style. He wanted to introduce classical columns, pediments, and the like, and to convert the hall into a two-storied suite of modern chambers. Mr. Weston was happily deterred by the formidable estimate of his advisers, and Sutton Place escaped a greater danger than it had ever run, even in the fire of 1561, or in all the commotions of the Civil War and the Revolution. The designs for the "improvements"—these truly atrocious monuments of Vandalism—are now in the possession of F. H. Salvin.

Mr. Webbe-Weston inherited in 1794, on the death of his cousin, Anne Monington, the estate of Sarnesfield Court, in Herefordshire. He himself died suddenly at Hereford in 1823, leaving by his wife, Elizabeth, only daughter of John, the third son of Sir John Lawson, Bart., of Brough Hall, York, a numerous family. Elizabeth Weston died in 1791, and is buried in Trinity Church, Guildford. The present owner of Sutton, Francis H. Salvin, is the son of Anna Maria (daughter of John Webbe-Weston and Elizabeth Lawson), who in 1800 married William Thomas Salvin of Croxdale, in Durham.[1]

[1] It is rather remarkable that in the 302 years which separate the grant of 1521 from the death of J. Webbe-Weston the estate had been held in

John Webbe-Weston, whose first wife died in 1791, at the age of thirty-four,[1] married secondly, in 1794, Mary, eldest daughter of William Haggerstone Constable, of Everingham, County York, by whom he had no issue. On his death, in 1823 (he is buried in Sarnesfield Church, County Hereford), he was succeeded by his eldest son, John Joseph Webbe-Weston, who in 1811 had married Caroline Graham, only daughter of Charles Graham. Charles Graham was great-grandson of Sir George Graham of Usk, and grandson of Sir Reginald Graham of Norton-Conyers. Caroline Graham, Mrs. John J. W. Weston, was thus a cousin of Sir James Graham, the statesman who died in 1861.

On the death of John Joseph Webbe-Weston, in 1840, he was succeeded by his only son, John Joseph Webbe-Weston, the second of that name, a captain in the imperial Austrian service. He in 1847 married Lady Horatia Elizabeth Waldegrave, daughter of John James, sixth Earl Waldegrave. Captain Weston served in the war between Austria and Hungary in 1848-49. Both he and his wife were taken prisoners by the Hungarian national troops, and detained in captivity some time. Captain Weston died *s.p.* of cholera during the siege of Comorn, on the Danube, 24th September 1849. Lady Horatia Weston, his widow, was in possession of the Sutton estates until her re-marriage. On 28th November 1854 she married John Wardlaw, brother of General Wardlaw. She died in June 1884.

---

possession by no more than nine owners, giving an average tenure of more than thirty-three years apiece. In the 400 years separating Domesday from the battle of Bosworth there had been about fifty owners with an average of eight years.

[1] See monument in Trinity Church, Guildford.

Upon her second marriage the Sutton estates passed to Thomas Monington Webbe-Weston,[1] uncle of the late Captain Weston, for his life. He married Mary Wright, and died without issue in 1857. Thereupon the male descendants of John Webbe-Weston were exhausted; and by the will of Captain J. J. W. Weston the estates passed to his cousin, the present owner, Francis Henry Salvin of Croxdale, County Durham, a grandson of John Webbe, the devisee from Melior Mary in 1782.

The windows with painted glass and coats of arms in the east and west staircases, on the south front, were placed by F. H. Salvin in 1857, from the designs of Charles Buckler. Those in the east window give the names and dates and arms of the six owners of the estate after Sir Henry Weston, who died in 1591. Those in the west window give the names, dates, and arms of the five owners since the estate passed to the Webbe-Westons in 1782. In each case they impale the arms of their respective wives. Hence we find the coats of *Dister* (married 1583); *Harper* (died 1669); *Copley* (married 1637); *Nevill* (about 1701); *Gage* (1730); *Lawson* (married 1778); *Constable* (married 1795); *Graham* (married 1811); *Waldegrave* (married 1847); *Wright* (about 1854); (*Salvin* 1857).

There are pictures in the house of the following members of the family—*Dorothy Arundell*, Lady Weston, 1575 and 1590; *William Copley*, 1620; *John Weston*, 1634, who married William Copley's granddaughter in 1637; *William Wolffe* of Haseley, died 1739—portrait by Giles Hussey; *Frances Weston*, his wife (about

---

[1] The Webbe-Westons inherited the Sarnesfield estate from Anne, surviving daughter and heiress of John Monington of Sarnesfield.

1720); *John Wolffe,* their eldest grandson (*ætat.* eleven, 1754), by Giles Hussey; *Thomas Webbe* (died 1780); *Anne Tancred,* his wife; *John Webbe-Weston,* their son, devisee of estates in 1782, and grandfather of F. H. Salvin. This picture is a pastel by Russell, R.A., of Guildford. It represents Mr. Webbe as a very young man: it was exhibited with many of Russell's works at Guildford in 1887.

Francis H. Salvin, on coming into possession of the estate, made no structural alterations in the house, except the insertion of two six-light windows with stone mullions, filled with painted glass, in the eastern and western staircases facing south. The eastern wing in its lower story had apparently been unused since the fire of 1561. But a portion of the upper story was fitted up as a chapel. In 1876 the Chapel of St. Edward was built on the site, it is believed, of the original mansion and castle of St. Edward. It was founded by the late Miss Salvin, who is there buried.[1]

The house stands thus very nearly the same on the outside as it was when raised by Sir Richard in 1525. It is indeed now far more like its original form since the twelve mullioned windows, destroyed in the last century, have been replaced. Of very few houses in England in the course of 370 years have the external walls been so little altered. That which has been so ruinous to the fortunes of the family has been the salvation of their

[1] At the same time the long gallery was restored, and the terra-cotta mullions of the windows were replaced from castings of the originals. The present drawing-room, formerly the kitchen, was arranged, and the dividing wall and chimney-stack removed under the plans of Norman Shaw, R.A., by Frederick Harrison, then lessee of the house. He died there in 1881, and the house has since been in the occupation of his widow and of his sons, Lawrence and Sidney Harrison.

house. As a Catholic family, constantly and stubbornly opposed to the Elizabethan, Parliamentarian, Cromwellian, Orange, and Hanoverian governments, the Westons were excluded from public life in England, and were constantly and heavily mulcted in their estates under the Test and Penal laws of the seventeenth and eighteenth centuries. They thus had no resources wherewith to modernise their family mansion, or to vie with their Protestant neighbours in converting Gothic or Jacobean piles into the style of Wren, Vanbrugh, or Soane—the ruthless destroyers of many a fine old court. A succession of very long tenures by some very quiet country gentlemen and that excellent old maid, Melior Mary, and since then a series of fortunate accidents, have prevented the owners of Sutton from destroying, as so many squires throughout the country have done, the venerable home of their forefathers. To touch it now, to add to it, to "restore" it, would be a social crime. Let us keep its bricks, its tiles, and its painted windows together as best we can, until the miserable day shall come when the elements shall have to themselves the proud house of Wolsey's "most humble servant," and the hall where Sir Richard was so careful of the "grete carpete to lay under the Kyng's fete."

CHAPTER VIII

THE HOUSE

THERE is reason to think that the house was built about 1523-25. The date is given by Manning (vol. i. p. 136) as 1529 or 1530; by Aubrey (vol. iii. p. 228) as 1521. It is exceedingly improbable that the house was built so late as 1529, the year of the divorce of Catherine of Aragon, since her device of a pomegranate appears in the spandrels of the arched chimney-piece in the great hall, and again in that of the panelled hall, and her arms are found in the hall (window north-east, VI. 1) impaled with the arms of England. As Catherine had lost the favour of Henry VIII. in 1527, it is hardly conceivable that her emblems and arms were placed at any later date in the hall of one of the King's ministers.[1] The better

---

[1] There are other things which also suggest the earlier date. The great bell, which is now removed to St. Edward's Chapel, would not have been erected till the whole pile was complete. It bears the legend—*Pierre Baude ma faicte* 1530. Also in the hall are the

conclusion seems to be that the house was erected between the date of the grant of the manor (1521) and 1527; probably on the return of Sir Richard Weston from the war in France in 1523.

The present house was built about a quarter of a mile from the site of the previous manor-house, which stood on the hill now occupied by St. Edward's Chapel and Vine Cottage. Here, it is said, originally was the hunting-lodge used by Edward the Confessor, when Lord of the Manors of Woking and of Sutton, and the mansion-house of Sutton subsequently took its place. The survey taken at the death of Philip Basset, the Lord of the Manor, in 1270, gives it as "a tenement, containing about one acre of land, of the yearly value of 1s."; in the surveys of 1329 and of 1410 it is spoken of as "a ruinous messuage, value £0:0:0." Traces of the old house have been found in the field south of the present chapel. A clump of birch trees marks the site of the old well, of which the remains have been recently examined. This very ancient well under the clump of birch trees has always been called St. Edward's Well. Old encaustic tiles have been there found. The field is still called the Manor Field. The decay of the village of Sutton, now only represented by a few cottages on Sutton Green, probably followed the removal of the manor-house eastwards to the banks of the Wey and the extension of the estates towards Clandon and Merrow, on the building of the new Sutton Place by Sir Richard Weston, say in 1525.

arms of second Lord Derby, died 1522; and second Duke of Norfolk, died 1524; also of Nicolas Lepton, the vicar of St. Nicholas, Guildford, who died 1527. Manning's date of 1529 could only refer to the final completion of an edifice which would require several years to erect and then to adorn with woodwork and glass.

The house, as originally built, consisted of a principal quadrangle, enclosing a space of 81 feet on each side, and fronted by an arched gateway with a tower flanked by lofty hexagonal turrets. On the western side is now also an inner quadrangle, enclosing a space of about 50 by 40 feet, with stabling and offices beyond. Careful examination shows that the smaller quadrangle on the west side is not part of the original edifice. The brickwork and terra-cotta moulding of the base are traceable all round the western wing, and the wall of the smaller quadrangle is merely built up to and on it, and is not worked in with the original brickwork, as is the case with the angle of the main quadrangle. This is observable both within the smaller quadrangle, at its north-east junction with the older building, as well as without. In the old pen-and-ink drawing in the possession of Mr. Salvin there is no second quadrangle. The whole house is built of brick and terra-cotta, no stone whatever having been used in the construction or ornamentation. This use of terra-cotta is one highly characteristic of the builder's age; it is found in one or two other contemporary examples,[1] but it was shortly afterwards abandoned, and did not reappear until very recent times.

Sutton is one of the very earliest existing specimens of the purely domestic mansion-house, entirely planned and constructed in an era when no purpose of defence was thought of, and when modern ideas of domestic economy had been fully developed. With Layer Marney Towers, in Essex, and Compton Winyates, in Warwickshire, both built about 1520, Sutton Place remains the earliest example of a non-castellated domestic residence. In all the examples of houses built before the sixteenth century,

[1] In particular, East Barsham, Norfolk, and Layer Marney, Essex.

of which Haddon Hall is a familiar instance, either an existing castellated work was adapted or incorporated with the house, or the house itself was planned with a view to military defence.[1] Down to the sixteenth century, mansion-houses consisted mainly of a great hall used for common purposes, and a few separate chambers for the master and his family, the rest of the edifice consisting of kitchen, buttery, guard-room, bakehouse, brewery, and other outbuildings. At this date the rooms were not regularly connected with each other. Access to them was only possible by passing across the quadrangle, and the stories were reached by a succession of winding stairs in turrets and projecting angles. So in Thornbury Castle and Sudeley Castle, in Gloucestershire, and other mansions of the fifteenth century. At Sutton Place we find a house planned with all the apartments recognised by modern habits, some forty in number, large, symmetrical, and unguarded windows, and all the chambers reached by passages and staircases, and not by circular stairs in turrets. The large staircases, however, are obviously more recent; and there are traces of circular staircases in the original work on the north wing only. It is accordingly an example of the modern mansion-house of the class of which Hatfield House and Longleat are splendid specimens. But it is much earlier in date, and of an order of architecture differing radically from any Elizabethan or Jacobean work. It is one of the very few extant complete examples of the Gothic Renascence style of the age of Henry VIII. and Francis I.

The revolution in habits and ideas implied in the

---

[1] Hever Castle, built by Sir Geoffrey Boleyn, Lord Mayor of London, and great-grandfather of Queen Anne Boleyn, and completed by her father, was strongly fortified.

building of a first-rate mansion on purely pacific principles, without any defensive character at all, is one of the most important in the history of manners. For five centuries perhaps no man of mark had ever built a residence in the country without providing for the case of its needing to be defended at least against an armed mob. Sir R. Weston, who was himself a soldier of experience and could remember the battle of Bosworth, builds a house in which no trace of war appears, even by way of ornament. The forty years of Tudor sovereignty had done their work. The "King's peace" was so perfectly a habit, that the minister of Henry VIII. takes no more heed of defending his house than would a minister of Victoria.

Every separate work of this age was the distinct creation of some particular artist. The charm of the Renascence in France especially is that each product of it is unique. At Sutton Place this blending of the Gothic and Renascence elements is treated in a way special to itself. In this age of transition each artist selected the parts of each style for himself, and himself devised the spirit in which they should combine.

In the house before us the elements of the Gothic and the Renascence are combined in a way that is perhaps without any exact counterpart. Was the designer of this house working under English, French, or Italian influence? Was he consciously undertaking a new method of building? Was he following a known model? Did he belong to the masters of the Gothic art or of the Renascence?

Seen from a distance, the house appears to be simply Gothic of the early Tudor age. But the details are in many cases purely Renascence, and Italian rather than

English in style; whilst there are occasional points of resemblance (arabesque and Raffaellesque) to some of the buildings of the age of Francis I. in France. Sir Francis Weston, the only son of the founder, who was born about 1511, was obviously named after the brilliant French king. He is the only Francis in the family. It was a great building age, and one when England was brought into close relations with the artistic work of France and of Italy. Henry's visit to Francis at the Field of the Cloth of Gold took place in 1520. As we have seen, Sir Richard Weston, the builder of the house, was one of the knights who attended him. In 1518 Weston had been one of the embassy sent to Paris to Francis I., and probably saw the châteaux of the Loire recently erected. Leonardo da Vinci was at this time living at Amboise.

On the other hand, Henry VIII. had employed many Italian workmen, both on the chapel of Henry VII. at Westminster Abbey, and elsewhere. Girolamo da Trevizi was the King's architect, and he is said to have introduced terra-cotta or moulded brickwork for ornaments. Mr. Hayward in his account of Layer Marney[1] quotes Dallaway in his notes to Walpole thus :—

"Girolamo da Trevizi and Holbein introduced both terra-cotta or moulded brickwork for rich ornaments and medallions, or bas-reliefs fixed against the walls, plasterwork laid over the brick wall, and sometimes painted, as at Norwich, and square bricks of two colours, highly glazed and placed in diagonal lines, as at Layer Marney."

---

[1] "Architectural Notes on Layer Marney Hall, Essex," by Charles Forster Hayward, F.R.I.B.A., 1862, in *Transactions of the Essex Archæological Society*, vol. iii. part i.

All of these devices are found at Sutton Place. And Mr. Hayward then quotes from a communication made to him by Mr. Digby Wyatt as follows :—

"Among other Italians in this country whose taste exercised a powerful influence upon architecture and the application of sculpture and painting to architecture were—John of Padua, Torrigiano, Girolamo da Trevizi (often called Trevisano), Tolo dell' Annunciata, a painter, Benedetto da Rovezzano, a very able Florentine sculptor who was associated with Holbein, Zucchero, the painter, Luca Penni. Of these Luca Penni, painter, Tolo dell' Annunciata, painter, and Trevisano, architect and engineer, all pupils or of the school of Raffaelle, were attached to the court of Henry VIII., and at work before Holbein came here. Layer Marney terra-cotta ornaments were very likely executed under the influence of Girolamo da Trevizi, the King's architect, with whom Sir Henry Marney, the founder of the house, must, as Captain of the Guard to Henry VIII., have come into occasional contact."

Holbein came to England first as a young man in 1526. It is more likely that Girolamo or one of the Maiani was the man whose influence gave to Sutton its marked Italian character.[1]

The house, therefore, is probably a work of builders trained in Gothic art, but working under directions of a designer familiar with the new domestic architecture of the Renascence, and possibly with designs for the details or moulds given by a foreign and no doubt Italian artist. There is no improbability in supposing that the general

[1] The famous terra-cotta medallions of the Cæsars at Hampton Court were executed by Giovanni Maiano. For these and an account of terra-cotta work by Italians for English palaces see *History of Hampton Court Palace in Tudor Times*, by Ernest Law, p. 50.

artistic superintendence and the finer ornamental work was given by Trevisano.

The parts where the different styles appear may be said to be as follows :—

The general plan of the house is that of the domestic architecture of the first half of the sixteenth century, and in its general outline and main characteristics it is Gothic. It is far more distinctly Gothic than the houses built in the second half of that century. The gateway and tower, the quadrangle, the great hall dividing the two wings with the principal chambers at the upper end, and the kitchen, buttery, and cellars at the lower end, are features invariably found in the centuries preceding, and in Gothic and castellated edifices. The pointed arch distinctly appears over the mullions of the upper lights in all the windows of the ground floor, in the small arcade of the parapet on the façade, and in the heads of the doors, large and small. The use of mullions, transoms, and labels for the windows, the trefoils and quatrefoils, the bays and gables, are essentially Gothic. The irregular disposition of the garden or south front is also essentially English and Perpendicular Gothic. The general disposition of the house, however, is Tudor rather than strictly Gothic, and entirely English in character.

On the other hand, the use of terra-cotta is almost always traceable to foreign influences, usually Flemish or Italian. The diaper pattern in dark brick is said to have been introduced by Holbein, but was probably earlier. The use of steps in the gables, as seen in the wings on the north end, is said by Mr. J. J. Stevenson[1] to be

---

[1] *House Architecture*, 1880, vol. i. p. 354. It is a special peculiarity of Scotch architecture, and was there called " corbie steps "—the name indicating its foreign origin. It is also seen at Stockbridge Hall, in Westmorland (see

originally a French artifice, and it is certainly rare in England, though occasionally seen in the Perpendicular style. It is very marked at Layer Marney, as is shown by Mr. Forster Hayward's drawings. Again, the quadrangle of Sutton shows a symmetry and careful disposition of parts so as to produce a regular façade, which is not characteristic of Gothic work, but is peculiarly a feature of Italian Renascence. The quadrangle would be exactly symmetrical in all its parts were it not that on the western side the windows are not all placed at regular intervals. There is perhaps no known example in England of a house of a date so early having a plan and façade so symmetrical as is the interior of the great quadrangle of Sutton. Nor will it escape notice that the ancient chimneys are carefully kept out of sight from the quadrangle, the fireplaces throughout the house being mostly in the outer and not in the inner walls. Some of the chimney-stacks are obviously more recent additions.

But the most distinct feature of Renascence work that the house contains will be found in the details of the ornament in terra-cotta. The amorini over the hall doors, north and south, and in the parapet above, the arabesque work in the mullions, the string-courses moulded with the "tun," the baluster ornament, the small arabesque moulding with it, and also the lozenge ornament, are all entirely in the taste of the Renascence, and are apparently of refined Italian design. Nothing in the least like any of them is to be found in Gothic work; and the perfect freedom and grace with which these Renascence details are adapted to the Gothic work, and

Parker, *Domestic Architecture*, vol. iv. 209), and at Hillfield, Warwickshire, 1560 (see *Old Warwickshire Houses*, by W. Niven, 1878).

even applied to pointed arches, is one of the peculiar features of this house.

Yet whilst many of the details of the ornament are of strictly Renascence character, there is no single example, even the smallest, of classical work.[1] The column, the round arch, the pilaster, the architrave, the cornice and baluster, and the pediment are nowhere seen; nor, on the other hand, are the broad scrolls, contorted gables, the lattice-work and fantastic parapets of the Elizabethan style proper. The spirit of the work is rather horizontal in its lines than perpendicular, but the number and disposition of the mullions over each other prevent the horizontal lines from being prominent.[2]

The house remains, the unique work of some unknown "Master of 1525," as one of the landmarks in the history of English architecture. It is so far modern that it has all the symmetry of a Palladian design, whilst it has no single classical feature such as occur at every point of a building of Renascence times. The work as a whole is truly Gothic, but Gothic treated with the eye for ornament of an Italian of the age of Raffaelle. The profuse ornamentation is of the most delicate kind, never obtruding itself, and in singular contrast with the coarse and florid decoration by which the Elizabethan and Jacobean builders sought to obtain effects of shadow and of contrast. It is interesting to speculate what might have been the future of English domestic architecture if it had

---

[1] The classical style was introduced into England by John Thorpe, at Longleat, in Wiltshire—date 1567-97. Every Elizabethan example has classical features: there is not one at Sutton.

[2] A good collection of views of Elizabethan houses is given in a recent work, *Architecture of the Renaissance in England*, 1560-1630, by J. Alfred Gotch and W. Talbot Brown, London, 1891. It will be seen how greatly all of these differ from Sutton, which remains Gothic.

sought to adapt and retain the Gothic forms to new uses in the refined and graceful spirit of the builder of Sutton.

The problem remains who was he, of what nation, of which school? The solution which seems the more probable is this—That the house was erected by English builders in the contemporary English style of domestic Gothic; that it was planned under the influence of men who had seen the great palaces which had recently risen in Italy and France, and who understood the new requirements which the modern life of the sixteenth century had introduced; and that the English builders were assisted in the symmetrical design and in the details of the ornamentation by Trevisano or some of his countrymen and companions.

Whatever may be its origin, it is a building of singular interest in the history of art, as well as of a rare and peculiar beauty. It is a significant example of the flexibility of the Gothic architecture, and of the vitality that remained in it just as it was about to be swept away. It is an evidence of the possibility of building a modern house entirely graceful and light without resorting to a single classical expedient. Lastly, it is a wonderful example of the resources and durability of terra-cotta in building. The brickwork and moulded terra-cotta, which was originally prepared in several shades of red and orange, has now been softened by age and exposure into a rich assemblage of different hues: red, brown, russet, chocolate, orange, salmon, and straw colour, but all harmonising with ordinary brick far better than would stone of any shade. The whole of the work, constructive and ornamental, is in brick and terra-cotta. The bases, doorways, windows, string-courses, labels, and other dripstones, parapets, angles, cornices, and finials are of moulded clay.[1]

In all, about forty or fifty different moulds appear to have been used. These are combined and arranged with great ingenuity and freedom. An elegant quatrefoil parapet ornament is obtained by uniting above and below two of the trefoil heads of the window lights. Beside this about six other moulded plaques are used in varied combinations. One consists of a lozenge and ball ornament, one is an arabesque balustrade, others are horizontal mouldings and string-courses; three others contain a "tun," R.W., and a conventional bunch of grapes, being a "rebus" or punning emblem of the builder.[2] The whole of this series of ornaments of the most delicate character is in a wonderful state of preservation. Not a single piece is wanting in the quadrangle; and after 370 years of exposure it is so sharp and perfect that casts have been recently taken from it and new mullions reproduced. It may be taken as certain that from the date of its erection till our own day those moulded ornaments have never been copied or reproduced, and that every piece now remaining in the building is the original work of Sir R. Weston, except the portions which have been quite recently renewed. In 1875 terra-

---

[1] I have not been able to discover in the original building a single piece of stone of any kind, except on the tops of the semi-octagonal turrets flanking the north door to the hall. The great gates of the main north gateway were of course hung in stone. Fragments of these sockets remain in front of the central door into the hall.

[2] Of course the vulgar story that the "tun" and the "bunch of hops" show that the builder was a brewer is an idle blunder. The grapes appear as an ornament at Layer Marney, and show a foreign rather than an English designer. The grapes at Layer Marney are certainly as much like "hops" as those at Sutton. One supposes that in Essex they say to this day that Lord Marney, Captain of the Bodyguard, was the King's "brewer."

cotta mullions and frames, taken in moulds from casts of the existing windows, were replaced in windows which had been altered to modern sash windows probably early in the eighteenth century. The new mullions then inserted were the following—Four windows in the east wing, at its southern end; eight windows in the garden front, at its western end; and two small windows were inserted when repairing the gables of the quadrangle. The terra-cottas for this work were made by Messrs. Blashfield of Stamford in 1875.

The age in which Sutton Place was built was fruitful in works of domestic architecture. Henry VIII. is called by Harrison (*Description of England*, p. 330) "the onlie phœnix of his time for fine and curious masonrie." Cardinal Wolsey was building Hampton Court, Christ Church, Oxford, and Trinity College, Cambridge; Edward Stafford, the princely Duke of Buckingham, built Thornbury Castle, in Gloucestershire, between 1511 and 1520. Grimsthorp, in Lincolnshire, was built by the Duke of Suffolk; Kenninghall, in Norfolk, by the Duke of Norfolk; and Layer Marney Towers, in Essex, by Lord Marney. The latter is the building which comes nearest to Sutton Place in character. It was built by Lord Marney about 1520, and is also remarkable for the use of terra-cotta combined with brick. Like Sutton Place, it is a Perpendicular Gothic building, the windows having mullions, transoms, and labels, pointed arch and fantastic Renascence ornaments in the Italian style. It was probably designed or decorated by Trevisano.

The points of resemblance between Layer Marney Towers and Sutton Place are these—Layer Marney was built about 1520, Sutton about 1525. Both are of brick and terra-cotta, and both are English Perpendicular, with

Italian Renascence details. In both the main brick walls are diapered. They both have in plan a symmetrical courtyard, hexagonal turrets, parapets, and circular staircases. But the details of the work at Layer Marney are far more distinctly Renascence than at Sutton; and this is especially visible in the parapet. There is nothing at Sutton so rococo as the parapet at Layer Marney.

Layer Marney Towers still exists about 8 miles from Colchester. A good account of it, with drawings by Charles F. Hayward, was published by the Essex Archæological Society in 1862 (*Transactions of the Essex Archæological Society*, vol. iii. part i.) An account also appears in the *Building News*, 19th September 1879.

Other buildings of the same date are Hengrave Hall, in Suffolk, built by Sir Thomas Kytson, 1525-38, and Boughton Malherbe, Kent, both built by courtiers of Henry VIII. The following are houses nearest in date to Sutton Place—East Barsham, Fakenham, Norfolk (temp. Henry VII.), also a brick building. It shows the H.R. and E.R., griffin and greyhound, crown and hawthorn bush as in the windows at Sutton. Also parts of Haddon Hall, 1545; Littlecotes, Wilts; Bramhall Hall, Cheshire (see accounts of this in Ormerod's *Cheshire*). Of Hengrave Hall, Suffolk, built by Sir Thomas Kytson, 1525-38, there is an excellent account (*History and Antiquities of Hengrave*, by John Gage, 203, 4to, 1822),[1] and see Parker's *Domestic Architecture of the Middle Ages*, and *House Architecture*, by J. J. Stevenson, 1882.

Terra-cotta is used profusely in the following contemporary buildings—Hampton Court, Layer Marney,

---

[1] Hengrave is built of freestone and white brick, but without terra-cotta. Its plan is not symmetrical, like that of Sutton; the entrance is not in the middle of the quadrangle.

East Barsham; but it seems to have disappeared almost immediately from English work until revived in this generation.

A plan of a house during the sixteenth century is described in a curious book, *A Dyetorie or Regiment of Health*, by Andrew Boorde of Physick Doctor, 1547 (edited by F. J. Furnivall, E. E. Text Soc., 1870). In chap. iv. he writes—"Make the hall under such a fasshyon that the parler be anexed to the heade of the hall, and the buttery and pantry be at the lower ende of the hall, the seller under the pantry, yette somewhat abase; the kychen set somewhat a base from the buttry and pantry commyng with an entry by the wall of the buttry, the pastry-house and the larder-howse anexed to the kychen. Then devyde the lodgynge by the cyrceute of the quadryngall courte, and let the gatehouse be opposyt or agaynst the hall-dore (not directly) but the hall-dore standing a base, and the gatehowse in the mydle of the front entry into the place: let the pryve chambre be anexed to the chambre of astate, with other chambres necessary for the buyldynge, so that many of the chambres maye have a prospecte in to the Chapell." And then he goes on to describe the proper position for the stables, the slaughter-house, half a mile from the mansion, also the bakehouse, how to keep the moat clean, the fruit garden, fish-pool, the park "with deer and conyes," butts, and a bowling-alley.

This is the plan followed at Sutton Place. The hall is in the centre, entirely dividing the east from the west wing, and occupying the height of two stories.[1] The

---

[1] A feature worthy of notice is that the hall door is precisely in the centre of the quadrangle, and hence in exact line with the gateway in the tower of the north front, and both are also in line with the garden door of the hall.

principal sitting-room was at the east end of the hall. The kitchen was in the west wing, the room now converted into the drawing-room. The principal apartments were in the east wing, the buttery and pantry at the west end of the hall, with the cellars underneath. As originally built, the north end of the quadrangle was occupied by a wing communicating across, and having in the middle a lofty tower with gateway. This wing, like the east wing, was externally 27 feet in width. It was, of course, in length exactly the same as the quadrangle, *i.e.* 81 feet. This front appears in three drawings in the possession of the present owner, one being about the beginning of the seventeenth century, say 1600; a second is dated 1750; and the third is 1779. An engraving of the latter was given in the *Gentleman's Magazine*, p. 108, February 1779. This tower and side of the quadrangle had long been in a ruinous condition, and it was removed by the then owner in 1782.[1] A careful architectural elevation taken previous to that date is now in Mr. Salvin's hands (1750). From these it would appear that the gate-tower rose to a height nearly double the existing house. It had a large gateway, apparently four-centred arch, with three entire stories over the gateway. The central windows were of four lights with transoms, the lowest window of eight lights; the mullions, labels, cornices, and medallion ornaments in

This is contrary to the directions given in the *Dyetorie* and apparently contrary to the universal practice. At least, I can find no plan of a Gothic house where a right line passes true through the external gateway and the inner and outer hall doors, and is at the same time the central axis of the principal court.

[1] The bills of the contractor for the pulling down the tower are now in the possession of Mr. Salvin. They are dated 1782. The receipts for the various works and alterations (£2445) are dated 1784.

terra-cotta, precisely similar to those of the present façade of the quadrangle. Beside the gateway were two turrets, obviously containing staircases, and giving access to the stories above. From the ends of each wing a high wall with a coping is shown in the older drawing (1600), terminating at the corners with hexagonal towers, similar to that one now remaining entire in the garden. Of these turrets in the curtilage there are said to have been eight.

With the exception of the removal of the north side, the quadrangle as seen externally remains in its original form. Whether the hall is internally in its original form, or whether it extended to the west so as to include another window, or even another bay, is very doubtful. The present partition at the west end of the hall is slight. We meet inside no solid and thick wall until we reach the west bay; and the height of the rooms adjoining the minstrels' gallery corresponds with the ceiling of the hall, and not with that of the other rooms.[1] Here stood the pantry and buttery, adjoining the kitchen, and close to the stairs descending on the garden side, under the present

[1] The fact that the west wall of the hall is a slight partition wall is not at all decisive against its being the original end of the hall. Although the hall as it stands might well be longer for its width, it would be highly unusual and inconsistent if the hall door stood anywhere near the middle, instead of the end of the hall. As it is, it occupies a very unusual place, one due probably to the desire of the designer to produce a symmetrical façade. It will be observed that in the inventory of 1542 there is next to the butler's chamber the "litle chambre bi the mydell entre." This must have occupied the site of the present passage which gives access to the hall at its north-west door. The hall, therefore, could not very well be longer than it is now. Besides, with the increase of living rooms in a mansion the great hall was reduced in size. It was no longer the general living and sleeping room of the retainers, as it had been in the thirteenth and fourteenth century (Parker, *Dom. Arch.* iii. 15).

staircase, to the cellars and vaults. In houses of this date the sets of rooms round a quadrangle do not communicate. As Mr. J. J. Stevenson says (*House Architecture*, ii. p. 34), "the house (of 1500-50) is only a collection of separate houses; access between them could only be got by going outside." And the fact that there are three doors together makes it evident that this was the plan adopted here. The present opening through the wall at the west angle into the corridor to the great hall is recent. Originally, it is probable that the rooms of the west wing did not communicate with the hall except through the kitchen; and it is probable that the rooms on the ground floor in the east wing did not communicate with the hall.

There is no reason to suppose that any of the three great staircases as now seen in the house belonged to the original work. They present the character of a later date. The north and east sides of the quadrangle were those chiefly injured by the fire of 1560; and they seem never to have been completely restored or adapted to use. What was the original character of the rooms, and whether the existing party walls were so planned, it seems impossible now to determine.

The present long gallery occupies the upper floor of the whole east wing. It was restored in its present form in 1878. About half of it had previously been used as a Catholic chapel during this century. Whether the original plan contained a long gallery at all resembling the present may well be doubted. No long gallery of the scale and completely developed character of the present can be found in England so early as 1525. That which we now see resembles the fully formed galleries of the Elizabethan and Jacobean age. It is certain that the gallery, if any such there were, was much shorter than the present one; otherwise it would have had windows on all four sides, and would have been hardly habitable in winter. There are now behind the panelling recesses for four fireplaces, not for one as we now see. They communicate with chimneys in the four double stacks visible in the eastern wall, all part of the original edifice. And it may be doubted if the builders of the early sixteenth century ever designed a single room to be warmed by four fires in place of one large one. In the inventory taken at the death of the builder in 1542 there is no description of a room which would correspond with the long gallery, as "the gret chambre" is undoubtedly the present hall. It is probable that three, if not four rooms, or even more, occupied the place of this gallery.

In the original plan the private rooms of the master were probably in the south end of the east wing, adjoining the head of the hall, the old *solar*, in fact. An opening, loft, or gallery may have existed on the upper story, whence the family could see what was going on in the hall after they had left it. The entrance door in the quadrangle to the east wing led to the set of chambers quite distinct from the rest of the house, and the entrance in the quadrangle to the west wing led to the offices and kitchen. The original chapel is said to have been in the western side of the inner court facing the stables, and the priest's room was till lately the low panelled room facing the garden at the extreme south-west angle of the house. This, at least, has been the disposition in the last century, when the family were under the pressure of the anti-Catholic laws. Whether there was any other chapel in the original design is not clear. No traces of it appear, and it may have been in the east wing.

The plan of the house will be made out best by following the inventory. It is possible that was drawn up in this way: beginning with the hall in the centre, it passes into the chambers in the east wing; so round the east wing to the gateway or northern front, and thence round to the west wing, the kitchen, pantry, offices, and stables. But the original chambers cannot now be identified; and doubtless the house as planned consisted of four sides of a great quadrangle, each side being practically separate, and having access without and within the quadrangle by separate entrances. Within these four distinct blocks of building, north, east, south, and west, the separate apartments were only divided by very slight, and perhaps variable partitions of panelling, or even screens of tapestry and canvas. The dimensions of the principal halls are as follows—The hall is 51 feet 6 inches long by 25 feet 6 inches, or between the bays 38 feet. It is 30 feet 9 inches high. The long gallery is 174 feet long by 23 feet wide, and 15 feet high.

The account given by Aubrey in his *Natural History of Antiquities of Surrey*, iii. 228, is as follows—"The place is a noble seat, built of brick, and has a stately gatehouse, with a very high Tower, bearing a turret at each angle. In it is a square court. The windows [? mullions and transoms] are made of baked earth, of whitish yellow colour (like Flanders bricks). The mouldings within the house are adorned with pendants of Fruits and Flowers of the same brick, where is R.W. and the Figure of a Tun, as a rebus of his name. In the hall (of the same sort of work as in King's College, Cambridge, if not by the same hand) is the crest of Weston. In the parlour is his coat of arms."

CHAPTER IX

THE QUADRANGLE

THE quadrangle, in its original form, as completed by the northern wing, measured within (above the moulded base) 81 feet 3 inches × 81 feet 3 inches.[1] It is remarkable for two essential features which distinguish it from the English architecture of the period; the first being its regular and symmetrical character, both in plan and in elevation; the second, that its scheme of ornament is in the low and delicate relief of the Italian style, rather than of the open cut and linear work of the late Gothic

[1] The exact line of the northern wing, both on its inside and outside walls, is easily traceable, the return of the moulding of the skirting or base being visible both on the east and west wings; and the foundations have recently been opened and discovered by Mr. Sidney Harrison.

manner. The quadrangle is in height on the east and west wings 32 feet 6 inches from the ground to the top of the parapet. It is divided into two stories by a string-course, the lower story being 16 feet from the ground to the string-course, the upper story 13 feet, and the parapet itself is 3 feet 6 inches. On the south wing, where the upper story is 2 feet 6 inches higher, the measurement from the ground to the top of the parapet is 35 feet. It appears from the mouldings and the bases on the two entrance doors of the hall north and south, and the two entrance doors in the east and west wings, that the level of the quadrangle is nearly, if not exactly, the original, as is the floor of the hall.[1] It is no doubt one of the peculiarities of the building, perhaps due to the extreme evenness and dryness of the situation, that the entire ground floor of the whole house in both quadrangles now stands on the exact level of the soil, both on the quadrangle and the garden side; so that no step of any kind is employed for entering the house on any side, and apparently none was ever designed.

The entrance doors to the hall and all the windows of the lower story throughout the house are protected by dripstone labels; the windows of the upper story have none. The windows of the upper story are sufficiently protected by the string-course and dripstone under the parapet, the upper story being 3 feet higher than the lower; thus the heads of the windows in the upper story come close up to the string-course. The windows of the lower story also have in their upper range of lights four

---

[1] The surrounding soil must have been raised somewhat in three centuries by the action of earth-worms; see Charles Darwin on the action of earth-worms, which raise open ground about 1 foot in each century (*The Formation of Vegetable Mould through the Action of Worms*, 1881).

cusps, forming at the top a pointed head. The other lights have two cusps, forming a round head. A base with moulding, at present 2 feet 6 inches from the level of the soil, runs round the building. Over the second story stands a parapet, and the whole building is covered by a high-pitched tiled roof.

The principal entrance, called in the inventory of 1542 "the mydell entre," opening into the west end of the hall, is in the centre of the south side of the quadrangle, and stood in exact line with the gateway in the north tower and wing, now removed. It is also in exact line with the similar entrance to the garden on the south side of the house. Thus the axis through the centre of the quadrangle passed through the centre of the outer gateway, and also through the two great doors of the hall, north and south.

At the upper end of the quadrangle in the west and east wings are two similar doorways, exactly facing each other. All of these are 11 feet high. Nearly in the centre of the west and east wings are two sloped bays, 13 feet by 3 feet, also facing each other, and in every way identical. North of each bay on the upper story are three windows, and south are two windows; all of them having six lights. The four windows, identical in design and corresponding with each other, on either side of the two side doors, east and west, have four lights each. The rows of windows on the two stories stand nearly, but not quite, regularly over each other, and are placed nearly, but not quite, at regular intervals. From the old pencil drawing by William Woolfe, signed and dated 1750, it would appear that the northern wing, then standing, as seen from the quadrangle, nearly corresponded with the existing southern wing, and had six windows of six lights each on either side of the gateway. The principal entrance door in the south wing is obviously planned with a view to a symmetrical façade, and is hardly the most convenient for the use of the hall itself. The quadrangle itself is an exact square. An arrangement of the quadrangle so symmetrical is quite contrary to all the methods of building adopted in earlier times, or in any building of a castellated kind. It may well be doubted if there is extant in England any earlier example of such a plan, and in any case it was due to foreign influence and reminiscences. It would probably be difficult to find in England a house so early as 1520 where, as at Sutton, the desire of symmetry in the external elevation entirely dominated the claims of convenience within.

The south side of the quadrangle, as seen from within it, is perfectly regular in plan and elevation. It is $2\frac{1}{2}$ feet higher than the wings on the side, east and west. The entrance in the centre is flanked by two regular half-octagonal turrets, 3.2 feet in diameter above the base, rising to a height of 48 feet. The string-courses and ornament of the parapet are carried round the turrets. They are completely covered from top to bottom with moulded ornaments, being the terra-cotta plaques with the R.W., the "tun," and the grape patterns set close together. At the top they are now capped with large finials of stone, and they are connected with an ornamental embattled parapet. It seems not improbable, from the way in which the parapet is built on to, and not into, the turrets, that it was a later addition, in spite of the use of the lozenge plaques between the embrasures. The fragments of stone before the main central doorway are probably pieces of the piers in which the great outer gates were hung. This is the only instance in the existing building where either stone or battlements are found. Both have been repaired at some unknown date; but there seems no means of ascertaining if they are precisely according to the original design. The change, if any there be, is very slight.

Over the entrance are two tiers of *amorini*, or winged cupids, handling apparently rosaries, or strings of beads with crosses. They are quite Italian in conception, but crudely executed and somewhat monotonous in arrangement, as though English artificers were working out an Italian sketch or suggestion. The amorini appear immediately over the entrance door, which is itself a very fair specimen of Tudor Gothic with geometric tracery and quatrefoils in the spandrels. Under the embattled parapet above, the rows of amorini appear again, each in a rather tame and awkward niche of low Gothic pattern, apparently formed by inserting a double cusp.

The parapet, which runs completely round the quadrangle, is fanciful and varied. It consists, in alternate spaces of about 10 feet each, arranged without precise regularity, of three distinct sets of ornaments—the lozenge pattern, the flat oblong plaque only used here, and the common English quatrefoil pattern, ingeniously contrived by inserting four of the cusps used in the window heads. Neither this nor any other part of the parapet is open or pierced. On the east and west wings the lozenge ornament is found also between the windows under the string-course. On the south wing there is a continuous band of the lozenge ornament over the windows and under the string-course. At the juncture of each of the patterns for the parapet is a finial, now much decayed, as it would seem, four finials in each wing. Enough remains of the finials to show that they were formed of plain and solid hexagonal blocks of terra-cotta, about 14 inches high, set on bases formed of hollow blocks of the same form. What now looks like stone is the decayed plaster backing for the hollow pieces of terra-cotta. The parapet above the bays is formed of the lozenge ornament in rows, capped by the coping of toy battlemented work characteristic of English Perpendicular. The finials were probably capped in the same way as the hexagonal turrets now are.

The north wing appears to have been of the same width as the east wing, viz. 27 feet (externally). A good idea is obtained by the pencil drawings of Mr. W. Woolfe, dated 1750, of its north and south front. The gate tower was about 70 feet high.[1] The large gateway in the centre was a four-centred Tudor arch with deep mouldings. Over this was a flat band of ornamental terra-cotta work, with the amorini similar to that over the entrance doors to the hall inside the quadrangle. Above the gateway were three stories, each lit by a large window, the lower one having transoms and eight lights, the two upper four lights in one row. All three windows were protected by labels. The gate tower was flanked by two large octagonal turrets, apparently 6 or 7 feet in diameter, and have six lights, one above the other, between which, at the top, ran a battlemented parapet. These turrets obviously served as staircases to reach the upper stories. The chimney-stacks are here, as elsewhere, on the outside, there being few chimneys on the

---

[1] The ground has been recently opened and trenched by Mr. Sidney Harrison, who has made careful measured plans. From these the exact line of the building can be followed.

quadrangle side throughout the house. The gateway as shown in several drawings is a Tudor arch with mouldings and no label. Though it was originally pointed, it is drawn as roughly rounded in the three independent drawings extant. The gateway, and indeed the windows, more nearly resemble those of Layer Marney, also a terra-cotta work of this date, than perhaps any other extant example of Tudor architecture.

The whole façade of the quadrangle is ornamented profusely with terra-cotta plaques and mouldings. The quoins are all worked with alternate squares of the R.W., "tun," and grape design, the black bricks forming a diaper pattern on the red bricks, and the terra-cotta being in two main colours, one deep brick-red, the other an orange-straw colour, several of the designs appearing alternately in the two colours. The brickwork and terra-cotta have by age acquired an immense variety of different tints, varied by the grays and greens of lichens, mosses, and wallflowers, so that the whole presents an extraordinary assemblage of warm and harmonious hues.

There seems to be but little attempt to cover brickwork with plaster, as at Layer Marney, the chief examples of this being on the parapet as a backing to the quatrefoil ornament, and again on the parapet on the garden front south of the house.

The elaborate scheme of ornamentation is confined to the quadrangle. The gateway front to the north, and the external walls of the house east and west, have no ornamental work beyond the mullions of the windows and the moulded base, and no parapet and no string-courses or dripstones. The garden front is of a very different character from the quadrangle. All attempt at symmetry is discarded, the parts are grouped in deep and irregular masses, and the chimney-stacks and gables characteristic of Tudor architecture are disposed irregularly. The garden door to the hall on the south side is ornamented similarly to that in the quadrangle on the north side, and the parapet is carried along the south side. No doubt the external south side of the building was protected by an outer wall.

It may be noted here that the large and ungainly *cross moline* made of coarse tiles, which is inserted three times under an ogee pattern in this parapet, is almost certainly a late addition, not earlier than 1640. The *cross moline* is the coat of Copley, whose heiress married John Weston in 1637. There is nothing in the family heraldry to account for the *cross moline* before the year 1652, when John Weston succeeded. It is plainly not the cross of St. John, to which Sir Richard Weston could have no claim. And though a *cross moline* is found in one of the quarters of the coats of Sir Francis and Sir Henry Weston, 1536-92, it is simply for *Longuevilliers*, one of the quarterings of *Pickering*. It could have no meaning as a bearing of Sir Richard Weston.

The external walls measure 3 feet in thickness; the north wall of the northern gateway wing measures 4 feet, as the broken return now shows. The roof over the east and west wings, and also that over the south wing, are similar, and form one continuous structure, open throughout, though on rather different levels. The roof is high-pitched and tiled, supported by immense arches of oak fastened by cross pieces, and bound together by huge horizontal transverse beams resting on the walls. There is no evidence that these were ever prepared so as to form an open roof, or that any room or dormitory ever existed in the roof; the few and irregular dormer windows are merely to light the roof. Beneath the transverse beams are now flat ceilings of lath and plaster, and the form of the ceiling in the roof, with a coving of about 1½ feet, is perhaps not far from the original form. The immense beams in the roof that cross the ceiling may easily have supported pendants in the hall, but there is nothing to show that they did. The action of fire is visible in the roof of the northern part of the east wing, as it is in the brickwork of the ground floor of the same wing. The roof of about half the east wing, at the northern end of it, is evidently a later and rather rude restoration. The two small double-light windows in the gables of the east and west wings are still visible on the north end. The mullions seem to have been early removed from the eight windows on the north ends of the east and west wings, as appears from the old pen-and-ink drawing, made apparently in the seventeenth century.

As originally built, the house appears to have consisted of this quadrangular court, with probably a chapel in the south-west corner, but without the second court on the west. The smaller quadrangle on the west does not contain any terra-cotta whatever. The inventory made on the founder's death mentions about thirty-two rooms. There are now more than this number in the house, without reckoning the north and east wings at all, and few of the existing rooms answer to the " lytell closets," which were merely bits enclosed from other rooms. No partition walls of any solidity appear in the house, except that the walls of the east and west wings are carried along across the south wing at a thickness of 2 feet 6 inches. These are probably the only partition walls in the original structure, as in accordance with the practice of the times the apartments would be separated only by panelling or other light division. The original staircases, either as external adjuncts or within, cannot now be positively traced.

There is no doubt that the house, as now and for a long period inhabited, has been completely transposed. The most pleasant part of the house must have been the east and south-east wings. The part of the house reserved for the family was doubtless in the north and east wings, one of which is now removed altogether, and the other practically abandoned as a residence. The west wing, in which the present residence is, was the quarter of the offices; the present drawing-room was the kitchen until about forty years ago; the present dining-room was probably once connected with the back buildings, on which it abuts. The west wing measures 1 foot less in width than the eastern and the north wings.

It is probable that from the time of Sir H. Weston (temp. Eliz.) down to that of the third Sir R. Weston (temp. Car. I.) Clandon and not Sutton was the principal residence of the family. Their baptisms and marriages are registered at West Clandon, and in existing deeds of the seventeenth century Sir R. Weston is described as of Clandon, not of Sutton. If so, the rooms injured by the fire in the time of Elizabeth, in the north and east wings, may never have been completely refitted and furnished. In 1641 Sir R. Weston sold the Clandon estate and mansion to Sir R. Onslow. It was then, probably, that the house at Sutton was refitted anew, and to this date we may attribute much of the carved panelling and oak doorways and staircases, and the Copley arms—a *cross moline*—on the parapet, etc., and in the panelling; and as Sir R. Weston devoted much of his fortune to the canal speculation, and ultimately embarrassed his estate, he may have lived at Sutton with less magnificence than did his grandfather, Sir Henry, eighty years before, and thus, after the sale of Clandon, he fitted up for his own residence the west wing. Aubrey calls the panelled hall the "parler," so that in his day (1673) the family apparently lived in the west wing; and at this epoch it is not improbable that the small quadrangle on the west side of the house was added.

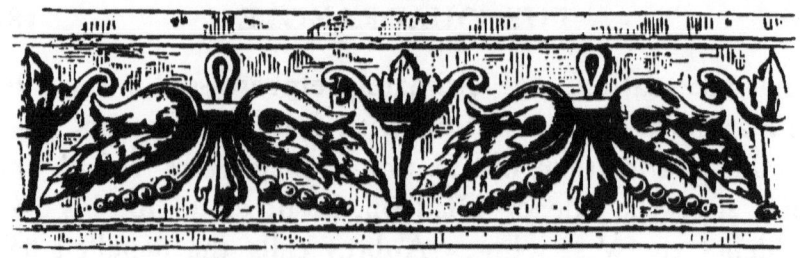

CHAPTER X

THE GREAT AND THE PANELLED HALL

THE smaller hall in the west wing, abutting on the west entrance from the court, now serves as the general entrance hall to the building. Aubrey, writing in 1673, speaks of it (iii. p. 228) as the "parler." It measures 24 feet by 19 feet 6 inches, excluding the bay. It is now completely panelled in old oak wainscotting. The whole of this was until recently covered with layers of old paint, whitewash, and canvas. The room had long been used as a lamp-room. In 1874 the screens and paint were removed and the panelling cleaned. Some pieces from other parts of the house were used in forming recesses and doors, but in general the panelling is in its original condition. These alterations or repairs were made by Frederick Harrison, then in occupation under a lease. The panelled hall has a Tudor four-centred arch for the fireplace of terra-cotta, similar to that in the great hall, and like it ornamented with the pomegranate, the badge of Catherine of Aragon.[1] This would show that the

---

[1] Ferdinand V. of Spain was engaged in the conquest of Granada, 1483-85, when he received news of the birth of Catherine, and she received the pomegranate (*granada*) as her badge, in commemoration of the issue of the

CH. X THE GREAT AND THE PANELLED HALL 183

fireplace itself was not later than 1527, the year of the disgrace of Catherine; and it would show that this room, if the fireplace is *in situ*, belonged to the more important parts of the house. The fireplace might possibly have been removed and placed here when the carved oak chimney-piece was fitted up, the date of which it is easy to fix.

Over the fireplace is a panel, and painted on the oak are the arms of Weston, impaling those of Copley. This was the coat borne by John Weston, who married Mary Copley in 1637, and who died 1690. Above this used to stand the large escutcheon of the arms of Sir Thomas Copley, with numerous quarterings. In 1874 the paintings and woodwork were restored by Mr. F. H. Salvin, and the escutcheon was removed and placed in the south end of the long gallery in the east wing. The woodwork and fittings of this hall are therefore to be attributed to about the middle of the seventeenth century, and the same is perhaps the date of much of the carved oak panelling in the hall and elsewhere in the house.

In this hall is an old picture of a large house of the Jacobean period, which has not been identified. The painted iron safe is of the same period. Both of these are supposed to have been part of the original furniture. The other pictures and furniture in this hall have no historical connection with the house, and have been recently placed there. This hall in the original plan may have served as a guard-room, armoury, or lower hall.

---

campaign. In the spandrels of the arch are the arms of Weston and of Camel, as they were quartered by Sir R. Weston, the founder, and appear in the original glass windows of the great hall.

THE GREAT HALL

The great hall, which occupies the larger part of the south wing, is a noble apartment, 51 feet 6 inches in length, 25 feet 6 inches in breadth, and nearly 31 feet in height. It has two principal entrances facing each other, the centre of both being now 12 feet from the west end of the hall—the one on the north opening into the court, the other on the south into the garden. The hall is warmed by an open fireplace on the south side, which, it will be observed, is one of the immense stack of chimneys 5 feet thick in the south wall. The other two chimneys in this stack must have belonged to the vaults. The hall occupies both stories, and is lit by the four windows of the two bays, north and south, and by six other windows on the north, and four on the south side.

The position of the entrance doors is certainly most unusual. Halls of this class usually are entered at their lower end, or if entered by the side, then the entrance is at the extreme end, and is protected by a screen of some kind. Here the main entrance, called in the inventory of 1542 the "mydell entre," is so far from the end of the hall that the passage running across the two doors cuts off exactly one-third of the whole length of the hall. It is extremely difficult to see how any screen could have crossed the hall without destroying its appearance and obscuring the view of the painted glass in the windows. It is equally difficult to see how the hall could have been either longer or shorter than it is at present. All the windows of the hall now have their painted glass, apparently in their original position, and contemporary with the house, at least those in the lower windows are (see the arms of Lord Derby in IV., and of Sir Walter Dennis in X. 3).

The inventory of 1542 mentions a room "bi the mydell entre," which could hardly have been so called if the hall were longer. Although an entrance at the side of the hall and so near its centre must always have been inconvenient, it seems to have been so used until the alterations of 1874, though by the removal of the north wing the court is now much more exposed to the weather. The entrance was probably protected by a small screen enclosing a few square feet round the door. Another peculiarity is that there is no trace of any dais in the hall, and the windows of the bays north and south are so near the level of the soil that probably none ever existed.[1] At the east end of the hall a solid party wall 2 feet 6 inches thick separates the hall from the east wing. At the lower or west end of the hall no solid partition of any kind is traceable. We find none until we reach the wall continuous with that of the west wing, which is 2 feet 6 inches thick. The cellars below show buttress work, as though designed to support the end of the existing stone floor.

The ceiling is now a flat plaster roof, which was painted for the owner in 1874. There is no trace of any pendant work, or of any other class of roofing. The beams in the roof over the hall were evidently not constructed to be shown as an open timber roof; they are perfectly equal to support any weight that might be hung from them, but there is no trace of anything of the kind. The dormer windows in the roof are too small and few for any other purpose except just to light the roof, and there is nothing to show that any habitable

[1] There is no *dais* in the great hall of Hampton Court. The dais was omitted about this period. As to this, and the reduced size of the mediæval hall, see Parker, *Dom. Arch.* iii. 15, 78.

rooms ever existed in it. Thus every examination leads to the belief that the hall, as we now see it, is not very far from its original appearance.

The general disposition of the hall appears to have been as follows—At the upper or east end, where the billiard table now is, the high table stood across between the bay windows north and south. Here was the "gret carpet to the table there" in the inventory; also in the wardrobe prepared for royal visits was the "grete carpete to lay under the Kyngs fete." Below this in the body of the hall stood the "bord in the gret chambre," where sat the officers, retainers, and strangers, for the inventory speaks of "a clothe of dyap for a square borde"; "xi fyne table clothes for the hawle for strangers." In a house of this kind, in a country at that time so thinly cultivated, something like open house was a necessity of the age. Round the walls were, no doubt, hangings of some kind of tapestry, for the inventory gives in "the gret chambere," "Ffyrst . . . peces of hangyngs of the Story of the Egypcyons." Behind the high table would be the door communicating with the principal rooms of the family in the east wing, and doubtless, as now, a gallery in the upper story from which they could survey the hall after leaving it. At the west end of the hall were the buttery, butler's pantry, and other offices, "the butler's chamb," and the "litle chamb bi the mydell entre." Adjoining the pantry was the staircase leading down to the cellarage, which is no doubt much in its original condition. The kitchen stood farther west, next to the garden, in the part now occupied by the inner drawing-room. This was still the kitchen within the last forty years. On the second floor, at the west end of the hall, stood, as is now to be seen, the minstrels' gallery.

The whole of the hall is vaulted underneath with an extensive system of cellars. The arches and jambs of these are made of hard chalk. The huge oak beams and doors are still in many places visible. It would appear that two of the chimneys in the great stack of three in the south wall were intended for these cellars.

The fireplace is of terra-cotta, and is apparently in its original place and form. It is a four-centre arch with Tudor-Gothic mouldings, the spandrels of the arch showing rudely-worked Saracens' heads, the crest of the Westons, and also branches of pomegranates with fruit and tendrils. As observed in the similar fireplace of the panelled hall, the pomegranate implies a date earlier than 1527, the year when Henry VIII. actively promoted the divorce of Catherine.

The wainscotting of the hall is no doubt of various dates, perhaps none of it contemporary with the house. No part of it seems earlier than the seventeenth century, the ornamental work over the two large doorways being apparently Jacobean and in its proper place. The carved work over the fireplace is obviously made up of seventeenth-century fragments, perhaps pieces from the ends of bedsteads or sides of chests; and it would be unsafe to assign any definite date to this rather artless concoction of stray fragments. The bulk of the panelling in the hall is probably of the seventeenth century, with perhaps some repairs, alterations, and refittings of the eighteenth century. It may be mentioned that the furniture, chandeliers, carved chairs, cabinets and chests, tables and tapestries, both in the hall and in the long gallery, have no historical connection with the house.

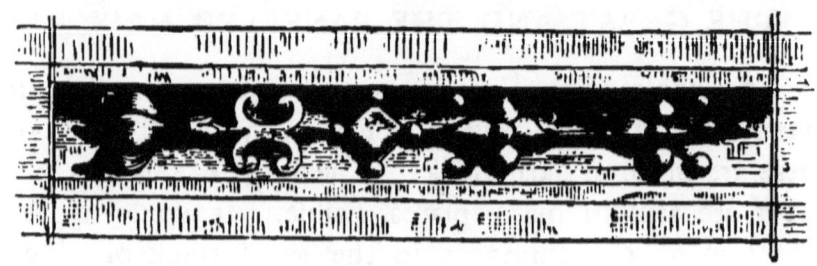

CHAPTER XI

THE LONG GALLERY, TAPESTRIES, PORTRAITS, AND ESCUTCHEONS

THE east wing of the house, in which with the northern or gateway wing were situated the principal apartments of the original building, was partially destroyed by the fire of 7th August 1560. The extent of the fire, which injured about one-third of the east wing on its northern end, can be distinctly traced in the roof, and also in the ground floor. And there is every reason to think that the whole of the east wing was never completely restored. A portion of it was formerly fitted up as a Catholic chapel, and the staircase and much of the woodwork evidently belongs to the last century.

In the year 1878 the gallery was restored in its present form by Frederick Harrison, the lessee. As now fitted up, somewhat short of the external length of the wing, the gallery measures internally, and including the staircase, 152 feet by 21 in width. Mr. Harrison replaced the terra-cotta mullions, frames, and mouldings in four of the windows there; reglazed the lights on the windows at the northern part of the gallery, and fitted up the panelling and tapestries. The panels were for the most part discovered by the owner, F. H. Salvin, in another house, and were replaced; the tapestries are the property of Mr. S. Harrison, and form part of the tenant's furniture. The windows, with stone mullions and painted glass arms and quarterings of the Westons, were placed there by F. H. Salvin in 1857.

It may be taken as certain that the house, as originally built, did not contain any such long gallery as we see. Many points in its construction, as well as the inventory, concur in leading to this conclusion. If the gallery be the original, its great size and early date would make it a more remarkable fact in the history of domestic architecture than anything else in the house; for thus two sides of the quadrangle of which the house then consisted would have been almost entirely occupied by two very large chambers. The panelling of the gallery is of a composite kind, none of it apparently earlier than the seventeenth century, and most of it of the eighteenth century, with some recent additions. There were not found any traces of ornamental ceilings or painted glass in the windows.

The Tapestries

The tapestries have no historical connection with the house, and are the property of Mr. Sidney Harrison. Most of them are very fine Brussels work of the sixteenth century. They bear the well-known marks for Brussels; also a castle *or* on a shield *gules*. Amongst the maker's cyphers are the following—for Herselin, a famous Brussels artist, 1530-40; for François Speering, about 1588. He made the famous tapestry of the *Armada* in the Houses of Parliament, burnt in the fire of 1834; apparently the mark of Jean Raes. Jean Raes was a famous Brussels artist who made the *Seven Capital Sins* and the *Battle of the Virtues and Vices.*

Another may be for W. Pannemaker, who made the *History of Abraham,* 1548. But the marks in the margin of the pieces are all more or less defaced by injury and repairs.

The tapestries are not all of the same class, but a pair of them are of the very finest work of the Brussels designers of the best age. The two tapestries representing the story of Joseph are the work of Herselin of Brussels about 1530-40, and must be from the designs of Bernard van Orlay, or some other master of that school. If these are compared with the grand pieces by Bernard van Orlay in Hampton Court, little doubt will exist that the designs are from his hand. The *Hercules between Pleasure and Wisdom* is almost equally fine in design, and is also possibly a work by Herselin, now in the dining-room. The finer tapestries are thus contemporary with Henry VIII. and Elizabeth. The Brussels pieces have the characteristic border of vines and pomegranates on a blue ground. One or two pieces are *verdures,* where the landscape is the principal subject.[1]

Window on Eastern Staircase, south

The two large six-light windows with stone mullions on the staircases east and west of the great hall were placed on the south or garden side of the house by F. H. Salvin in 1857. They had in them painted glass coats of arms from the designs of C. A. Buckler. They give,

---

[1] See Jacquemart, *Old Furniture,* English ed. pp. 97-99; A. Pinchart, *Les Tapisseries dans les Pays-Bas,* Bruxelles, 1859-64; Jules Houdoy, *Les Tapisseries de Haute Lisse,* Lille, 1871; J. J. Guiffrey, *Histoire de la Tapisserie,* Tours, 1886.

with names and dates, the coats of the Westons and their wives from Sir R. Weston the second, died 1611, to Melior Mary, died 1782. In each case but the last the arms of Weston impale those of the wife. They are as follows—

1. *Weston*, *ermine* on a chief *azure*, five bezants, impaling *Dister*, *gules*, a chevron *ermine* between three eagles displayed *argent*; for Sir Richard Weston, died 1611, married Jane Dister of Bergholt, Essex.

2. *Weston* impaling *Harper*, *sable*, a chevron and canton *ermine*; for Sir R. Weston, the agriculturist, married Grace Harper of Cheshunt, Herts, died 1652.

3. *Weston* impaling *Copley*, *argent*, a cross moline *sable*; for John Weston, died 1690, married Mary Copley of Gatton.

4. *Weston* impaling *Nevill* of Holt, *gules*, a saltire *argent*; for Richard Weston, married Melior Nevill of Holt.

5. *Weston* impaling *Gage*, per saltire *azure* and *argent*, a saltire *gules*; for John Weston, died 1730, married Elizabeth, sister of Thomas, Viscount Gage.

6. Melior Mary *Weston*, died 1782, the last lineal descendant of the founder.

Window on Western Staircase, south

The window on the south-western staircase, facing garden, has also six coats for the owners of the Webbe-Weston family.

1. *Weston* impaling *Lawson*, *argent*, a chevron between three martlets *sable*; for John Webbe-Weston, married (1778) Elizabeth Lawson.

2. *Weston* impaling *Constable*, quarterly *gules* and *vairé*, over all a bend *or*; for John Webbe-Weston, married (1795) Mary Constable.

3. *Weston* impaling *Graham*, *or* on a bend *sable*, three escallops of the first; for John Joshua Webbe-Weston, married (1811) Caroline Graham.

4. *Weston* impaling *Waldegrave*, per pale *argent* and *gules*; for John J. Webbe-Weston, married (1847) Lady Horatia Waldegrave.

5. *Weston* impaling *Wright*, *azure*, two bars *argent*, in chief a leopard's head *or*; for Thomas Donnington Webbe-Weston, married (1854) Mary Wright.

6. *Salvin*, *argent* on a chief *sable*, two mullets of the first, a mullet for difference; for Francis Henry Salvin of Croxdale, County Durham, succeeded 1857; present owner.

The Escutcheons

There are three large ancient escutcheons painted on panel, each about 4 × 5 feet, forming very complete specimens of the armorial blazonry of the sixteenth century. They are all for Sir Thomas Copley; one is dated 1568, and two are dated 1567. They were, no doubt, brought to Sutton Place from Gatton some time after the marriage of John Weston with Mary Copley in 1637. They consist of elaborate marshalling of the Copley coats and quarterings with arms, mantling, crest, motto, cords, tassels, and the like within a marble colonnade. The three are nearly the same design, and bear the monogram T.C., the dates 1567-68, and for motto *Medium tenere beatum*.

The principal escutcheon is now placed between the windows on the eastern staircase going up to the long gallery. It was removed from the panelled hall, where Aubrey saw it. It is thus blazoned in four grand quarters.

First grand quarter. COPLEY.—*Argent*, a cross moline *sable*, in the centre of the cross, a crescent *or* for difference.

Second grand quarter. WELLES.—*Or*, a lion rampant, double-queued *sable* quartering *gules*, a fesse dancettée between six crosses crosslet *or*.

This is for *Engaine* of Essex.

Third grand quarter. *Hoo.*—Quarterly *sable* and *argent*.

Fourth grand quarter. *Waterton*. Barry of six, *ermine* and *gules*, over all three crescents *sable*.

On this shield is an escutcheon of pretence for *Luttrell*. *Or*, a bend between six martlets *sable*.

Sir Thomas Copley, born 1535, died 1584, married Catherine, daughter and heiress of Sir Thomas Luttrell.

Supporters. Lion rampant *sable*. Swan *proper*, ducally crowned and gorged *or*.

Crest. On a knight's helmet, wreathed *sable* and *argent*, a griffin segreant *or*.

On separate shields are: (1) *Copley* impaling *Hoo*; (2) *Copley* impaling *Shelley*, *sable*, a fesse between three whelks, *or*; (3) *Hoo* impaling *Welles*; (4) *Hoo* impaling *St. Leger*, *azure*, fretty *argent*, a canton *gules*; (5) *Hoo* impaling *Scotland*, differenced, *or*, within a tressure flory-counter-flory, a lion rampant *gules*; (6) *Hoo* impaling *Welles* and *Waterton* quarterly.

All of these arms occur constantly in the glass in the hall (see chap. xii.), the arms of Copley and the crest alone in lower north bay No. 8. Also a shield *ermine* on a chief *sable*, three crosses crosslet *argent*, for *Wychinghon* or *Wickingham*.

The two escutcheons or hatchments dated 1567 are at the top of the western staircase.

Small Escutcheons in Great Hall

There are also in the great hall several small escutcheons, apparently modern.

They are as follows:—

1. *Weston.* 2. *Copley.* 3. *Luttrell.* 4. *Engaine of Essex.* 5. *Barrow*, *sable*, two swords in saltire between four fleur de lys *or*, within a bordure *or*. William Webbe of Salisbury, *temp.* Henry VIII., an ancestor of J. Webbe-Weston, married Catherine, daughter and co-heir of John Barrow. 6. *Pinchyon* of Writtle, County Essex. Per bend *argent* and *sable*, three roundels within a bordure engrailed counter-changed. John Wolffe of Great Haseley married Ann, daughter and co-heir of John, son of Sir Edward Pincheon. Their daughter Bridget married John Webbe, and was by him grandmother of John Webbe-Weston. 7. *Wolffe, gules*, a chevron between three wolves' heads erased *or*. 8. Webbe, *gules*, a cross between three falcons *or*. 9. *Salvin, argent*, on a chief *sable*, two mullets of the first, a mullet for difference.

Portraits

In the two halls are many historical portraits, which have been mainly identified from information supplied by the owner.

1. HENRY VIII. (on panel)—The well-known portrait after Holbein, small half length.

2. QUEEN ELIZABETH (on panel)—The well-known portrait after Zucchero, small half length.

3. QUEEN MARY (on panel)—Full length, about 70 by 45 inches; standing in black robe, holding a miniature in frame, apparently after Antonio More.

4. DOROTHY ARUNDELL, wife of Sir Henry Weston, said to be by Federigo Zucchero. Exhibited by the Royal Academy at the collection of old masters, 1884. It was described thus in the catalogue—" Painted probably about 1575, when Zucchero was in England. Full-length figure standing to right, lace head-dress and collar, rich dress, feather fan in her right hand, the left hand rests on a chair, dark background, canvas 71 by 40 inches."

This very fine portrait gives us the likeness of the noble lady who entertained Queen Elizabeth so frequently at Sutton (see chap. v.). She was cousin of Queen Anne Boleyn, Queen Elizabeth, Queen Catherine Howard, and Lady Jane Grey; being great-granddaughter of Thomas, second Duke of Norfolk, and of Thomas Grey, Marquis of Dorset. The picture must have been painted by Zucchero about 1575; he was in England 1574-78, when he painted, amongst others, the portrait of Lord Howard of Effingham, Lady Weston's cousin and neighbour. At that time Lady Weston was about thirty-five; and her husband, who had been High Sheriff for the county in 1569 and M.P. in 1571, was at the height of his splendour and popularity. The expression of noble stateliness and power, with the wonderful mastery over the details of jewellery, lace, embroideries, and brocade, mark this portrait as a characteristic and excellent specimen of the painter's qualities.

5. WILLIAM COPLEY, with date and inscription—

ÆTATIS·SUÆ·55·1620.

William Copley, born 1565, died 1643, was the son of Sir Thomas Copley, whose escutcheons stand on the staircase, by Catherine Luttrell. He married Magdalen Prideaux, and was grandfather of Mary Copley, married John Weston in 1637. The picture, a half-length life size, is perhaps by one of the Janssens (Corneliez Janssens, born 1590, died 1665).

6. Portrait of DOROTHY ARUNDELL, Lady Weston, in Marie Stuart ruff, about *ætat.* sixty-five. This now hangs in the great hall. The likeness to the large Zucchero portrait (No. 4) is very marked.

7. Portrait of JOHN WESTON, husband of Mary Copley, 1637.

8. Portrait of FRANCES WESTON, youngest sister of John Weston, died 1730, last male descendant of the name and family of the founder. She married William Wolffe of Great Haseley, and their issue became extinct in the second generation. She was aunt of Melior Mary (No. 11); painted about 1700 (*ætat.* thirty) in the manner of Kneller (born 1648, died 1723).

9. WILLIAM WOLFFE of Great Haseley, married Frances Weston, died 1739. He was son of John Wolffe by Ann, granddaughter of Dorothy, sister of Richard Weston, Earl of Portland. Picture by Hussey.

10. JOHN WOLFFE, died 1758, s.p.; inscribed on back, Joann Woolfe, *ætat.* eleven, 1754. *Ægid. Hussey pinxit.* Portrait by Hussey. John Wolffe was the grandson of Frances Weston (No. 8) and William Wolffe (No. 9), and was equally descended from the Westons of Sutton and the Westons of Prested Hall. By his death, and that of his brothers, all s.p., the blood of the founder became extinct, with the exception of Melior Mary.

11. MELIOR MARY WESTON, born 1703, died unmarried 1782; half length, in the style of Kneller, painted about 1723 (*ætat.* twenty).

12. THOMAS WEBBE of Fulham, died 1780, father of John Webbe-Weston; full length, in rich lace coat.

13. ANNE, his wife, daughter of Thomas Tancred, full length.

14. JOHN WEBBE-WESTON, devisee of the Sutton estate, 1782, son of Nos. 12 and 13, grandfather of F. H. Salvin. Pastel by J. Russell, R.A., of Guildford, born 1774, died 1806, exhibited at the Guildford Exhibition, 1879.

15. On staircase in western wing—Portrait of Rev. FATHER LEANDER A ST. MARTINO (J. Jones, D.D.), a Catholic Bishop, 1618, and President of the Benedictine Order 1633-35, died 1635, *ætat.* sixty-one. He was much esteemed by Queen Henrietta Maria, and was one of her advisers. He was in England during the time of Sir Richard Weston, the agriculturist, who was doubtless his host.

16. Portrait of a young lady, dated 1610, *ætat.* eighteen. This may be Jane Weston, daughter of Sir Richard Weston the second, and sister of the agriculturist. She married Sir Thomas Bishop, Bart.

Other historical portraits of ecclesiastics have not been

identified. The landscapes and pictures on the staircases and passages seem to be without interest or history. There are a set of old engravings of French and Dutch towns of the age of Sir Richard Weston, the agriculturist, and doubtless brought by him from abroad.

The pictures in the living-rooms of the family are the property of Mr. Harrison, the lessee, and have no historical connection with the house.

CHAPTER XII

THE PAINTED GLASS

THE most interesting feature in the hall is to be found in the fine painted glass with which it abounds.[1] The whole of the fourteen windows, having ninety-two separate lights in all, are adorned with shields and quarries of painted glass, one coat or set of devices in each light. They are of different dates and of various quality, but they seem to belong to about three different epochs, and hardly one of them is without some relation to the founder or his family. Some specimens are of extraordinary beauty and rarity; in some cases they seem to be older than the house itself,[2] and from the remarkable number

---

[1] For painted glass refer to Charles Winston, *Memoirs on the Art of Glass-Painting* (1865), *Difference of Style in Ancient Glass-Painting* (1847), and his other *Memoirs*; also see A. W. Franks (of the Brit. Mus.), *Ornamental Glazing Quarries* (1849), and *Principles of Glass-making* (1883), by H. J. Powell, etc.

[2] As Winston tells us, glass-painting in England reached its perfection between 1530-50, and had begun to decline in 1545.—Winston, *Art of Glass-Painting*, p. 248.

The original glass in the hall is almost exactly of the date 1530. The glass in Henry VII.'s Chapel was begun 1502, finished about 1510; the glass

of royal and historical characters whose arms and devices are shown, they are of unusual interest. If we take the historical associations of the hall itself, and follow up the suggestions of the many heraldic coats and emblems, we are carried into the strange and revolving picture of the sixteenth century in Europe.

The hall is profusely decorated with emblems of the Roses, both White and Red, the badge of the union of the rival houses of York and Lancaster under the first Tudor king; it has the arms in full of Richard III. as Duke of Gloucester, and the emblems of the battle of Bosworth. During the fifteenth century the manors of Woking and of Sutton had passed with strange rapidity from one family to another, and had reverted to and been held by every king from Henry IV. down to Henry VIII. The estate was actually won back at the battle of Bosworth to the Red Rose, and Woking was the residence of Margaret, Countess of Richmond, during the latter part of her life.[1] It is most probable that the fine glass of this age anterior to the house was brought either from the earlier house that stood on the same manor, or from the mansion at Woking.

---

was so fine that it was taken as a model for King's College, Cambridge, finished 1516.

For glass in King's College, Cambridge, see *History of Cambridge and its Colleges*, by Professor Willis and J. W. Clark, 1880, vol. i. chap. xi. "Glass in King's College, begun by Bernard Flower, the King's glazier, 1515." It contained portcullis, red and white rose, white rose *en soleil*, hawthorn, H.K., H.E., pomegranate, as seen at Sutton. Bernard Flower died in 1526, and he doubtless executed the pieces anterior to that date.

[1] About 1497 Margaret of Richmond "retired to her patrimony of Woking in Surrey, the manor-house of which had been recently enlarged and repaired by Henry VII. She there fixed her abode, and there she continued to dwell with little intermission for the remainder of her life."—Halsted, *Life of Margaret Beaufort*, p. 195.

The different epochs at which the glass was designed are as follows :—

1. There are some magnificent specimens of the finest painted glass of the time of Henry VIII. Some of these are identical with pieces still to be found in Henry VII.'s Chapel at Westminster, and some others are exactly similar to designs now in the stone or metal work in the chapel.

2. Much of the original glass placed here by the founder, and of his date, still remains. This is as fine in execution as any extant of the period, and is probably by the same hand or from the same works as the glass in the chapel of King's College, Cambridge.

3. Another series of heraldic coats and emblems belongs to the Copley family, and was probably brought from their mansions and inserted here about 1637, when other restorations took place.

4. From time to time additions were made in the upper windows, possibly from neighbouring houses or from dilapidated chapels in Guildford. Many of these are connected with the Onslow and allied families.

5. Lastly, it appears from inscriptions cut with a diamond in some of the upper windows that the glass was repaired first by John Weston in 1724, and secondly in 1844.

Amongst the most noteworthy of the coats and emblems in the windows of the hall are the following :—

1. A series of coats of arms, crowns, crests, and badges for Henry VII., the battle of Bosworth, Sir Reginald Bray, Lord Bourchier, Archbishop Bourchier, the Beaufort portcullis crowned, and the badges of Henry VII. and Elizabeth of York, red and white rose united.

2. White rose *en soleil*, and arms of Richard, Duke of Gloucester.

3. Arms of Henry VIII. impaling those of Catherine of Aragon; also arms of King Arthur and badge of Catherine.

4. Arms of Thomas, second Duke of Norfolk, the victor of Flodden; of Thomas, second Earl of Derby, and Edward, third Earl of Derby; the arms of William Fitzalan, thirteenth Earl of Arundel, 1524; of Stephen Gardiner, Bishop of Winchester, and Bishop White of Winchester.

All of these are very fine specimens of the best work of the early sixteenth century.

5. The arms, crests, and devices of Sir R. Weston, the founder, and others of his family, also of his son-in-law, Sir Walter Dennys, quartering Berkeley—all very fine specimens of glass of 1530.

6. The badge and crown of Jane Seymour (a splendid specimen), the arms of Philip and Mary impaled, and a portrait of Charles II. in painted glass.

7. A series of coats of the Copley, Cecil, Shirley, Paulet, and Onslow families of the seventeenth century.

8. A series of Dutch emblems, grotesques, and scenes, scriptural and rustic, of the middle of the seventeenth century. The dates 1630, 1629, and reference to a book published in 1635, occur here.

The following is an exact account of the glass now found in the hall. For purposes of reference the windows are referred to by a large Roman figure, the lights in each window by a large Arabic numeral. (For convenience, the lights *below* the transoms are numbered as distinct lights). The numbering of the windows begins from the west end of the upper story of the north side of the hall.

I., II., III. are the upper windows on the north side from west to east.

IV., V., VI. are the lower windows on the north side from west to east.

VII., VIII. are the upper windows on the south side from east to west.

IX., X. are the lower windows on the south side from east to west.

The bays are described as north and south bays, upper or lower story. Thus :—

North bay, upper and lower, are the two windows on the side of the court.

South bay, upper and lower, are the two windows on the side of the garden.

The lights are numbered 1-6, or in case of the bays, 1-8, beginning at the top left-hand corner (as looked at), and passing horizontally—in the same way as the quarterings in a heraldic shield are read.

Thus :—

III.

1	2	3
4	5	6

Accordingly, III. 6 stands for the light in the lower right-hand corner of the upper story window next to the bay on the north side of the hall.

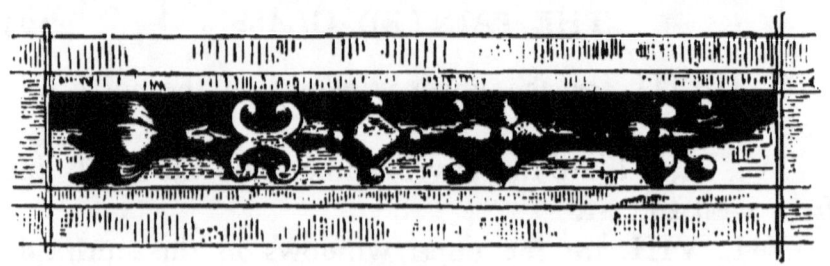

COATS OF ARMS, ETC., IN WINDOWS

Window No. I

I. 1.—HERE was originally the white and red rose united, as in **I. 5, II. 1**, etc. In the centre the portcullis chained *or*, for the Beaufort family or Henry VII. In place of coronet or crown is the head of a king crowned in aureole, probably for Edward the Confessor. This is fine old glass of the beginning of the sixteenth century. This piece has been repaired with old fragments representing flowers and other devices, obviously used in quarries in lower windows, but the pieces are all original, if not earlier than the house. In the sides of this piece are two coats of arms, not visible from the floor, and evidently late additions. They are not in full colours, and are apparently intended for the following :—

A. HOLCROFT quartering CULCHETH, County Lancaster, impaling JENNINGS. Sir T. Holcroft, 1538, married daughter and heiress of N. Jennings of Poynton.

1 and 4. *Argent*, a cross and bordure engrailed *sable*, for HOLCROFT of Holcroft, County Lancaster.

2. *Argent*, an eagle displayed preying on an infant ppr., swaddled *gules*, banded *or*, CULCHETH of Lancaster.

3. *Argent*, a griffin segreant *azure*, armed *or*, CULCHETH of Chester.—See Baines's *Hist. of Lancashire*, iii..129. HOLCROFT impales JENNINGS.

1 and 4. *Argent,* on a fesse *gules,* three bezants, JENNINGS.

2 and 3. *Argent,* a bull's head cabossed *sable,* armed *or,* for DUNSTON. Same as in II. 1.—See J. P. Rylands, *Genealogy of Holcroft,* 1877.

B. The second coat appears to be for NICHOLSON quartering FROMONDE.

1 and 4. *Ermine,* on a pale *sable,* three martlets *argent.*

2 and 3. *Ermine,* a chevron between three fleurs de lys *or.*

FROMONDE—William Copley, born 1565, whose portrait is in the hall, married Margaret Fromonde, and was grandfather of Mary Copley, who married John Weston.

I. 2.—The arms of the See of Winchester impaled with those of JOHN WHITE, Bishop of Winchester, 1557-59, viz. party per chevron, embattled *or* and *gules,* three roses counterchanged, slipped *vert.* On a chief of the second, three hour-glasses, *argent,* framed of the first. The whole surrounded with the Garter. The mitre has been injured and replaced by fragments. These arms were granted by Dethick, Garter King in 1557.

John White was a Marian Bishop, who resigned on the accession of Elizabeth. Sutton Place is in the diocese of Winchester.

This piece of glass is very fine, and the date is fixed by the family arms of the Bishop (see R. Bedford, *The Blazon of Episcopacy,* p. 103, and Warren, *Arms of the English Episcopate*).

I. 3.—Portcullis chained *or,* similar to I. 1, and of date of the house. Remains of a Red Rose with fragments from lower windows, flowers and devices from the original quarries, oak leaves, roses, and daisies of same period. Also two shields A and B (not in colours).

A. Crown and two crosses pattée in pale.

B. *Ermine,* a chevron between three fleurs de lys *or,* FROMONDE.

In the place of the crown over the portcullis is now the

head of an angel, corresponding with the crowned head in aureole in **I. 1**.

I. 4.—Entirely made up of fragments, principally architectural canopies, late Gothic, with some pieces of fleur de lys, Garter, etc., of seventeenth-century work.

I. 5.—A very grand White and Red Rose united with the Crown of Henry VII. This is identical in colour and drawing with the similar rose in Henry VII.'s Chapel at Westminster, and may be taken to be from the workshop of Bernard Flower or his successors, 1515-25. Doubtless this specimen, compared with similar united roses in **II. 3** and **III. 5**, gives us a good idea of the original design in the upper windows.

In one of the lozenge panes below this there is the following inscription cut with a diamond:—

"This Hall was reglazed by Painter James Cruikshank, Mr. D. Laing of 2 Villiers Street, Strand, London, in April 1844."

I. 6.—This light contains an elaborate coat with ornamental mantling, apparently of sixteenth-century work (Elizabethan), and many pieces of different dates, evidently collected from other windows. The most remarkable are four devices of the Crown in Hawthorn Bush, and the initials H. and E. for Henry VII. and Elizabeth of York. These are better seen in the lower south bay, and will be described there. There are other devices from the original work. Besides there are several coats, A, B, C.

A. *Azure*, three saltires *argent* in pale, for LANE quartering MALMAYNES, STRETLEY of Northampton, HUSSEY of Dorset. These are as follows:—

1. *Azure*, three saltires *argent* in pale, possibly meant for LANE.

2. *Azure*, a fesse between six cross crosslets *or*, possibly also for LANE.

3. *Azure*, three sinister gauntlets couped *argent*, MALMAYNES.

4. Gyronny of eight, *or* and *sable*, on a canton *gules*, a covered cup *or*, STRETLEY of Northampton and Oxon.

5. Barry of six, *ermine* and *gules*, HUSSEY of Dorset.

B. Same as I. 1, B.   C. Same as I. 3, B.

The original design for both I. 4 and I. 6 has been completely lost, and it has been replaced in a very careless and unmeaning manner.

Window No. II

II. 1.—Fragments of a White Rose and Crown, similar to I. 5, but imperfect. The crown is exactly similar to examples in Henry VII.'s Chapel.

In a small shield are the arms with names inscribed, apparently PILE and JENNINGS of Hayes, Middlesex. The family of Pile also took the name of GERNON.

PILE—*Gules*, three Piles wavy *argent*, impaling :—

1 and 4. JENNINGS—*Argent*, on a fesse *gules*, three bezants.

2 and 3. DUNSTON—*Or*, a bull's head cabossed *sable*.

II. 2.—This very interesting fragment shows two heads, A and B, of fifteenth-century costume, both with helmets or caps bearing crests or badges. The helmets have been injured and repaired with fragments of mantling.

A. Has a crest with swan's head gorged with a ducal coronet.

B. Has a crest, apparently a bear muzzled. Between them are two White Roses *en soleil*. The *swan* and the *bear* were well-known badges of the Beauchamps, Earls of Warwick, and their descendants. See both together in the seal of Sir Richard de Beauchamp, K.G., fifth Earl of Warwick, died 1439, in Boutell, *English Heraldry*, frontispiece.

These heads are fine and interesting, and are apparently older than the house. One bears some resemblance to the portraits of Richard III. They evidently belong to the White Rose (York), and may have come from the house at Woking.

II. 3.—Remains of a magnificent Red and White united Rose and Crown, similar to that in **I. 5**, evidently from the same workshop as the Rose and Crown in the next window.

In the sides are two shields, both alike, being the arms of ONSLOW, *argent*, a fesse *gules* between six Cornish choughs proper, 3, 2, and 1, impaling a coat, three bucks' head cabossed (2 and 1), a canton *or*, not otherwise tinctured.

II. 4.—In this large shield, similar in shape originally to **I. 4** and **I. 6**, are some very old fragments. Two have the monogram H., crowned in the form of the Dragon, the badge of Henry VII. It is better seen in **V. 5**, a lower window; also the Crown in Hawthorn Bush, and some fine fragments of mantling (original). In the midst of this is inserted a shield of much inferior and later work, being the arms of ONSLOW with their quarterings.

CARR—*Gules*, on a chevron *or*, three mullets *sable*.

HAUGHTON of Chester—*Argent*, three bars *sable*. This coat impales—*sable*, a chevron between three elephants' heads erased *argent*, tusked *or*, a chief *or*; possibly for HUSKISSON of Earth, Sussex, but the tinctures are indistinct and very doubtful.

II. 5.—This very interesting piece gives the arms of Archbishop BOURCHIER. Above is a mitre. Archbishop Bourchier crowned Henry VII. in Westminster Abbey, October 1485, and married Henry VII. to Elizabeth of York, January 1486.

This may have come from an older house, perhaps the Royal Manor of Woking, long the residence of Margaret Beaufort, Henry's mother. The coat shows:—

i. First grand quarter, quarterly—

1 and 4. *Argent*, a cross engrailed *gules* between four water bougets *sable*, BOURCHIER.

2 and 3. *Gules*, billettée *or*, a fesse *argent*, LOVAIN, over all a label of three points *gules*, on each point three lioncels rampant *or*.

ii. Second grand quarter, quarterly—*Or* and *vert*, BERNERS.

iii. as ii.; iv. as i.

Also in small shields, carelessly mended, are—ONSLOW impaling three stags' heads cabossed *sable*, a canton *or* (?).

In this very fine old design there are many of the original ornamental pieces, fleur de lys, devices of birds, and ornamental initials and monograms.

One of these is 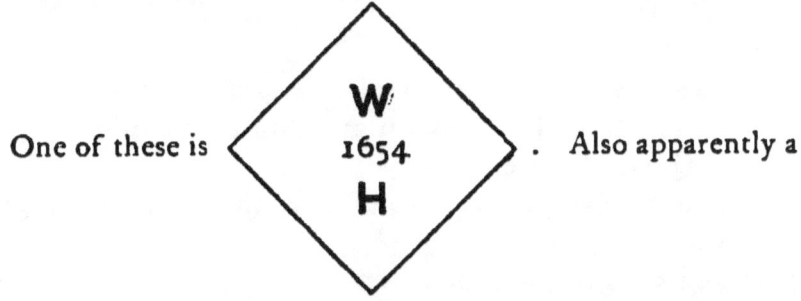 . Also apparently a merchant's or artist's monogram [? James.Nicholson]  .

There is also T. C., doubtless for Sir Thomas Copley, and I. P., both with string ornaments in the Henri II. French manner (1550).

There are also, apparently of later date, two small shields of eight quarterings. These are (A) apparently for William Cecil, second Earl of Exeter, 1613, married Lady Elizabeth Manners, Baroness Roos, only daughter of Edward, third Earl of Rutland.—See J. Doyle, *Official Baronage of England*, i. 716, and iii. 190.

These coats are (A) CECIL impaling MANNERS.

(A) 1. Barry of ten, *argent* and *azure*, over all six escutcheons, 3, 2, 1, *sable*, each charged with a lioncel rampant of the first, CECIL.

2. Per pale *gules* and *azure*, a lion rampant *argent*, holding a tree eradicated *vert*, WYNSTON of Hereford.

3. *Or*, two bars *azure*, a chief quarterly *azure* and *gules*, 1 and 4 charged with two fleurs de lys, 2 and 3 with a lion passant guardant, all *or*, MANNERS.

4. *Gules*, three water bougets *argent*, DE ROOS.

5. (Broken) ? *gules*, a saltire *argent*, NEVILL.

6. *Or*, fretty *gules*, on a canton *argent*, a ship *sable*, NEVILL of Bulmer.

7. *Gules*, a lion passant guardant *argent*, crowned *or*.

8. *Gules*, three lions passant guardant *or*, a bordure *argent*.

(B) Quarterly of eight—

1 and 6. *Ermine*, on a pale *sable*, three martlets *argent*, NICHOLSON.

2 and 5. *Gules*, a chevron cottised between three trefoils, slipped *or*.

3. *Argent*, on a bend *sable* (or *azure*), between two eagles' heads erased, a rose *argent*, a bordure engrailed *sable* (or *azure*).

4. *Gules*, on a bend wavy *argent*, three martlets *sable*.

7. *Argent*, a fesse between three boars' heads erased *sable*.

8. *Argent*, a chevron engrailed *gules* between three bugle horns *sable*, stringed *or*, PETIT.

II. 6.—The design in this light has been much injured, and the centre replaced with a very poor and late Rose in Garter with Crown. There are four initial letters

| H | W |

(twice), apparently for Sir Henry Weston, 1560. There is also an M. crowned, and H. E. with the Crown in the Hawthorn Tree. These are of earlier date. The M. may stand for Queen Mary, but probably is for Margaret, Queen of Scotland, or Mary, Queen of France, both sisters of Henry VIII. Sir Richard Weston was one of the knights who went with Mary Tudor to France on her marriage with Louis XII. in 1514.

Window No. III

III. 1.—This light originally contained a Red and White Rose, of which only the extremities remain, with the ornamental devices of flowers, animals, etc., of original glass.

In place of the Rose has been inserted an old inscription of which all we now see is—O PRETIU EST DAT HONORES MICITIAS IBIQUE. IA. Probably not later than the house.

It may be noted that at King's College, Cambridge, are similar mottoes—*Sola salus servire Deo*—*Sapientiae et felicitatis* (Willis and Clark, i. 578).

There are also two shields of later date.

A. 1. *Argent*, a fesse *gules* between two crescents and a bugle horn, stringed *vert*, NEALE, Hants, 1579, impaling *sable*, two bars *or*, in chief three mullets *or*, FREKE of Dorset.

B. 1 and 4. *Argent*, on a fesse *sable*, three mullets *or*, in chief two dragons' heads couped, in base a cross formée fitchée *sable*, POUND.

2. *Argent*, three fleurs de lys, two and one *sable*, ARDEN.

3. *Argent*, a chevron between three eagles' legs erased *sable*, BRAY.

III. 2.—Here has been an original White and Red Rose, crowned, with fragments of the Garter. Pieces have been inserted badly. The fragments show—

1. *Vair*, 4. *gules*, a saltire *argent*, for NEVILL, very fine in colour.

Also fragments of a coat *sable*, two lions passant *or*.

III. 3.—Remains of an original Rose, with floral designs surrounding it. In the place of the Rose has been inserted an inscription similar to that in **III. 1**—NON EST MIHI SAPIE RE VIVAM SERA NIM ASTINA DIE. Beside this is a shield, ENGLAND, in a garter, and the following device— 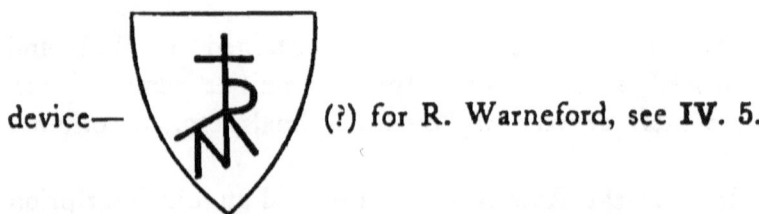 (?) for R. Warneford, see **IV. 5.**

III. 4.—This light contains, with fragments of original devices, a large and much more recent coat of STRANGEWAYS quartering RATCLIFFE, and impaling HOWSON of London (1605). The crest, a lion passant paly *argent* and *gules*, has been reversed in repairs.

STRANGEWAYS is *sable*, two lions passant in pale, paly of six, *argent* and *gules*.

RATCLIFFE of Essex is *argent*, a bend engrailed *sable*, an escallop in chief *sable*.

HOWSON, quarterly *argent* and *sable*, four roundels counter-changed.

The date below is 1621.

Sir R. Onslow, M.P., temp. Charles I., married Elizabeth, daughter and heiress of Richard Strangeways, County Durham.

There are also two small coats at side.

A. Same as I. 1, B., crest, a leopard pierced through with an arrow.

B. ONSLOW impaling SWAN, a crescent for difference.

III. 5.—Here is a magnificent specimen of the old Red and White Rose united, seeded *or*, with the crown of Henry VII. This is doubtless from the same artist who produced the Roses in Westminster Abbey (compare **I. 5**).

III. 6.—This light is uninjured. In it is a fine specimen of the coat of STRANGEWAYS quartering RATCLIFFE, with mantling, crest complete, a lion as in the arms, and also dated 1621. Same as dexter side of coat **III. 4**, which see.

1 and 4. STRANGEWAYS.

2 and 3. *Argent*, a bend engrailed *sable*, in chief an escallop *sable*, RATCLIFFE of Essex.

Compare the Onslow quarterings in the ancient glass windows of West Clandon Church, and the fine illuminated pedigree of the family in the possession of the Earl of Onslow.

Window No. IV

IV. 1.—We have here, nearly perfect, a very fine design contemporary with the house, and of the finest glass of the period.[1]

It is the coat of arms of Edward, third Earl of Derby, K.G., impaling those of his first wife, Dorothy, daughter of Thomas, second Duke of Norfolk. The coronet is wanting. He may not at this time have succeeded to the title, if the glass is earlier than 1522.

The arms of this Duke of Norfolk, his father-in-law, are found in **IV. 3**, and those of Thomas, second Earl of Derby, his father, are in **IV. 3**.

This Edward, Earl of Derby, succeeded his father in 1522, and was third in descent from the Lord Derby who contributed to the victory at Bosworth. He was High Steward at the coronation of Queen Mary, and was Chamberlain of Chester under Elizabeth. He was celebrated for his magnificence. He died in 1572. This coat may date from any year after his marriage (see *Memoirs of the House of Stanley*, 4to, 1767).

The quarters for Howard on the feme side are quite similar to those of the Duke of Norfolk in **IV. 3**, and are no doubt of the same age.

It will be observed that the coats of the Lords Derby here

---

[1] It will be noticed that in the coats *gules* (both here in **IV. 1**, as in **IV. 3**, **V. 1**, **V. 3**, **VI. 3**, and in south bay) the pattern is produced by grinding off the ruby glass so as to produce white or yellow objects on a red ground. This is now effected by fluoric acid. The use of the diamond was not known before the seventeenth century. The ruby glass became gradually thinner in successive ages. The effect of this process is that of an intaglio, the charge being engraved like a seal on the field.—See Winston, *Style in Ancient Glass-Painting*, 1847, p. 119; H. J. Powell, *Principles of Glass-Painting*, p. 99.

and in **V. 1** differ very slightly, and are both nearly the same as those represented on the bronze tomb of Margaret, Countess of Richmond, in Westminster Abbey, for their ancestor, her third husband.

The coat of Edward, third Earl of Derby, is :—

i. First grand quarter, quarterly—

1 and 4. STANLEY—*Argent*, on a bend *azure*, three bucks' heads cabossed *or*.

2 and 3. LATHOM—*Or*, on a chief indented *azure*, three plates.

ii. and iii. ISLE OF MAN, of which Earl of Derby was king. *Gules*, three legs conjoined in the fesse point in armour proper, garnished and spurred *or*.

iv. Quarterly—

1 and 4. STRANGE—*Gules*, two lions passant guardant in pale *argent*.

2. WIDVILLE—*Argent*, a fesse and canton *gules*.

3. MOHUN—*Or*, a cross engrailed *sable*.

On an escutcheon of pretence is DE MONTALT, *azure*, a lion rampant *argent*.

See Brayley, *Westminster Abbey*, Tomb of Margaret of Richmond; J. Doyle, *Baronage*, i. 553.

The only difference between these coats is that the coat of the father, **V. 1**, quarters WARREN; that of the son, **IV. 1**, quarters also MOHUN.

It will be observed that the quartering of Widville in **IV. 1** is *or*, a fesse and canton *gules*. *Or* is evidently an error for *argent*. It is correctly shown in **V. 1**, and in upper south bay **3**.

It will be noticed that neither this coat, **VI. 1**, nor that of the Duke of Norfolk, **IV. 3**, nor that of the second Earl of Derby, **V. 1**, show any traces of the Garter, as they all impale the arms of their wives.

The arms of Dorothy, daughter of Thomas, Duke of Norfolk, are given on the feme side. They are as follows :—

1. Lost and replaced by a fragment of mantling; 2. Howard; 3. Warren; 4. Mowbray, damaged. The peculiarity that Howard is in the second place in this coat, as it is in **IV. 3**, will be noticed presently.

IV. 2.—A magnificent shield of the arms of COPLEY, probably the coat of Sir Roger Copley of Roffey, about 1530. The quarterings are similar to those in the painted panel in the gallery dated 1567, with initials R. C.; but this glass has no escutcheon for Luttrell, the wife of Sir T. Copley. It shows in six quarterings, badly re-set and broken.

1. COPLEY; 2 and 5, WATERTON.

3. Has been removed, and in its place we have a fine fragment of the lions from some coat of ENGLAND,[1] and a fragment of what is intended for ST. OMER, *azure*, a fesse between six cross crosslets *or*.

4. Is Leo, LORD WELLES; 6 is LORD HOO AND HASTINGS. Compare the Copley coats in **VI. 2**, and in the upper south bay.

These coats belong to the family of Copley about the time of the founder, and are of glass of that date. A question arises how they came here. John Weston married the heiress of Copley in 1637, a hundred years later. Possibly these Copley coats were brought and inserted here about that date at the same time as the three panels or escutcheons of Sir T. Copley, 1567, or they were inserted in the hall at the building. Sir Roger Copley (1540) was a grandson of Sir G. Boleyn, and the Copley and Weston families were connected long before the marriage. Sir R. Copley was High-Sheriff of Surrey at the time of the building of the house.[2]

IV. 3. We have here a magnificent piece of glass of the

---

[1] See the corresponding fleurs de lys, which have slipped into the Copley coat in **VI. 2**.

[2] Note on **IV. 2** as to pedigree of Copley, communicated to F. H. Salvin by D. G. C. Elwes, Esq. "LEO, LORD WELLS, married for his first wife Joan, daughter and heiress of SIR ROBERT WATERTON, Knight. His second wife was Margaret, daughter and heiress of SIR JOHN BEAUCHAMP of Bletsoe. His daughter Eleanor married Thomas, LORD HOO AND HASTINGS. The

date of the foundation. The coronet is damaged. Note that the field of ruby glass is deeply incised, to show the charges. This is the coat of Thomas, second Duke of Norfolk, Earl Marshal, K.G., and Lord Treasurer (1514), died 1524, at the age of eighty. He commanded the English at the battle of Flodden, where James IV. of Scotland was killed, 1513. He was Treasurer of England whilst Sir R. Weston was Under-Treasurer. He was grandfather of the Queens Catherine Howard and Anne Boleyn, and also of Margaret Howard, Lady Arundell, and thus he was great-grandfather of Dorothy, Lady Weston (1560). On the feme side are the arms of Tilney. TILNEY—*Argent*, a chevron between three griffins' heads erased *gules*, beaked *or*. The Duke married successively Elizabeth, daughter and heiress of Sir Frederick Tilney, and Agnes, sister and heiress of Sir Philip Tilney. This coat is for the second wife, who was mother of Dorothy, Countess of Derby, in **IV. 1.**

This coat of the Duke of Norfolk, and also that for Dorothy, his daughter, **IV. 1,** show a very great and interesting peculiarity. The arms borne by the Dukes of Norfolk are, as is well known :—

1. *Howard*.
2. *England* (*differenced*), for Thomas de Brotherton, son of Edward I.
3. *Warren*.
4. *Mowbray* (or recently *Fitzalan*). The two coats in these lights (about which there cannot be the least doubt that they represent the Norfolk arms at the date 1530), show —1. Blank (lost) in both cases ; 2. *Howard;* 3. *Warren;*

latter married first Elizabeth, daughter and heiress of Sir Thomas Felton, Knight ; second, Elizabeth, daughter and heiress of SIR NICHOLAS WICKINGHAM, Knight, by whom he had an only daughter, Anne, married to Sir Geoffrey Bullen or Boleyn, Knight, Lord Mayor of London ; third, Eleanor, daughter of Leo, Lord Wells, sister and at length co-heir to Richard, Lord Wells. The daughter of Thomas, Lord Hoo and Hastings, by Eleanor, daughter of Lord Wells, was Anne (or Jane), married to Sir Roger Copley."

4. *Mowbray.* Examination shows that in both cases the glass bearing the arms of Howard was painted for the second, and not for the first quarter. Unquestionably, the first quarter in both was occupied by the missing arms of *de Brotherton*, possibly without the label of cadency. It is well known that Lord Surrey, the grandson of this Thomas, second Duke of Norfolk, was executed, and also Thomas, the third Duke, the son of the second Duke, was attainted in 1546 on charges of high treason, one of the proofs being that they had improperly borne the royal arms. The Duke, upon his trial, admitted that he had borne the arms of De Brotherton in the first quarter (see Howell's *State Trials*, vol. i. p. 457, Confession of Thomas, Duke of Norfolk, 38 Hen. VIII. 1546). "I do likewise confess," he says, "that to the peril, slander, and disinherison of the King's Majesty and his noble son, Prince Edward, his son and heir apparent, I have against all right unjustly and without authority borne in the first quarter of my arms ever since the death of my father the arms of England, with a difference of the labels of silver * * *, which I know and confess by the laws of the realm to be High Treason." There is said to be no extant example of this peculiar quartering in the case of the Duke himself. But the royal lions were borne in the first quarter by some families at that date, *e.g.* by Stafford, Duke of Buckingham. It is found in seals of William Berkeley:—dexter side, *de Brotherton;* sinister side, *Berkeley.* Also of Elizabeth, Duchess of Norfolk, which is:—dexter side, *de Brotherton;* sinister side, *Howard* and *Warren*, quarterly. In the *Memorials of Howard*, by Henry Howard, 1834, folio, p. 9, in a portrait of the victor of Flodden, from a book of heraldry, 1597, the arms are quartered—1. Brotherton; 2. Howard; 3. Warren; 4. Mowbray.[1]

---

[1] An example of the arms of John Howard, first Duke of Norfolk, with the royal arms of *De Brotherton* in the first quarter, is to be found in MS. E., Philpott's Press, in the College of Arms (MS. Letter of Charles A. Buckler).

Doubtless they were shown so here originally. But on the attainder of Lord Surrey and the Duke, in 1546, the compromising lions of England were rudely removed by the widow, Lady Weston, or by the Anne Pickering whose husband, Sir Francis Weston, had been executed ten years before. These windows, if we assume, as we must, that the first quarter contained originally the royal arms, are quite independent evidence that the Howards, Dukes of Norfolk, had borne their coat in that form in a preceding generation, and twenty-two years before the attainder. And it will be noticed that they were so shown in the hall of a colleague, in which it is certain that Henry VIII., Wolsey, Cromwell, and other ministers of the king were frequently in council with him. It throws new light on the monstrous absurdity and iniquity of this particular charge against the Duke and the Earl of Surrey.

In the brass effigy of this Duke of Norfolk, on his tomb at Thetford, his arms are given impaling those of Tilney for his wife, Agnes (see H. Howard, *Memorials*, p. 29).

IV. 4.—Fragments of heads, rudely mended, the Stafford knot, and a bit of the Garter.

IV. 5.—A quarry of four curious devices of original glass; two are the well-known Bourchier knot forming a double B. Sir John Bourchier, Lord Berners, the famous soldier, author and statesman, was Lieutenant of Calais 1521-32, and there he died in 1532. Sir R. Weston was at that date Treasurer of Calais. Sir John Bourchier, Lord Berners, was Chancellor of the Exchequer whilst Sir R. Weston was Under-Treasurer. He was the friend of Caxton, the translator of Froissart, and one of the foremost of those who in the age of Henry VIII. promoted the extension of European culture.

Here is also a coat—Party per fesse embattled *argent* and *sable* [sic], six crosses pattée, 3 and 3 counterchanged, a crescent for difference. A motto, DA MIHI FERRE CRVCES. At each side are the initials R.W. This must be for one of the family of WARNEFORD of Warneford Place, Wilts. Above, in place of crest, is a Latin cross. The family crest is a garb proper.

IV. 6.—Fragments badly replaced and unintelligible.

Window No. V

V. 1.—A very fine coat of the date of the house. It gives the arms of Thomas, second Earl of Derby, grandson of the first Earl, husband of Margaret Beaufort. He impales the arms of Anne, daughter of Lord Hastings of Hungerford, whom he married, 1507. This Lord Derby succeeded his grandfather in 1504, and died in 1522 (see J. Doyle, *Official Baronage*, i. 553).

The coat of this Lord Derby is almost identical with that of his son, the third Earl, Window IV. 1, except that in the first grand quarter, No. 3, he quarters WARREN, checky *or* and *azure*, and in fourth grand quarter, No. 3, he omits MOHUN and repeats WIDVILLE, as in No. 2. The coat impales HASTINGS of Hungerford, as he married Anne, the daughter of Edward, Lord Hastings of Hungerford. On the feme side the coat displays quarterly—

1. HASTINGS—*Argent*, a maunch *sable*.
2. HUNGERFORD—*Sable*, two bars *argent*, in chief three plates.
3. BOTREAUX—*Argent*, a griffin segreant *gules*.
4. MOLEYNS—Paly wavy of six, *or* and *gules*.

It will be observed that this glass, like that in IV. 1, IV. 3, and others, is of "pot metal," the colour being run in the glass (see Winston, *Memoirs*, 1865, p. 79), and in the ruby pieces the charge is produced by grinding the surface. Owing to this, the charge on the Hastings coat, No. 3, looks like two garbs, and is not like a griffin at all. Compare COMYN of York, *argent*, three garbs *gules*, banded *or*. This was, however, the designer's intention (see J. Doyle, *Baronage*, ii. 150 ;

Papworth and Morant; Banks's *Dormant Baronage*, vol. ii. etc.) The coat, No. 4, is sometimes attributed to MOELS, also a bearing of HASTINGS. This Lord Derby, according to Collins, iii., was Viscount Kynton, Lord Stanley and Strange, Lord of Knokyn, Mohun, Basset, Burnal, and Lacy, Lord of Man and the Isles. His wife, Anne, sister of George Hastings, Earl of Huntingdon, was daughter of Lord Hastings, who was, in right of his wife, Lord Hungerford, Botreaux, Moleyns, Moels, and de Homet. Hence these quarterings. They are explained by reference to the pedigree on page 221.

V. 2.—A magnificent head of Saracen, the crest of SIR RICHARD WESTON (see chap. iii. p. 88, and chap. vii. p. 144), with wreath and "tun," green, blue, and red. This seems nearly perfect, and is one of the original pieces *in situ*. Doubtless several of the lower windows were filled with these heads. Compare lower south bay No. 5, and X. 2.

V. 3.—A very fine coat of COPLEY, nearly perfect, the quarterings of which are all shown in the painted escutcheons dated 1568 (see chap. xi.) But this coat is evidently earlier, and of the date of the house, or shortly afterwards. It is quarterly of six—

1. COPLEY—*Argent*, a cross moline *sable*, a crescent for difference.

2. Hoo—Quarterly *sable* and *argent*.

3. ST. OMER—*Azure*, a fesse between six crosses crosslet *or*, a quartering of Hoo (see Banks's *Dormant Baronage*, iii. 376; and also the seal of Sir W. de Hungerford, died 1410, *Archæological Journal*, xiii. 195). This piece has been broken and badly mended. The fesse in ST. OMER has been replaced by a fragment of SHELLEY, turned on its side in a very clumsy way. The marriage of Sir Roger Copley with Elizabeth Shelley was after 1530.

4. WELLES—*Or*, a lion rampant double queued *sable*.

5. ENGAINE—*Gules*, a fesse dancettée between six crosses crosslet *or*.

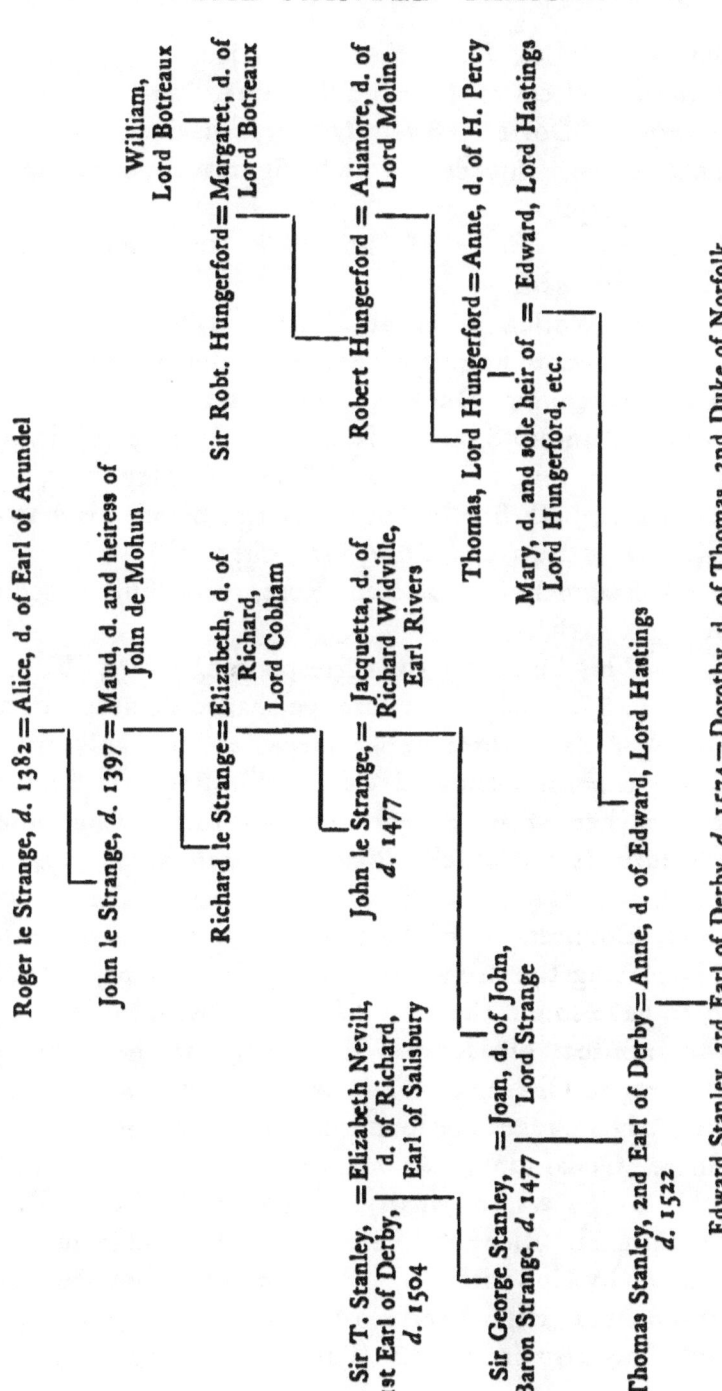

Adam de Welles, Lord Welles, married, 1299, Margaret, daughter and heiress of John de Engaine, Lord of Grimsby before 1295 (J. Doyle, *Official Baronage*, iii. 605).

Hence comes this coat which figures so often in the Copley quarterings.

6. WATERTON—Barry of six, *ermine* and *gules*, over all three crescents *sable*.

Leo, Lord Welles, killed at Towton, 1461, married, first, Joan, daughter and heiress of Sir R. Waterton, and, second, Margaret Beauchamp, Duchess of Somerset.

This coat, unless SHELLEY is improperly inserted in it, as seems probable, might be for Sir Thomas Copley, born 1535, the son of Elizabeth Shelley, but of course before his marriage with Katherine Luttrell (*Escutcheons*, chap. xi.)

V. 4.—Fragments of a Red Rose, very fine in colour, restored.

V. 5.—This light, like the corresponding lights, **IV. 5, VI. 5, IX. 5, X. 5**, contains four lozenge-shaped devices, arranged in a lozenge. The three upper pieces are probably original, two of them being curious devices of Sir Reginald Bray, one a hemp-crusher, *bray*, of very curious form; the other a *Hawk's* lure (see Boutell, *English Heraldry*, p. 104, and Manning, pp. 514-525). Sir R. Bray was in the service of Margaret, Countess of Richmond, and was an active instrument in placing the crown on the head of Henry VII., and is said to have found the crown in the hawthorn bush. He was the architect of Henry VII.'s Chapel in the Abbey, and of St. George's Chapel at Windsor. He laid the first stone in 1502. His badges are found in many churches in Surrey, *e.g.* Shere, Godalming. As he died in 1504, it is unlikely that this badge was originally placed in the hall. But he served with Sir Richard Weston; or the badge may have been used by inheritance. Sir Edmond Bray of Stoke d'Abernon was High-Sheriff of Surrey in 1521, and Sir Edward Bray also in 1538. The third lozenge contains an initial H. crowned, formed by a dragon, probably for Henry VII. This occurs also in **II. 4.** See it in A. W. Franks's *Ornamental Glazing Quarries*, p. 98.

The fourth lozenge contains a crest—a demi-bull, collared and chained, a crest of HASTINGS.

V. 6.—Fragments of a Red Rose, badly restored.

Window No. VI

VI. 1.—This is a fine coat of arms, being the arms of Henry VIII. impaling those of Catherine of Aragon. This is probably nearly perfect, but is without the Crown. He was king at his marriage. Part of a lion passant remains. The coat shows on baron side France and England; on feme side—

1 and 4. Grand quarters—LEON and CASTILE, quarterly.

2 and 3. Grand quarters—ARAGON impaling SICILY, per saltire, BRABANT (Willement, *Royal Heraldry*, p. 67; Jenkins, *Heraldry*, 1886, p. 83, where these quarterings are shown and explained; see H. Woodward and Burnett, *Heraldry*, 1892, p. 495).

VI. 2.—A fine shield for the COPLEY family, somewhat transposed, but probably for Sir Thomas Copley, about 1560.

It is much injured and badly restored.

It may have been originally quarterly of eight.

1. COPLEY; 4. (?) broken, *azure*, fretty *argent* (?) ETCHINGHAM.

5. WELLES; 8. HOO.

2, 3, 6, 7, appear to have been badly repaired and transposed, and have a fragment, as it were in chief, *azure*, three fleurs de lys *or*, from some older royal coat.

There are also BELKNAP, *azure*, three eagles in bend between two cottises *argent*, quartered with SHELLEY, *sable*, a fesse engrailed between three whelk shells *or*. Sir W. Shelley, Chief-Justice of the King's Bench, 1521, married

Alice, daughter of Sir H. Belknap of Essex. Their daughter, Elizabeth, married Sir Roger Copley. Also there seem to be coats—*or*, two bendlets *gules*, SUDELEY, and *azure*, on a bend flanché *or*, a hawk *argent*.

VI. 3.—A grand coat of the finest glass, contemporary with the house or older, being probably a fanciful coat for the ancient kings of Wales, and representing Henry VII. or Henry VIII. as hereditary King of Wales or England by descent from the Britons. It is quarterly.

1 and 4. *Or*, lion statant regardant *gules*.

2 and 3. *Azure*, three ducal coronets in bend *or*.

The traditional arms of WALES are—

Quarterly, 1 and 4. *Gules*, a lion passant guardant *or*.

2 and 3. *Or*, a lion passant guardant *gules*.

The piece is surrounded with a wreath in fine old work, and above is a lion passant. The ruby glass is deeply incised. See Heylin's *Help to History of England*, pp. 7, 20; Papworth, p. 593. *Azure*, three crowns *or*, for King Arthur (Sandford, *Royal Genealogies*, p. 277).

VI. 4.—A circular piece enclosing the arms of England and France, and crown, with fragments of the Garter. R. with crown, from device H.R., and apparently another *bray*, device of Sir Reginald Bray (see **V. 5**, badly restored).

VI. 5.—The lozenge piece enclosing four lozenge devices—

1. Arms of England and France quarterly.
2. A tulip, finely drawn, see the same in **X. 5**.
3. A parrot.
4. Grotesque, more recent, a man shearing a pig, or a pig in ram's fleece.

VI. 6.—This interesting circular piece encloses, with fragments of royal arms and the Garter, a portrait of Charles II., probably at the date of his restoration, ætat. 30, 1660. He wears the ribbon of the Garter. The portrait has the Crown and C.R. Though the portrait is not very life-like, and is apparently that of a younger man, it is hardly probable that this piece, to which the iron bar of the window is adapted, could have been placed here during the Commonwealth. Brayley (*History of Surrey*, ii. p. 20) calls this a portrait of Charles I., and indeed it is almost as much like him as his son.

Upper North Bay

U. N. Bay 1.—This light has a magnificent specimen of a Red and White Rose, dimidiated with green petals, the Rose being party per pale *argent* and *gules*, with the Tudor Crown, and probably with a wreath and monogram, H.R., as in upper south bay 1.

This glass is evidently identical with similar roses and crowns in Henry VII.'s Chapel in the Abbey.

U. N. Bay 2.—Here is a very fine coat, contemporary with the founder, for a Bishop of Winchester, with Garter and Mitre. But the piece has been broken and badly repaired.

The dexter side gives the arms of the see imperfectly, *gules*, a sword and *one* key in saltire *argent*, badly mended.

The sinister side seems to be—

Azure, on a chief *argent*, a saltire *gules* (? St. Patrick), or this may be that *azure* is a restoration or clumsy repair.

Round, with fragments of Garter, are some letters, apparently ABP-OS-T·E., or APS-OS-A·T·S. Doubtless, this once contained the arms of Cardinal Wolsey.

U. N. Bay 3.—Another magnificent coat of arms for Gardiner, Bishop of Winchester.

On the dexter side is, in chief—

Gules, two keys in bend, *argent* and *or*, between them a sword of the second.

And in base is—

Gules, three crescents *argent* (?), careless restoration, taken from another coat.

On the sinister side are the arms of GARDINER. *Azure*, on a cross *or*, between four griffins' heads erased, a cinquefoil *gules*, pierced of the second (see Rev. R. Bedford, *Blazon of Episcopacy*, 1858, p. 103).

Stephen Gardiner, 1483-1555, was Bishop of Winchester from 1531-52; he was in France with Wolsey, 1527; and ambassador to the Pope, 1528. He was Master of Trinity Hall, Cambridge, from 1525-49, and again, 1553-55. He was also Archdeacon of Norfolk.

U. N. BAY 4.—A splendid Red and White Rose with Tudor Crown. The crown and wreath are almost perfect. The rose has been broken.

These are doubtless contemporary with the house, and from the factory of Bernard Flower. Henry VII.'s Chapel was filled with pieces from the same workmanship.

Upper North Bay (Lower Half)

Windows **5, 6, 7, 8** are apparently ONSLOW coats, and their quarterings of seventeenth or late sixteenth-century work.

U. N. BAY 5.—Quarterly of six.

1, 2, 3 are apparently removed and replaced by a large hand, the sleeve striped *or*, holding a fish *vert*. But this is not heraldic, nor from a coat.

4. CARR—*Gules*, on a chevron *or*, three mullets *sable*. Edward Carr married Jane, daughter of Sir Edward Onslow, who died 1571. (?) COBHAM of Kent.

5. Now simply *azure*.

6. *Argent, gouttée du sang*, a lion rampant *sable*, KYNASTON. John de Onslow, 8 Henry VI., married Margaret, daughter and heiress of Madoc Kynaston of Shropshire (Collins, *Hist. Peerage*, v. 462).

This impales the coat of SHIRLEY of Sussex quartering BREWSE or BRAOSE, *azure*, semée of crosslets, a lion rampant *or*, langued *gules*.

Sir Edward Onslow, died 1571, married Elizabeth, daughter of Sir Thomas Shirley of Sussex. The coat shows—

1 and 4. SHIRLEY—Paly of six, *or* and *azure*, a canton *ermine*.

2 and 3. BRAOSE, as above.

U. N. BAY 6.—COKE impaling PILLETT.

Quarterly—

1 and 4. COKE—Party per pale *gules* and *azure*, three eagles displayed *argent*.

2 and 3. *Argent*, a chevron *azure* between three torteaux, on each a saltire of the first : (?) wreaths.

Feme side is PILLETT—*Sable*, a chevron *argent* between three covered cups *or*.

U. N. BAY 7.—Broken fragments, badly replaced and unintelligible.

U. N. BAY 8.—ONSLOW—Quarterly of six. Same as dexter side of Window **II. 4.**

1 and 6. ONSLOW—*Argent*, a fesse *gules* between six Cornish choughs proper, a crescent for difference.

N.B. The piece above the fesse is broken and lost.

2. KYNASTON—*Argent, gouttée du sang*, a lion rampant *sable*, langued *gules*.

3. CARR—*Gules*, on a chevron *or*, three mullets *sable*.

4. *Argent*, on a chevron *sable*, three bezants. (?) BOND, County Devon.

5. Barry of six, *sable* and *argent*, a canton *argent*. Underneath is the date 1639, which may be transposed. HOUGHTON.

Lower North Bay

L. N. BAY 1.—A magnificent original piece, the device of the founder, the tun with wreaths. Quite perfect and very brilliant.

L. N. BAY 2.—A fine old coat, damaged, but apparently party per bend *sable* and *or;* it may be *or*, a greyhound, monkey, or monster *sable*, on a chief *sable*, three bezants.

Above is an old White Rose *en soleil*, the badge of the house of York, also in the next light.

L. N. BAY 3.—This very magnificent and interesting piece gives us the coat of Richard, Duke of Gloucester, being the royal arms, with a label of three points *ermine*, on each point a canton *gules* (see Boutell's *Heraldry*, Royal Cadency, p. 222), with the White Rose *en soleil*. The colouring and design of this splendid specimen of the coat of Richard as Duke is singularly fine. It remains a doubt how the coat, which must be older than the house by forty years, came in so conspicuous a position in the hall where Henry VIII. was undoubtedly entertained by his Minister. After his accession, June 1483, the coat of Richard, as Duke of Gloucester, could not have been shown thus. It has no doubt been reset. It may have come from the older house, or from the hall at Woking. Both this manor of Sutton and that of Woking undoubtedly were in the possession of Richard III. as king.

L. N. BAY 4.—Here was the device of the "tun," with a wreath similar to No. 1. In lieu of the tun we now see architectural fragments of Perpendicular style, beginning of sixteenth century.

L. N. BAY 5.—Picture of sheep-shearing—seventeenth century; poor work; pigs and bullocks at the side; an owl holding a mirror, a fox and some flowers and birds are of original and much finer glass.

Lights 6 and 7, both here and in lower south bay, are filled with lozenge ornaments made up of nine lozenges. Many of these are original.

L. N. BAY 6.—A portcullis crowned, a grasshopper, and a fox are fine original designs and very interesting. Then come grotesques, a monkey playing on a guitar, and an eagle playing on the same, with a crest, a horse's head couped (now *brown*, probably *or* and *gules*, armed and plumed), and a crescent for difference. Then a curious and interesting monogram design dated

```
   ┌─────────────┐
   │      W      │
   │  I.    A.   │
   │    1567     │
   └─────────────┘
```

intertwined with a true lover's knot. It is uncertain for which of the Weston family this is.

Sir Henry Weston, an only child, and Dorothy Arundell had been married apparently in 1560; Lady Anne (Pickering) was now Lady Knyvett, and at least forty-five. Richard, the eldest son of Sir Henry, was born in 1564, and married Jane Dister in 1583. This may have been for the betrothal of the infants.

There is also twice repeated a later design, a book with a ducal coronet above it; on the dexter page a heart and three stars above; on the sinister, a key. Motto, *Respice, Suspice*, 1630.

L. N. BAY 7.—Here is another quarry of nine lozenges; many of them are original and very finely drawn.[1]

The first is a marguerite or double daisy rising out of a tun. This is undoubtedly a rebus for Margaret, the daughter of the founder, the wife of Sir Walter Dennys, whose magnificent coat of arms is seen in **X. 3**. Below this is a camel, probably from the arms of CAMELL, borne by the founder, but certainly later in date; the White Rose *en soleil*, same as in **2** and **3**, is fine; an eagle's head erased, a mushroom, a design of an eye in the sun, the crest of BLUNT of Maple-Durham. A shield *argent*, a chevron between three fleurs de lys (?) *gules* (now brown), a crest, a white hart lodged, attired and hoofed *or*, collared with oak leaves and acorns *vert*, a crescent for difference, BELLASIS, Yorkshire, or BELASYSE, County Lincoln.

---

[1] As to *quarries* (from quarrel, *quadrellum*, low Latin) see A. W. Franks, *Ornamental Glazing Quarries*, 1849, where several of these specimens are given.

In the centre is a complete coat of arms of Spain, impaling those of England, being no doubt for Philip of Spain and Mary, 1554. Sir Henry Weston, the then owner of the estate, defended Calais for the Queen. This coat, which is contemporary, is merely drawn, and not coloured. The arms of Philip are nearly the same as those of Catherine of Aragon in **VI. 1**, except that they quarter FRANCE within a bordure gobonated for BURGUNDY, and FLANDERS—*Or*, a lion rampant crowned *sable*. See Woodward and Burnett, p. 495.

L. N. BAY 8.—The arms of COPLEY, with mantling and crest complete, probably of late sixteenth-century work, far inferior to the original design.

Here is a fragment also seen in **VIII. 4**; a circular enclosure, with palisade.

Upper South Bay

This contains in its upper lights some splendid examples of glass of the date of the house, uniform with the upper tier of lights in upper north bay. The lower lights, as in north bay, have later (Copley) coats.

U. S. BAY 1.—A magnificent Red Rose crowned and in wreath. This is very rich in colour and quite perfect. The wreath bears the monogram HR.

U. S. BAY 2.—Royal arms of England with Crown and Garter; perfect, and very fine in colour and design.

U. S. BAY 3.—The arms of William Fitzalan, thirteenth Earl of Arundel, K.G., succeeded to the earldom 1524, died 1544. He was Lieutenant of Calais, 1541. He was the son of Margaret Widville, daughter of Earl Rivers, and was cousin of Henry VIII. (see *History of Arundel*, by M. A. Tierney, 1834, vol. i.; Doyle, *Official Baronage*, vol. i.) His coat, which has the Coronet and Garter, shows—

1. FITZALAN of Arundel—*Gules*, a lion rampant *or*. The brilliancy of this in the mid-day sun is extraordinary.

2. FITZALAN of Bedale—Barry of eight *or* and *gules*.
3. WIDVILLE—*Argent*, a fesse and canton *gules*.
4. Quarterly, being—
    1 and 4. MALTRAVERS—*Sable*, a fret *or*.
    2 and 3. FITZALAN of Clun—*Argent*, a chief *azure*.

U. S. BAY 4.—A very fine Red Rose with Crown and motto—DIEU ET MON DROIT.

All these are unquestionably of the date of the house, and the finest work of 1530.

U. S. BAY 5.—A very elaborate, but rather later coat of COPLEY, in eight quarters, with an escutcheon of pretence for LUTTRELL (see *Escutcheons*, chap. xi.) Surrey Archæol. Coll. iii.

1. COPLEY—*Argent*, a cross moline *sable*, a crescent for difference.
2. WELLES and ENGAINE—Quarterly, see Window **V. 3**.
3. WATERTON—Barry of six *ermine* and *gules*, over all three crescents *sable*.
4. Hoo—Quarterly, *sable* and *argent*.
5. ST. OMER—*Azure*, a fesse between six crosses crosslet *or*.
6. MALMAYNS—*Azure*, three sinister hands couped *argent*.
7. WYCHINGHAM—*Ermine* on a chief *sable*, three crosses pattée *argent*.
8. ST. LEGER—*Azure*, fretty *argent*, a chief *or*.

On an escutcheon of pretence is—

LUTTRELL—*Or*, a bend between six martlets *sable*.

This coat is doubtless for Sir Thomas Copley, died 1584, great-grandfather of Mary, wife of John Weston, 1637.

ST. OMER, MALMAYNS, and ST. LEGER were quarterings of Hoo. The first Lord Hoo, 1446, was the son of Alice St. Maur, whose mother was Jane, daughter of Nicolas Malmayns. His second wife was Elizabeth Wickingham.

U. S. BAY 6.—The coats in Nos. 6, 7, 8 are all COPLEY coats with nearly the same quarterings, apparently of the same date, and for the same Sir Thomas Copley. They have been injured and badly repaired, especially No. 6, the lower quarters of which, 5 to 10, are not intelligible.

U. S. BAY 7.—7, *sable*, three talbots' heads erased *argent*, HALL, County Lincoln ; *argent*, a lion rampant.

U. S. BAY 8.—*Azure* (?) FAUCONBERG. In **8** appears NEVILLE—*Gules*, a saltire *argent*, and MOWBRAY—*Gules*, a lion rampant *argent*. These are probably misplaced during repairs.

In **8** are two very fine monograms. R. with crown, and H.E. with crown and hawthorn bush, fleur de lys, etc.

Here are also two of the original grotesques, a monkey and a griffin, both finely drawn ; also the device of Henry VII., H.E., and the crown and hawthorn bush, with some fine original emblems.

Lower South Bay

L. S. BAY 1.—Fragments of Tudor crown, very fine old glass, not of one coat. There is a grand fragment from the arms of Catherine of Aragon, Leon and Castile, with arms of England, also the following :—

i. *Azure*, upon a chevron between three harts at gaze *or*, as many crowns *sable*. (?) GREEN, Norfolk. This seems to impale—

ii. 1. *Or*, three fleurs de lys *azure* in pale.

2. *Vairé*, BEAUCHAMP of Hache.

3. *Gules*, two lions' heads erased *or*.

4. Quarterly, 1 and 4. *Gules*, a castle *or ;* 2 and 3. *Argent*, a lion rampant *gules*, crowned *or*.

But the whole coat has been transposed and entirely confused in the resetting.

L. S. BAY 2.—A magnificent original design, happily quite perfect, the arms of the founder.

1 and 4. WESTON—*Ermine*, on a chief *azure*, 5 bezants.

2 and 3. CAMELL—*Argent*, three camels trippant *sable*.

Sir R. Weston was the son of Catherine Camell, heiress of John Camell of Shapwick, Dorset.

L. S. BAY 3.—A splendid head of Saracen for the crest of Weston, with mantling (compare V. 2).

This and the last light enable us to judge of the appearance of the hall as originally completed, and shows most noble examples of the work of the glass-makers of 1530.

L. S. BAY 4.—This design is much mutilated. It shows us the portrait of a king crowned, apparently Henry VII., certainly not Henry VIII. Below are the arms of England impaling those of Catherine of Aragon, White and Red Roses. Fragment *argent*, a saltire *gules*. (?) St. Patrick.

This and a fragment vairé are found together in III. 2, and are fine and original; also in upper north bay 2.

L. S. BAY 5.—Remains of a Tudor crown, apparently with wreath; now in the place of the arms is a circular niche of late Gothic work; within (not in colours) a shield, being—

Arms of the *Aaventurers or Hambrough Merchants*. This society was incorporated 24 Edward I., 1296, and obtained ample privileges and a confirmation of their charter from Queen Elizabeth. See Cunningham, *English Industry*, i. 372.

ARMS—Barry undée of six, *argent* and *azure*. A chief quarterly *gules* and *or*, on the first and fourth quarters a lion passant guardant of the fourth; on the second and third two roses *gules*, barbed *vert* (Boutell, Plate 13, p. 328; and Edmondson, *Heraldry;* Gwillim, *Heraldry*). Sir Richard may have been a member, see p. 47.

L. S. BAY 6.—The lozenge, with nine lozenge devices.

1. Castle crowned. Castile.

2 and 3. Two Roses *argent*, seeded *gules*, crowned. Two crown-and-hawthorn with monogram H.E., a bird with buckle, and the punning rebus LEP above a tun, for Lepton.

The quarries of Lepton are cut with a diamond and inscribed thus—" W.E. 1704," and " A. 1702."

Rev. Radulph or Christopher Lepton, Canon of Wells, was Rector of Alresford and St. Nicholas, Guildford, 1504-27 (Manning, i. 65, 69).

L. S. BAY 7.—Another lozenge quarry of nine pieces; three appear to be original; an eagle apparently saying grace before sitting down to table; a fox with bird, and the crown and hawthorn. Two are figures of late seventeenth-century work, apparently Dutch—Christ before Pilate, two sea monsters, dolphin and dragon; also *Respice, Suspice*, 1630. The book and crown as in lower north bay.

L. S. BAY 8.—Here is a splendid and apparently perfect royal device, a fine Tudor crown, uninjured, which supports a wreath of magnificent blues and orange. Within are the following devices:—

A donjon of a castle with two wards and a gate with portcullis forms a bed for flowers; out of the castle rise two roses and two marigolds, apparently counterchanged—a heart and cross are in flames; out of the flames rises an eagle, hawk, or phœnix crowned, with wings outspread. This is for Jane Seymour, and it was also borne at times by her son, Edward VI. (Willement, p. 71, Plate 17). The same appears in Hampton Court Palace (see *History* by Ernest Law, vol. i. p. 181).

The work is apparently contemporary with the house. Jane Seymour was married 1536, and died 1537. It is singular that the personal badge of Jane Seymour should be put in the hall of the father whose only son had been executed just before her marriage as one of the lovers of Anne Boleyn. But Sir Richard Weston attended the court ceremonies of Jane Seymour, as we see in chap. iii. pp. 73, 74.

Window No. VII

VII. 1.—The Garter encloses a crest, a falcon displayed belled and gorged with a ducal coronet, the crest of PAULET,

Marquis of Winchester. This light is much injured and badly mended with modern fragments. It contains the portcullis chained, and a coat for ONSLOW impaling SWAN, same as in II. 2, II. 3; *azure*, three swans *argent*, a chief *or*.

VII. 2.—Here was a magnificent original Tudor crown and Red Rose of the Abbey design, apparently encircled by the Garter.

VII. 3.—The Garter as in No. 1, HONY SOYT QUY MAL Y PENSE, enclosing a coat of ten quarterings for PAULET.

1. PAULET—*Sable*, three swords in pile *argent*, points to bases, pommels and hilts *or*, a crescent for difference.

2. ROOS—*Gules*, three water bougets *argent*.

3. POYNINGS—Barry of six, *or* and *vert*, a bendlet *gules*, a crescent for difference.

4. ST. JOHN—*Or*, on a chief *gules*, three mullets pierced *argent*.

5. DELAMARE—*Gules*, two lions passant guardant *argent*.

6. HUSSEY—Barry of six, *ermine* and *gules*.

7. SKELTON—*Azure*, a fesse between three fleurs de lys *argent*.

8. IREBY—*Argent*, a fret *sable*, a canton of the second.

9. DELAMERE—*Argent*, six martlets (3, 2, 1) *sable* (see Baigent, *Practical Manual*, p. 35, where these quarterings are given from a monument in Croxdale Church).

These are the arms of William Paulet, K.G., first Marquis of Winchester, 1551, created by Henry VIII. Lord St. John, 1539, and one of his executors. He succeeded Sir Richard Weston as Master of the Court of Wards and Liveries, 1540-54 (J. Doyle, *Official Baronage*, iii. 700). He was Lord Treasurer during the reigns of Edward VI., Mary, and Elizabeth, and he explained his long tenure of office by saying that he was "the willow, not the oak." He was the builder of Basing House, about twenty-five miles from Sutton, and must have been well known both to the founder and to his grandson, Sir Henry Weston. He died 1572, aged eighty-seven. The crescent for cadency marks the fact that the elder branch is represented by Earl Poulett.

The crest, falcon gorged with a ducal coronet and belled, appears also in **VIII. 1.** Below is a coat, *gules*, five leopards rampant in cross *or*, for BYNTWORTH, and the word *Bentsworth*.

VII. 4.—Here are two devices or *rebus*, a circular enclosure surrounded by a stockade, in front a five-barred gate, inside trees, above J., below R.

A late sixteenth-century coat with mantling and crest *sable*, four or six lions rampant in cross *argent*, langued and armed *gules*, a scutcheon of pretence *ermine* (?) ST. MARTIN.

Crest on a knight's helmet, a lion statant *argent*, langued *gules*, armed *or*, on a cap of maintenance. The whole is a complete piece of seventeenth-century work.

VII. 5.—This light has been injured and badly mended. Several pieces of the original devices, birds and animals, remain.

VII. 6.—This light has been injured and badly mended. Also the original hawthorn crowned and rose-tree crowned with H.R. In the centre of the design is a large shield of four quarters impaling *sable*, three pickaxes *argent*, for PIGOTT.

The coat shows:—

1 and 4. *Sable*, a buck's head cabossed attired *or*, between the antlers a cross crosslet fitchée *or*, langued *or*, and pierced through the nose with an arrow *or*.

2. *Argent*, a chevron between three rooks' heads erased *sable*, the chevron charged with an annulet *or*. (?) NORREYS.

3. *Argent*, a chevron *gules* between three squirrels siegant *sable*, each holding a nut *or* SCOBINGTON.

Window No. VIII

VIII. 1.—Original wreath from Saracen's head, badly mended; within is a large crest, falcon gorged and belled as in **VII. 1**, for PAULET, Marquis of Winchester.

VIII. 2.—Very fine original Red Rose with crown above, similar to that in **VI. 4**, but much damaged.

VIII. 3.—Fragments of original wreath from Saracen's head, badly mended, three fleurs de lys, one quarter of royal arms, original glass of 1530.

VIII. 4.—Original quarries of birds, grotesques, and mantling. Three birds sitting down to dinner. In the centre a shield, sixteenth century, of four quarters.

1 and 4. BABINGTON of East Brigford, Notts—*Argent*, ten torteaux, 4, 3, 2, 1, a label of three points *azure*.

2. DETHICK of Derby—*Argent*, a fesse vairé *or* and *gules* between three water bougets *sable*.

3. *Argent*, a chevron (?) between two compasses and a globe *or* (?). Company of CARPENTERS, who had a grant of arms, 1466 (Boutell, 331). Transposed in mending.

The family of BABINGTON of Notts, from Sir John de Babington, chief Captain of Morlaix, in Bretagne, under Edward III., intermarried with family of DETHICK, County Derby. Of this family was Anthony Babington, executed 1586.

VIII. 5.—Birds, grotesques, and fragments of original glass, the H.E. and H.R. with hawthorn and crown, and a large coat of six quarters.

1. *Ermine* on two bars *sable*, three fleurs de lys *or*.

2. *Sable*, six lioncels rampant *or*, 3, 2, 1. (?) ST. MARTIN of Wilts.

3. *Sable*, a griffin segreant between three cross crosslets *argent*. (?) FROXMORE.

4 and 5. Quarterly (unintelligible and transposed)—(1) goat's head erased, horned *or*; (2) leopard's head cabossed; (3) two leopards' heads cabossed; (4) two goats. An escutcheon of pretence *argent*, three crescents *sable*.

6. Fleur de lys, from original royal arms.

VIII. 6.—Late sixteenth-century shield, nearly complete, supporters two camels. This has been transposed; originally it contained arms, crest, and supporters of the Merchant Taylors' Company with their motto (incorp. 1466 and 1503). Crest, on a knight's helmet a lamb *en soleil argent*, on a cap *vert*. The shield below has been apparently filled with the royal arms as borne by James I., and is a good deal injured.

1. In the first quarter of the royal coat is now a rabbit, with the letters W.T. *In sole posuit tabernaculum suum.* See Psalm xix. v. 4.

2. In the second a White and Red Rose.

3. The harp, for Ireland.

4. England and France quarterly. Below the motto, *Concordia res parvæ crescunt*, motto of the Merchant Taylors' Company. See Burke, *General Armoury*, under "London, Companies of." Also motto of United Provinces.

In this window, light 3, is an inscription with a diamond—"John Weston Esquire putt in this painted glass, August ye 28, 1724," apparently done by a workman during some repair.

Window No. IX

IX. 1 and 3.—Very fine original designs of the arms of the founder. Both the same. WESTON quartering CAMELL, same as in lower south bay No. **2**, and in **X. 1**. These are fortunately complete, with their mantling, and give an excellent conception of the best armorial decoration of the period.

IX. 2.—The rebus of the "tun" for the founder, as in lower north bay No. **1**, and probably similar, surrounded with wreathing.

IX. 4.—Here are curious sixteenth-century fragments, heads of kings, birds, grotesques, and two fleurs de lys.

In the centre is a sundial, marked from 10 to 8. This very curious piece is probably *in situ*, and by a metal rod or bracket, placed outside, it apparently indicates the time.

IX. 5.—Here is a lozenge-shaped quarry of old grotesques; an eagle or hawk is wheeling in a barrow a smaller bird. It looks like an illustration of the Burial of Cock Robin; also an eagle, hawk, or rook on two staffs, crutches, or stilts, with a pack on his back, apparently disguised as a pedlar. Also a demi-virgin couped below the shoulders, issuant out of clouds, vested and crowned *or*, the crest of the Mercers' Company, 1394. The motto *Virtutis laus actio* is for CORBET, one of the quarterings of ONSLOW. This motto was also used by William Howard, Earl of Arundel, whose family occupied Sutton Place 1615-25.

IX. 6.—Here are later fragments, not now intelligible; in the centre a Madonna and Child.

Window No. X

Here are, no doubt *in situ*, in the upper tier of lights, the arms and crest of the founder and the arms of his son-in-law.

X. 1.—The arms of WESTON quartering CAMELL, as in IX. 1 and 3.

X. 2.—The Saracen's head with wreath, much injured.

X. 3.—Here is a magnificent coat of arms, contemporary with the hall, and almost perfect. This splendid specimen gives a vivid impression of the command over the resources of colouring possessed by the glass-painters of 1530. It gives the arms of Sir W. Dennys quartering the arms of Berkeley in right of his mother.

This beautiful coat is thus blazoned :—

1 and 4. Grand quarters—

DENNYS—*Gules*, three leopards' heads *or*, jessant de lys *azure* (*sic*); over all a bend engrailed of the last.

2 and 3. Grand quarters, quarterly—

1. BERKELEY—*Gules*, a chevron between ten crosses pattée, six in chief and four in base, *argent*.

2. BROTHERTON—*Gules*, three lions passant guardant in pale *or*, a label of three points *argent*.

3. WARREN—Checky *or* and *azure*.

4. MOWBRAY—*Gules*, a lion rampant *argent*.

These are the arms in contemporary glass of Sir Walter Dennys, who married Margaret, daughter of Sir Richard Weston (see her *rebus* in lower north bay, No. 7). Sir Walter was the son of Sir William Dennys of Dyrham, Gloucestershire, by Anne, daughter and co-heir of Maurice (Lord) Berkeley, descended from James, Lord Berkeley, 1421, who married Isabel, second daughter of Thomas Mowbray, Duke of Norfolk. Hence the MOWBRAY and WARREN quarterings.

A communication from Mr. Charles A. Buckler, 10th August 1880, himself descended from a sister of Sir Walter Dennys, who married Sir Richard Buckler, County Dorset, states as follows—"The royal coat of BROTHERTON is, in the first place, in the seals of William Berkeley and Elizabeth, Duchess of Norfolk. It is curious that, at Sutton Place, as the royal quarter had precedence in the HOWARD shield, it was not similarly treated in the BERKELEY quarterings, two sisters and co-heirs having transmitted it to both families. At Sutton Place the fleurs de lys in the coat of DENNYS are *azure*. This occurs in the earlier instances. Later they were leopards' faces, jessant de lys *or*, in order to avoid the *azure* bend."

X. 4, 5.—Fragments, apparently of fine sixteenth-century work. A fleur de lys, White Rose, *rose en soleil*, etc.

X. 6.—A quarry in lozenge of four designs, apparently all of the seventeenth century, and much inferior to the original work.

(1) A woman nursing an infant swaddled with bands; (2) an elephant; (3) tulip, as in **VI. 5**; (4) a curious and amusing design from George Withers's *Emblems*, published 1636. G. Withers was a Guildford man, a stout Puritan,

and a Commissioner under the Commonwealth. His *Emblems* had a great success.

> "A fool sent forth to fetch the goslings home,
> When they unto the river's bank were come,
> (Through which their passage lay) conceived a feare
> His dame's best brood might have been drown'd there,
> Which to avoyd he thus do show his wit
> And his good nature in preventing it,
> He underneath his girdle thrusts their heads,
> And the coxcomb through the water wades.
> Here learne that, when a fool his help intends,
> It rather does a mischief than befriends."

INDEX

Agriculture, works on, 121-124
   at Sutton Place, 122, 130
   Sir R. Weston on, 122-127
Anne of Cleves, 74, 103
Aragon, Catherine of, 4, 151, 183, 223
Architecture, debased, 145
   domestic, 153, 168
   Gothic, 155-158
   Jacobean, 160, 168
   Palladian, 160
   Renascence, 157, 161
Arms of Arden, 211
   Arundel, 121, 230
   Babington, 237
   Barrow, 194
   Beauchamp, 207
   Belknap, 124
   Bellasis, 229
   Berkeley, 239
   Berners, 208
   Botreaux, 219
   Bourchier, 208, 218
   Braose, 226
   Bray, 211, 222
   Byntworth, 236
   Camell, 232
   Carpenters' Company, 237
   Carr, 226
   Catherine of Aragon, 223
   Cecil, 209
   Coke, 227
   Constable, 192
   Copley, 135, 183, 191, 192, 193, 215, 220, 223, 231
   Culcheth, 204

De Brotherton, 216, 240
Dennys of Dyrham, 80, 229, 239
De Roos, 210
Dethick, 237
Dister, 148, 191
Dunston, 205
Engaine, 193, 220
Fenwick, 109
Fitzalan, 231
Freke, 211
Fromonde, 205
Gage, 191
Gardiner, 225
Graham, 192
Hambrough Merchants, 233
Harper, 191
Hastings, 215, 219
Holcroft, 204
Hoo, 193, 215, 220
Howard, 215
Howson, 212
Hussey, 207
Jennings, 204, 207
Kynaston, 226
Lane, 206
Lascelles, 108
Lawson, 191
Luttrell, 193, 231
Malmayns, 206
Maltravers, 231
Manners, 209
Mercers' Company, 239
Merchant Taylors, 238
Mohun, 214
Moleyns, 219

Montalt, 214
Moresby, 109
Mowbray, 217
Neale, 212
Nevill, 191, 210
Nicholson, 205
Onslow, 208, 212, 226
Paulet, 234
Philip II., 230
Pickering, 95, 108
Pigott, 236
Pile, 207
Pillett, 227
Pinchyon, 194
Pound, 211
Ratcliffe, 212
Richard, Duke of Gloucester, 228
Rogers of Brianston, 81
Saint Leger, 193
Salvin, 148, 192
Scotland, 193
Shelley, 193, 223
Shirley, 226
Stanley, 214, 220
St. Omer, 220, 231
Strange, 214, 220
Strangeways, 212
Stretley, 206
Tilney, 218
Waldegrave, 192
Wales, 224
Warneford, 212, 219
Warren, 215, 216
Waterton, 193, 215, 222
Webbe, 194
Welles, 193, 215, 222
Weston, 49, 52, 55, 88, 143, 191, 192, 220, 232
White, Bishop, 205
Wickingham, 193
Widville, 214, 231
Winchester, Bishop of, 225
Woolfe, 143, 194
Wright, 192
Arundel, Countess of, 121
   Earl of, 121, 230
Arundell, Dorothy, 11, 109-114
   Portrait of, 11, 113, 195
   Lady, 11, 110
   Lord, 109
   Sir Thomas, 11, 74, 110

Aubrey, John, 170, 181
   Hist. of Surrey, 170, 181

Baker, Sir John, 67, 76
Basset, family of, 26, 152
Beaufort, family of, 31-34
   Margaret, 32-34, 200
Bell, the chapel, 151
Bigod, Earl Marshal, 26, 27
Boleyn, Anne, 65, 66, 70, 72, 93
   coronation of, 94
   execution of, 96-103
   Sir Thomas, Earl of Wiltshire, 53, 103
   Lord Rochford, 70, 103
Boorde, Andrew, Dyetorie, 165
Boston, Lincolnshire, 44, 83
Bosworth, battle of, 19, 33, 45
Brandon, Duke of Suffolk, 58
Bray, Sir Reginald, 222
Brianston, Rogers of, 80
Browne, 49, 93
Buckingham, Duke of, 56, 57
Buckler, C. A., xvi., 190, 240
Building, of Henry VIII, 1-5, 151-164
   of Sutton Place, 1-5, 151-168
Brussels, tapestries, 189, 190
Bryan, Sir Francis, 93

Calais, 60-63, 108
Canals, introduced at Sutton, 13, 16, 128
Carew, Sir N., 73, 93
Carrack, the *Great*, 88
Catherine of Aragon, 4, 53, 63, 65, 151, 183, 223
Cavendish, *Life of Wolsey*, 105
Charles I., 131
Charles II., 224
Charles V., Emperor, 36
Chute, Chaloner, 60, 69
Civil Wars, 128, 131
Clandon, 13, 16, 68, 121, 137, 180
Clerkenwell, History of, 87
Clover, introduced at Sutton, 122, 130
Copley, arms of, 135, 178, 183, 223, 231
   family of, 135
   John, 137

INDEX

245

Mary, 116, 135, 138
Sir Roger, 215
Sir Thomas, 13, 116, 135, 192, 193, 215
William, 137, 196
Crapelet, *Lettres de Henry VIII.*, 103
Cromwell, Oliver, 133, 139
Sir Richard, 40
Thomas, 41, 65, 66, 71, 96
executed, 74
Cross, moline, 178
of St. John, 81

Darwin, C., on Worms, 172
Daunay, Sir W., 84
family of, 43, 84
Dennys, Lady, 77, 80, 239
Sir Walter, 74, 239
Derby, Earls of, 213-221
Despenser, Hugh, 27
Dingley, Sir Thomas, 86
Dinteville, ambassador of Francis I., 99, 105
Dixon, Mr. Hepworth, 104
Domesday Survey, 16, 22, 23

Edward I., 28
Edward II., 26
Edward III., 28
Edward IV., 32
Edward VI., 73, 108
Edward, St., Confessor, 21, 22, 149, 152, 204
Elizabeth, Queen, 11, 70, 108, 113, 195
Embassy to France, 50
to Scotland, 46
to Spain, 46
Escutcheons, armorial, 192-194

Ferdinand, King of Spain, 48, 183
Field of the Cloth of Gold, 5, 55, 156
Fitzwilliam, Sir W., 70, 76
Flower, Bernard, 200, 206, 226
France, 50, 90
art in, 1, 5, 6, 156
Francis I. of France, 5, 50, 51, 55, 86, 90
Francis, the name, 90
Froude, Mr., 105

Gage, Viscount, 139
Elizabeth, 139
Gardiner, Bishop, 66, 226
Gatton, manor of, 14, 134, 136
Gentleman's Magazine, 166
George III. at Sutton, 145
Glass, painted, 190, 191
Gresham, Sir W., 78
Grey, family of, 11, 111, 113
Guernsey, island of, 45, 47
governorship of, 73
Guildford, 1, 3, 14, 16, 18, 73, 130

Hall at Sutton, 182-187
Hampton Court, 1, 85, 157, 185, 190
Harrison, Frederick, 149, 182, 188
Sidney, 149, 171, 176, 189
William, on England, 163
Hartlib, Samuel, 123
Harvell, Edmund, 72
Harvey, William, at Sutton, 121
Hayward, C. F., on Layer Marney, 157, 159, 164
Henry I., 22
Henry II., 24
Henry VII., 33, 39, 44, 233
Henry VIII., 1-10, 35, 39, 45, 156, 195, 223
Herselin of Brussels, 189
Holbein in England, 157
Holland, family of, 29, 30
Howard, family of, 12, 109, 113, 216
Lord Edmund, 109
Lord, of Effingham, 114, 115
Husee, J., letter of, 101
Hussey, portraits by, 143, 197

Inventory at Sutton, 60, 78, 185
at the Vyne, 60
Italian art, 2, 6, 157

Joan of Kent, 29
John, King, 26

Kent, Earls of, 29-31
Joan of, 29
Kingston, Sir W., 77, 97
Lady, wife of, 77, 97
Knyvett, Sir Henry, 93, 103

Law, Ernest, on Hampton Court, 157
Layer Marney Towers, 156
Leander, Father, 197
Lepton, Rev. Chr., 233
Letters—
  Cromwell to Weston, 71
  E. Harvell to T. Starkey, 72
  J. Husee to Lord Lisle, 101
  Kingston to Cromwell, 97
  Lord Sandys to Lord Lisle, 69
  of Gontier to Chabot, 86
  of Sir Henry Weston, 115
  Sir Francis to his family, 99
  Sir J. Russell to Lord Lisle, 69
  Sir R. Weston to Cromwell, 68
  Sir R. Weston to Wolsey, 61, 63
  Sir T. Copley to Weston, 115
  Sir W. Weston to Cromwell, 72, 73
  to Sir Henry Weston, 115
Leonardo da Vinci, 156
Lisle, Lord, 69
Locks, canal, 13, 16, 127
Loseley, 77, 78, 115
Loseley, MSS. at, 114
Lytton of Knebworth, 54

Machyn's *Diary*, 114
Maiano, G., 157
Malet, Robert, 19, 22-25
  William, 24
Malta, Knights of, 82-88
Manor Field, the, 22, 152
Manor of Clandon, 13, 16, 36, 68, 121, 180
  of Gatton, 14, 134, 136
  of Hampton Court, 85
  of Loseley, 57
  of Sutton, 7, 18-38, 57, 152
Margaret Beaufort, 19, 32, 200
Marney, Lord, 163
Marvell, Andrew, 101
Mary, Princess, 50, 80
Mary, Queen, 195
Mary, Queen of Scots, 115
Mary Tudor, Queen of France, 49, 210
Merrow, grant of, 36
Monasteries, dissolution of, 74, 75, 87

More, Sir Christopher, 8, 77
  Sir William, 115
Morette, French ambassador, 85
Mortimer, Roger, 28

Nevill, William, of Holt, 138
  Melior, 138
Noreys, H., 96, 97
Norfolk, Duke of, 97, 103, 110, 213, 214, 216

Onslow, Earl of, 121
  family of, 211, 227
  Sir Richard, 14, 121, 180
Orlay, Bernard von, 190

Pace, Richard, 56
Page, Sir Richard, 93
Painted glass at Sutton, 15, 38, 199-241
Patch, the King's fool, 92
Paulet, W., Marquis of Winchester, 234
Pavia, battle of, 60
Pedigree of Weston, 42, 134
Penruddock, Colonel, 139
Pickering, Anne, 67, 94
  family of, 94
  Sir Christopher, 94
Pitson, James, 128
Portland, Weston, Earl of, 128
Portraits at Sutton Place, 15, 195

Quadrangle, the, 171-181
Quarries, 229

Raes, Jean, of Brussels, 189
Reformation, the, 65-75
Renascence in Europe, 1-8, 155, 159
Rhodes, defence of, 59, 85
  knights of, 82-88
Richard I., 25
Richard II., 30
Richard III., 19, 32, 207, 228
Richmond, Countess of, 31-33, 200
Roberts, Sir Nicholas, 59
Rochford, Lord, 70
Rogers, Lady, 78, 80
  family of, 80
  Sir John, 80
Rose, an emblem, 204, 212, 225, 228

INDEX

Roses, Wars of, 32, 200
Russell, Sir John, 8, 69, 70, 77, 93
  John, R.A., 197

Saint John, Knights of, 43-45, 48, 59, 82-88
Salvin, F. H., 36, 37, 146-149, 189, 192
Sands, family of, 47, 79
  Anne, 47, 79
Sandys, Lord, 60, 69
Seymour, Jane, badge of, 234
  death of, 74
  marriage of, 72
Smeaton, Mark, 92, 96
Speering, François, 189
Star Chamber, 54
Step gables, 158
Stephen, King, 19, 25
Stevenson, J. J., on architecture, 158, 168
Suffolk, Brandon, Duke of, 58, 110
  Henry, Duke of, 110
Sutton, manor of, 1, 2, 18-38
  Alexander Pope at, 112
  always Catholic, 21
  Cromwell at, 6, 73
  Elizabeth at, 11, 37, 114
  furniture and stock at, 79
  George III. at, 145
  grant of, 7, 35, 57
  Henry VII. at, 34
  Henry VIII. at, 37, 38, 68, 70
  inventory at, 78, 169
  portraits at, 195
  William Harvey at, 121
  Wolsey at, 6, 35, 36
Sutton Place, 58, 152
  canals and locks introduced at, 13, 16, 121, 127
  fire at, 114
  grasses introduced at, 122
  turnips introduced at, 122

Tapestries, 188-190
Terra-cotta, 156-164
  fireplaces, 187
Trevisano in England, 157
Turkopolier, office of, 61, 84
Turnips introduced at Sutton, 122
Villiers, de Lisle-Adam, 59, 85

Vine Cottage, 22, 152
Vine, The, Hampshire, 60, 69

Waldegrave, Lady Horatia, 147
Walls of Sutton Place, 178
Wards, Court of, 54, 74
Warren, William of, 25
Webbe, John, 194
Webbe-Weston, J., 144
  arms of, 144, 191
  family of, 144-150, 192
  J. J., 147, 192
  T. M., 148, 192
Wenesi, 22
Westminster Abbey, 33, 201, 206, 225
Weston, Sir R. (1), 6-10, 39-81
  death of, 76
  his arms, 232
  his executors, 8, 70, 76
  his will, 77-79
  letters by, 61, 63, 68
  surrenders treasurership, 76
Weston, Lady Anne, 47, 79
Weston, Sir F., 8-10, 67, 89-106
  execution of, 101
  letter of, 99
  will of, 100
Weston, Sir H., 11, 12, 107-119
  his will, 118
  letters of, 115
Weston, Sir R. (2), 120
  Sir R. (3), 13, 16, 120-133
  Richard, 138
  Katherine, 80
  Margaret, 80, 229, 240
Weston family, 41-44, 83
  arms of, 49, 52, 55, 232, 240
Weston, Earl of Portland, 14, 131
  John (1), 134
  John (2), 138
  Melior Mary, 141-144, 195
  Sir John, 83
  Sir William, 62, 75, 82-88
Wey, the river, 10, 14, 16, 128
Will of Sir R. Weston, 77
  of Sir F. Weston, 100
  of Sir H. Weston, 118
  of Melior Mary Weston, 144
William, Conqueror, 22-25
Wilson, Mr. J., 122

Windows, *see* Painted Glass
Wingfield, Sir R., 53, 77
Winston, Charles, 199
Withers, George, 240
Woking, 34, 37, 200
Wolffe, family of, 142, 143
    William, 142, 176

Wolsey, Cardinal, 6, 35, 37, 41, 66
Woodstock, Edmund of, 28
Worplesdon, 130

Zucchero, Federigo, portrait by, 113, 195

THE END

Printed by R. & R. CLARK, LIMITED, *Edinburgh*

BY THE SAME AUTHOR.

THE MEANING OF HISTORY, and other Historical Pieces. By FREDERIC HARRISON. Extra Crown 8vo. 8s. 6d. net.

STANDARD.—"The plea for the synthetic interpretation of history has seldom been urged with more conspicuous force and beauty."
DAILY CHRONICLE.—"All these and other qualities are not only discernible; they penetrate through and through the texture of the deeply interesting, wise, and eloquent volume before us."
SCOTSMAN.—"Brilliant, vigorous, stimulating."

ANNALS OF AN OLD MANOR-HOUSE, SUTTON PLACE, GUILDFORD. By FREDERIC HARRISON. Illustrated from the original Drawings by WM. LUKER, Jun., W. NIVEN, and C. FORSTER HAYWARD. Printed on hand-made paper, and illustrated with numerous plates after original drawings, facsimiles, head and tail-pieces, etc. Medium 4to. 42s. net.

∴ Also an Abridged Edition. Extra Crown 8vo.

STANDARD.—"The book is written with scholarly care, as well as with imaginative insight, and everywhere there is a sense of space about the narrative, for Mr. Harrison never allows us to forget the changing social and political characteristics of each succeeding reign."
DAILY CHRONICLE.—"Externally, one of the handsomest books we have seen for a long time, and in contents a very charming labour of love."
SATURDAY REVIEW.—"Mr. Harrison would, no doubt, write well upon any house which had a history worth the tracing out. But his work upon this particular manor-house has all the additional charm of a labour of love."

THE CHOICE OF BOOKS, and other literary pieces. By FREDERIC HARRISON. Second Edition. Globe 8vo. 5s.
[*Eversley Series.*]

Mr. JOHN MORLEY.—"Those who are curious as to what they should read in the region of pure literature will do well to peruse my friend Frederic Harrison's volume called *The Choice of Books*. You will find there as much wise thought, eloquently and brilliantly put, as in any volume of its size."
TIMES.—". . . It is full of suggestiveness and shrewd analytical criticism."

OLIVER CROMWELL. By FREDERIC HARRISON. Crown 8vo. 2s. 6d. [*Twelve English Statesmen Series.*]

TIMES.—"He gives a wonderfully vivid picture of events, nor does he shrink from speculating on the incidents which history has left most obscure. As for the grand subject of his monograph, he paints him as Cromwell desired to be painted."

EDITED BY THE SAME.

THE NEW CALENDAR OF GREAT MEN. Biographies of the 558 Worthies of all Ages and Countries in the Positivist Calendar of Auguste Comte. Edited by FREDERIC HARRISON. Extra Crown 8vo. 7s. 6d. net.

Mr. JOHN MORLEY in the *NINETEENTH CENTURY.*—"These little lives are marvels of condensation. . . . The merit could not be expected to be absolutely equal in a team of fifteen; but one can only admire the skill and success with which the unity of the central idea has been preserved."
ATHENÆUM.—"Well-written and accurate sketches."

MACMILLAN AND CO., LTD., LONDON.

www.ingramcontent.com/pod-product-compliance
Lightning Source LLC
Chambersburg PA
CBHW032133230426
43672CB00011B/2318